"LISTEN CAREFULLY TO ME"

"Listen Carefully to Me"

Sue and Hugh O'Donnell

YOUCAXTON PUBLICATIONS
OXFORD & SHREWSBURY

ISBN 978-1-912419-37-1
Printed and bound in Great Britain.
Published by YouCaxton Publications 2018

First published in 2013 by Onwards and Upwards Publishers

YouCaxton Publications
enquiries@youcaxton.co.uk

Nihil Obstat:

Reverend Peter Phillips DD,
Censor Deptatus

Imprimatur:

Right Reverend Mark Davies,
RC Bishop of Shrewsbury

Isaiah 55:2-3

Why do you spend money for what is not bread,

And your wages for what does not satisfy?

Listen carefully to Me, and eat what is good,

And let your soul delight itself in abundance.

Incline your ear, and come to Me.

Hear, and your soul shall live;

And I will make an everlasting covenant with you—

The sure mercies of David.

Endorsements

I have in my Breviary the book which contains the Daily Office of the Church, a card which has a quotation from the writings of Dag Hammarskjold, who was Secretary-General of the United Nations from 1953 until his death in a plane crash in 1961. This quotation has been a great inspiration to me over many years and says, quite simply: "The more faithfully you listen to the voice within you, the better you will hear what is sounding outside."

This book is very much the product of many years of faithful listening to that still, small voice and understanding the implications of the understanding brought by that listening. It is not a book to be rushed through but savoured and pondered while the meaning is interpreted afresh for each reader. It is truly a book to be prayed with, and like all true prayer will change the pray-er in ways that may not be expected.

The habit of journaling our spiritual pilgrimage is one which is to be commended because it gives us the opportunity to look back at our journey up to the present time and perhaps see what has happened in perspective. In this remarkable book we can see the fruit of a growing personal relationship with the Father who knows us even better than we know ourselves.

We can all find inspiration and encouragement in 'Listen Carefully to Me', but we must do all those things: listen – carefully – to Him.

The Revd David Mawson

RC Priest

Personal Ordinariate of Our Lady of Walsingham

Shortly after my Confirmation, nearly sixty years ago, I was given a tuppenny tract on prayer entitled 'Think of Our Lord speaking – to You'. Its fresh, direct, personal approach changed both my perception and experience of praying. In a telling moment I realised that praying was much more about quietly listening to the 'still small voice of God' speaking intimately into my heart than it was about me talking to God. 'Listen Carefully to Me', compiled by Sue and Hugh O'Donnell, offers a daily experience of our Father God giving inspiration, instruction, wisdom and counsel to "my beloved child". We are invited, like pilgrims on a journey with God, through the days, weeks and months of the year, each offering steeped in Scripture, by the power of the Spirit flowing directly into our waiting hearts. What a divine treasury of loving inspiration, reassurance, and joy!

Rev Roger Bruce Balkwill

Retired Anglican Priest; part time Interim Minister in Telford, Shropshire

'Listen Carefully to Me' gives words of comfort, assurance and encouragement for each day. From someone who has been soaked in the scriptures, the passages read with the directness and urgency of prophetic utterance. Full of hope in God's goodness and the fulfilment of His Kingdom, the author's plea is that we stay close to the living God, the source of all life and being. Indeed, if we are not close to Him, how can He guide us and His Church in His way? Here is hope and wisdom for our journey with Jesus Christ.

The Rt Revd Mark Rylands

Anglican Bishop of Shrewsbury

God's Dream can unfold in our own everyday lives. This gentle, invitational book encourages us to tune in daily to the movements of divine love in our lives and to dance to its music resonating in our hearts.

Margaret Silf

Renowned Christian author, writer, broadcaster and retreat leader

When we believe the Lord is speaking to us and asking us to share what he says with others, we must carefully record every word. Sue O'Donnell has done this, and 'Listen Carefully To Me' is an inspiring devotional book, filled with words of wisdom and encouragement she received in prayer.

Charles Whitehead

International speaker, author and leader in Catholic Charismatic Renewal.

In his Letter to the Romans, chapter 1 verse 12, the Apostle Paul speaks about Christians being "mutually encouraged by each other's faith". Sue and Hugh O'Donnell share their positive, hopeful and encouraging faith with us in this deeply devotional book of meditations, helping us to open our lives to God and to be channels for His Good News to others. "Listen Carefully to Me" is filled with the tender care of God, the loving purposes of God and the healing touch of God, who longs to give His peace, wholeness and delight to all who will simply receive these blessings.

Revd Tim Harwood

Minister

Shrewsbury United Reformed Church

This is an inspiring, refreshing and timely book. It reveals the way to God's peace in a noisy, disturbed and confused world. Mother Teresa said, "The essential thing is not what we say but what God says to us and through us." This book leads its readers to an encounter with God, who is not absent but really present here and now. It leads directly to the discovery that God is not silent; if we truly listen, we will hear Him speak. The beautiful words of this book will help many to hear and know His voice.

Dennis Wrigley

Leader and Co-founder, Maranatha Community

About the Authors

Tel: 01743 244083
Email: maranatha@talktalk.net
Web: a-zchristianpoetry

Corinthians 2 v 12

Now we have received, not the spirit of the world, but the Spirit who is from God that we might know the things that have been freely given to us by God.

Sue and Hugh were married in 1968 and have four children and two grandchildren. They worship at the RC Cathedral in Shrewsbury where Hugh is an eucharistic minister and both run a house group and are chaplaincy team members at a local nursing home. They also belong to the ecumenical Maranatha Community.

In the 1990s they were inspired by the Catholic Charismatic Renewal movement, and subsequently Sue has consistently listened to (and written down) the Lord's promptings, resulting in the ever present truths contained in 'Listen Carefully to Me'.

For the last several years Sue has written at least a poem every day – these often coming in the twinkling of an eye – and a selection of these were published in her first book 'In Short', a collection of short, rich, intimate Christian poems.

Acknowledgements

With acknowledgements and warmest thanks to:

Bob Fowke and Steve Edwards of YouCaxton.co.uk for their professional help and expertise to publish the Second Edition.

Marian for her efficient and prompt typing;

Jean and **Susan** for their meticulous and timely filing;

Stanton and **Steve** for valued help with IT;

Jeremy and **Florence** for their careful proof-reading and encouragement.

Publisher's Preface

In this inspiring and heartfelt devotional, Sue and Hugh O'Donnell have captured insights received in prayer, sharing them to challenge and encourage us in our daily lives.

In order to preserve the original meanings and intentions, editing has been kept to a minimum; we have focused mainly on using punctuation to aid interpretation and to ease readability. However, in some places changes to the underlying text have been necessary, and these are indicated using square brackets for additions/modifications and ellipses where there are omissions in sentences.

Whilst the insights were originally for the benefit of the authors themselves and shared with their family and friends, they believe that many in the wider body of Christ will also benefit from them. Sometimes the text speaks to the reader individually but also in the plural, e.g. "My child" or "My children." In general the original words have been retained including some unusual phrasings (and even suspect grammar!) as these add richness and authenticity.

Omissions have been made primarily if a phrase or paragraph refers specifically to the immediate recipients of the word rather than all members of the body of Christ.

Sometimes the authors had asked a question in prayer and the original text was a response. These questions are shown in italics.

The authors have chosen to begin many words that refer to God with capital letters (e.g. My, Our, His Name) out of respect. Similarly, the name 'satan' is written in lower case.

Although this book has been laid out as a devotional, with a different message for every day of the year, it should be noted that the dates have been added by the publisher and the order of the messages does not correspond to the order in which they were received. The words offer insights into general truths that can be applied at any time. In addition, the various titles to the daily meditations were chosen by Hugh O'Donnell to reflect their content.

Introduction

In some ways this must be one of the easiest books ever written. You see, the words are not mine, they are the fruits of prayer. I felt that all I had to do was to write them down!

Of course, I had to be faithful and accurate in listening and writing, but this was easy once I had decided to be obedient, still and quiet before the Lord. It still thrills me that this has happened, and I am convinced these words were not just for my husband and me, but also are for a wider audience – hence this book.

'Listen Carefully to Me' is not unique; there have been several other devotionals or diaries where others have sought to hear what our Lord has spoken for our contemporary world, and indeed to many individuals to teach, to guide, to encourage and especially to show His love, compassion and care for us. He is real and He is here *now* – and He speaks to us still.

So, how did it all begin? My husband, Hugh, and I were invited to a Christian dinner where the speaker had just flown in from Africa. A total stranger to us all, he spoke about his own faith and then said that whilst praying in preparation for his talk he had been given three messages for different people in the room.

"The third message," he said, "I do not really understand." Then, to my spine-chilling astonishment, he described accurately circumstances in my life and work known only to me.

With the description there was no doubt that the message was for me. "Listen to the Lord," I was told. To my excited amazement I then knew that God was real and he was interested in my personal circumstances. I also realised that I was being asked not to be too busy but to allow sufficient time to be not only asking but *listening* in prayer. I decided to read around the subject of listening prayer.

I have a debt of gratitude to two authors: Joyce Huggett, writing in 'Listening to God', and Leanne Payne, the author of 'Listening Prayer'. They convinced me that it is possible for *any of us to hear God* – in His ways, circumstances and timing. Indeed, He wants to continually help and guide each one of us if only we would let Him! Any blockage is ours, not His! So let us be still and invite Him in. He is too polite to come as an uninvited guest!

So, I *expected* to hear. I ensured a silent place of prayer each day, sometimes reading the Bible, some passages riveting my attention, speaking into the circumstances of my life. I was listening and hearing! *And so can you!*

Then I realised words were coming into my mind unaccountably, not from my head but from deep within, during times of heartfelt prayer. I recorded without alteration or deviation (sometimes with the help of Hugh) these insights I received over a period of several years. It was quite clear when each dialogue in prayer started and finished, but there was no pattern as to which days I received and which I did not – *the Spirit blows where He wills.*

These passages have been selected and used in the daily reflections of 'Listen Carefully to Me'. May our Lord speak to you also in them so that you, too, will be blessed.

Sue O'Donnell

References:

Listening to God, Joyce Huggett, an omnibus edition, together with *Finding Freedom and a Listening to Others*, published 1998 Hodder and Stoughton. ISBN 0 340 678968

Listening Prayer, Leanne Payne, published 1996 Kingsway Publications. ISBN 0 85476 558 1

Ask Jesus' Spirit to speak to you
in these Daily Devotions

Backtrack - I

1st January

Backtrack. Look at your past to go forward. Look not with the eyes of condemnation, but with My eyes of love. Look to see all I am doing in your life. It is when you reflect – stop and reflect – you will see your progress in Me. Come, let us talk about this together.

The measure of faith is your progress in Me: how much you are prepared to receive; how much you are prepared to believe, to believe all I say to you; then, of course, how willing you are, how desirous you are, of wanting to put this into action.

Your efforts are rewarded to the extent that you allow Me to use you, but you need to see where you have been to understand something of where you are going. I will lead you according to that understanding developing, and you implementing it. Keep asking of Me to show you more but always letting Me handle the 'whys' and 'wherefores'.

You must not presume nor jump to conclusions for these may be in gross error outside My sovereign plan. What a waste of time, your precious time, My precious time! Ask Me, always ask Me, to show you what to do. Then wait for the answer for it will surely come, but you can help prepare the way by looking at yourself, where you have been and where you have learnt to move forward so far.

Ask Me to teach you more by My Spirit. Ask for the fullness of My Spirit and plead the triumph of My †, setting you free to be entirely in Me, completely within the bounds, working within the bounds of My sovereign power.

Backtrack - II

2nd January

Our success – yours and Mine together – comes when we serve according to our Father's will. He has a plan of fruition, specific to your life, for each and every one of you. He will take every aspect of your life, if only you let Him, and turn it into something good. That is why you must look back to look forward.

You have to ask, "What did I learn from this? What happened? How by God's grace can I implement this truth, the truth of God's love, that has been revealed to me?" There is an aspect of the fullness of God's truth given in Me, through My Spirit revealed to each of you who stops to reflect.

That is why I say to you, "Be still and know that I am God."[1] Be still sufficiently long and sufficiently often to do this. Stop and reflect; connect the past to the future and ask God what He is showing you, exactly what He is revealing to you. Then take the learning forward in My Name of grace. Great things will come from this, I promise you – great benefits to you and others; many blessings of the grace of My presence, the purpose of My teaching you, teaching as God our Father wants you to be taught.

To be taught you have to be a willing scholar, attentive and listening at all times, receptive to My Word, willing and wanting to put it into practice. Have you done this? Look back and ask the question. If not, why not? Repent before Me and determine to walk a better way into the future. *Listen to Me, Listen to Me, Listen to Me!*

---

1 Psalm 46:10

Backtrack - III

3rd January

The words that I speak are life to you and to those to whom I send you. Look to whom I am sending you and wonder why. Ask Me, "Why?"

High on My agenda is your understanding – your full, fullest understanding – of what I am commanding you to do. Understanding opens out the reason why. When you accept the reason why, you can see more of My purpose, My plan, and how I work in you and through you. When you go back, you see how I am taking you forward using your own personal experience for growth. Experience the experience you have had in Me, with Me and through Me. This is your best teacher for it is grounded upon My truth, the truth [of] who you are, who I want you to be, who you will be, will become, as you grow in Me, My child. Go back with Me to go forward with Me, and live in Me entirely.

Admit of no other influence, however seemingly exciting, enticing or rewarding. I am the wholeness of the Father manifest here upon earth. I am your teacher. My Way is the only way of being certain of pleasing your Father. My Truth is the only truth you can depend upon to the extent that you can stake your life upon it.

Your life – the fullness of your life – depends upon you recognising Me. Look back and see where I was with you. Look back and see where you walked your own wilful way, whatever the good intentions. What happened? Did all your plans come to fruition? No! Learn from this and move forward in Me. To be in Me, only in Me, entirely in Me, is to be free to know God's plan and purpose and follow it. Will you do this? Will you do this for Me? I ask you to! I ask you now to look back that you may go forward in Me.

Ask for My Spirit's enlightening. He will guide you. Ask Him often, and if you don't understand, ask Him again to open up, to open out, what He is showing you. If in doubt, ask Me and wait for the answer. Pay Me this courtesy of waiting. You may not yet be ready to receive all that I want to give you. Giving of Myself to you is a means by which you will grow. I want you to grow by looking back to move forwards. This is My will for you and is to be undertaken seriously with a committed heart. I always honour commitment, so make the time for this; find the time for this and you will be richly rewarded in Me.

Guidance

4th January

Letting go is letting Me take charge of your vision, that together we enlarge My purpose, My holy purpose. Love must be the token of exchange in all your dealings. Love means giving to others beyond yourself. By this I intend that you should work, overcoming any resistance of doubt.

Keep asking me for clearance and guidance and I will show you clearly the way forward in My timing which may not be yours in the immediacy of your worldly thinking. The point about seeking Me is that I enlarge your vision of Me, enabling Me therefore to change your decision, and this can actually change the direction of your life.

Life is full of strife – yes, particularly when you fail to consult Me. Do better on this, and you will see much unfolding that formerly you thought impossible. Be in conversation with Me as much as you can and wait, for My clearance is given when you are ready to receive, when you have made ready to receive by sufficient prayer. Prayer enables you to move forward successfully under the blessing, simply because we talked together.

Earnestly you must want to find out what I say, for what I say will always be according to God our Father's greater plan and purpose to bless. Do you not want to bless others?

Listen to Me and follow the advice. Do not fail Me in this. There is much at stake for yourself and others. Do you not yet realise the very great difference I came to make?

Put this now into practice in your own life and then rejoice. Rejoice in the choice – or choices – we have made together.

Let My Spirit work through you together with you. Then you can bless others in all that you do.

Come Away with Me

5th January

Fulfil My obligation to those people I give you. No more for this present time lest you slip back. My peace is My desire for you, not My burden of care overwrought.

Wait on Me and My telling. In the meantime serve where you have been already sent. Strengthen and succour yourselves and each other.

Come away with Me to those quiet places where your heart finds repose. There you can become My little child in the calm as you trust again, trust in all that is happening to you by My hand.

My Spirit is breaking you in ... This is My desire and longing, that you may know more of Me and work in My power. In My time you will know and understand all that I am working for in you, My children.

Come away with Me and let your hearts and minds be restored to gladness, refreshed by My Spirit. He it is who brings you life and love to the full, My very energy of being as you intend towards Me.

Teaching as taught, learning as of Me, knowing and understanding in My Name, strengthened and restored, you will be Mine again in a new way of revealing, a new certainty, My blessed assurance.

As your heart burns with longing for Me, your desire will be met by My closeness, My security. Come, My children, together we walk life's way, its twisting paths. Come and claim Me as your own, each day enfolded in My love and life source.

My Plans Are for You

6th January

My truth is My truth. It cannot fail you. My promise holds fast. Believe Me. No problems are insurmountable in My Name. I do for you what you want Me to do, if only you believe and ask.

Listen to My voice again. Listen and learn of Me. My heart's desire is to please you, to bring you My peace, for that was My promise. Do not be afraid, but turn all things over to Me in this situation, in every situation, knowing I am at work. Believe Me, My child. I am yours.

What you have is of Me. What you will be is of Me. Guard it prayerfully and with My hope. Take your stand and hold fast on to that which I give you, My Word, My promise that all will be well in spite of the appearances. This will help you know Me in a greater way as you see My power at work, My love manifest.

Be of Me and in Me; absorbed into My truth, at one with My being, totally committed; no shadow between us, no shadow of doubt nor plane of worry.

My plans are for you unfolding in My Name and cause. Continue to tread My path. Where it leads I will follow, making everything smooth enough. Do not give up on the way. I need you there beside Me. I am calling out to you as never before to believe in Me, with urgency. Do not be disheartened.

Praise My Name and sing of My glory as you become awakened to My power. Dear children, I hold you safe. Your plans are My plans and will not fail nor disappoint you. Wait patiently for My working, My promise to come to fruition.

My dream is not shattered; it is merely bending with the will of the world; but I came to overcome all forces contrary to good. You know that. Believe Me and claim My healing promise. I make all things well in My Name.

Mine it is to appoint, Mine to give and take away. I give you now My promise that all is not lost. This is the truth of My speaking.

Glad I am that you listened. Seek Me more that I may commune with you until we meet face to face.

My Gentle Spirit of Peace

7th January

It is my Spirit of peace come upon you. My longing to give you My life and My rest and My calm. My gentle Spirit of peace: peace in your hearts and minds; peace in your lives. Peace in your dealings with other people, that you may calm their troubled hearts because you believe in Me and bring peace, My peace into their situation. They can be healed once more in My Name of righteousness.

My justice will prevail where and when men walk in My peace claiming My promise to them: "My peace I bring you." This is no small promise but the foundation upon which security is built and you are strengthened. It is peace that binds, peace that holds, peace that mends those hearts and emotions torn asunder. Only My peace brings true healing and wholeness. Peace is My everlasting gift to those who believe in Me and act upon it.

Spread My Good News, for in as much as you do men can be made whole, recovered from doubt and despair. My gift is for the giving, yours for the receiving and sharing amongst those I put you with. This is My mission to you: "As you are Mine share Me out gladly, teaching in My Name of all that I have shown and told you." My peace will descend as you pray into men's hearts.

The Bread of Life - I

8th January

Taste and see that the Lord is good, bringing you the bread of life which will allow you the taste of My freedom. Come and sup with Me as often as you can, for thereby you will be strengthened and upbuilt in Me in My great mystery of transformation.

My life is [expressed][2] by the bread and wine offered for you on Calvary – My life poured out not in vain but in triumph to bring you back to the Father. As you eat this bread and drink this wine you become Our children again, for you and Me become as one body journeying together to the Father.

My bread is that which strengthens all of you, for it is the grain of true life and meaning. It sprouts within you when watered by My love and intentions which you allow. As the ears of corn grow tall, the sunlight imparts strength and the rain swells the grain into fullness of heart. So it is with Me.

I am the light and the warmth. I provide the nourishment which fertilizes growth. Germination can only take place when the soil of your heart is ready to be planted. This involves tilling, reaping and sowing in cycle. As the furrows lengthen and deepen, the seed of My word penetrates deeper into the heart soil. It will grow to fullness, true fullness only when you believe completely in all that I tell and show you.

Your belief must grow, must flower under the strain of the everyday burden of tasks, for in forming you I will show you what is of Me and what is not, what is of value and what you can jettison.

Clearing the clutter was the plan. You need My help on this for I see the way ahead, your heart's desire at the rainbow's end.

You will be granted My strength to succeed in all of those tasks given of Me and directed in My Name of righteousness. Seeking, you are finding My will, My plan, My purpose for you ...

Longing to serve, you too will be served by Me. My wish is that you know Me more thoroughly that you may use of My power as you reach out to others, those in search looking for Me.

---

2 symbolised

The Bread of Life - II

9th January

Plant in your heart's poor soil that which you know is truly of Me and My teaching. I came not to serve alone but to be in men's hearts, to be their strength, their sustenance, their soul's search, their destiny. It is life's mystery that you must seek Me every day in the 'everywhere' until you find My substance deep in your own heart and with others, as well as entirely beyond man's imagining.

You cannot comprehend Me nor contain Me, but can diffuse yourself, yourselves, into My being. Become as one with Me. This is how you were created to be, complete and wholly alive in Me.

I fill you now with My warmth of life, My love in riotous bloom, beautiful as the blossom you behold, breathtaking, breathing life into every fibre of your being.

Unite with Me in bread and wine. Drink of My cup. It is the cup of eternal salvation. Eat of My body. It is the bread of life-giving truth; it stands for all time.

My table stands ready for the banquet to which you are invited by Me. My children come and dance before Me with joy in My house forever.

It Is Not by Chance That Things Happen

10th January

Come unto Me, you who are heavily burdened. Come unto Me, My child, where you can rest secure in My arms as they enfold you in love. Encompassed about, you will be strengthened in Me. You will be held fast in My certainty, My belonging, My beckoning.

When I use you it will be with authority of My giving, My sustaining, your initiating. You must ask Me for guidance first. How else can you know the way I wish you to go? It is not by chance that things happen. Refer all unto Me for My direction and sanction.

Slowly you are learning about My strength given to you. To you too I will share power – My saving, healing power – that men might know Me and believe in My promises, My promise of fullness of life.

All authority in heaven and earth is given to Me. But I share it with those whom I choose and select. You are one such as this, one together and one apart. But you must remain one in Me, in My truth.

Shouldered high you will be by My protection, called into the marketplace of men's souls where bartering takes place. Your bid is for Me. Make it a strong one for I deliver you My gifts.

Learn of Me more and never stop trusting, longing for Me, reaching out expectantly, hopefully, joyfully. As you praise Me you set My heart alight. My love for you knows no boundaries, no decline, no restrictions. It is as wide and deep as the ocean. Avail yourself, yourselves, of it, receiving and giving of Me.

Select in My Name your times, places and peoples with whom to work ... The preparation is long and sometimes hard-fought, but the prize is beyond telling. My goal is clear: you must all be made ready.

Be patient in Me, choosing to use each day in the best way you can in readiness. All will be well; that is My promise to you all.

Seek, Seek and Again I Say, Seek

11th January

My child, I am with you always as I said I would be. Why do you sometimes doubt Me, My power and influence? Why do you think things escape My notice? It is not so, for in Me all things have their being. They cannot therefore be without Me. Only you can lose hold your grasp on the reality of Me when we fail to spend time together, to grow in our relationship.

Come unto Me, My child, seeking, yearning, knowing I am with you in men's hearts, in their lives, within and without, with form and substance but also in deeds and intentions, indeed everywhere, above and below your heart, that place of My making, My throne.

The heart is a beautiful vessel. It can hold all that is pure in Me, all that is worthy, all that is wholesome. Your heart's praises are My delight and solace in a sorrowing world. Those praises resound in heaven with joy – the joy of knowing Me, believing Me.

My child, learn of Me little by little until you become Mine entirely, enabled to walk and breathe Me every step of the way where I take you in Me. Resuscitate men's lives for Me. Give them new life, My new life of knowing peace sublime, tranquillity and serenity.

I prepare you now ... Learn of each other as of Me. Seek, seek and again I say, seek. For in seeking you will surely find Me each day – alive and active in you all.

Come to Me, My children, you will be well rewarded. Incline your ear and your heart to My voice.

I speak often to you in many ways. Do not miss what I have to say, what I am telling you, what I am showing you, for it forms part of the pattern I weave. The intricacies are many, closely woven by Me, tightly knitted together by prayer from your heart, your hearts, as you become one in Me.

Take of Me. Take and see that the Lord is good.

I Am the Master Weaver

12th January

I was thinking about us being so insignificant as human beings. I asked: 'Why Lord? Why are we so little, so lost in time and space?'

Because all are part of My Father's plan of unity in love, each one providing and supporting the other. You were made fragments of love that I may combine you together into one beautiful whole, an intricate pattern woven by My hands into a rich tapestry of delights, a sampler of great beauty and intricacy where if only one thread is pulled away, the beauty of the whole picture is somewhat tarnished.

I am the Master Weaver, pulling together all those threads in a tight skein. As the tapestry unfolds, you will see more of My hand at work in life's colour and variety, its opportunities and peoples.

I love to create, to create life and love, for all power is given to Me by My Father. And as I create, I share My power with you ... to do your part for Me. That is why there are so many of you in all places, each to do your part for Me, in Me and through Me. Together we can make a place of great beauty. This was My Father's plan in place for all times and seasons, all peoples and places. Not one is excluded.

All are in My tapestry of life, My rich and beautiful tapestry. That is why you are given senses to use in Me. Use them wisely, creatively, longingly to share in My power of creation.

I call you Mine for that is what you are, dearly beloved children: alive in Me, brought to fulfilment by My life in you. Go now and believe in My Name, My power, My plan in you.

I Embrace Your Calling

13th January

Trust in Me, believe in Me and go forward from where you now are. I embrace your calling. In My Name you will succeed in My endeavours, walking in the truth which sets you free to grow, be, see yourself as I made you. My child, listen to the beat of My heart telling, guiding your principles. Claim these as your own for they will strengthen you for the fight of progress.

Address some of the wrongs in My world, those where I take you to be – My ambassador bringing alive those who slumber in ignorance. Curtail your interests only when I say so, indicate, for I have plans for you not of your making. For I see the whole picture: the beginning from the end; the fine weave in between; places, people not yet dreamed of. Have no fear; I will not send you where you are not to go.

I know the child I made for Me: your delights, your desires, your fears, your failures. My weakness is your strength for I give to you what is good for you and that which I intended. You will not be sent beyond your expectations or scope.

Rest in Me

14th January

Rest in Me to test your obedience. I want you still and reflective until you understand My truths of life.

Life is given that you may enjoy it. This does not involve being worn out by doing what you think you should do but rather resting in Me who knows all things until I give you your marching orders.

You cannot, will not, run anywhere on empty. But ground to a halt, you will see and understand My commands to simply be still in Me. There you will see, understand, far more than in the busy-ness of this world, however worthwhile that busy exuberance is. Yes, you may want to partake of it, but I am making you quietly reflective, introspective so you can grow in My awareness of your planned destiny.

... Remain at rest with Me. Rest is not laziness but rather a full recharge of quiet life given to prayer and praise. You'll amaze at what you can achieve.

Be Still and Know That I Am God

15th January

Rest in Me to be set free from the temptation to overload unnecessarily. Rest is replenishment lent, sent to restore aching hearts and minds, for it is there in the stillness you find Me. You cannot see Me easily in the crowd. I'm shrouded out by noise, clamour, distraction, the attraction of worldly goods you do not need. Heed My promise of rest's replenishment lent on a daily basis to restore.

More of Me becomes more of you when you are ready to receive by waiting, listening, looking, coming to know My truths. Set apart, this is easier, more fruitful, more eventful because you give it your closer attention to live out My calling of "faithful scribe."

The release of peace is, as you know, dependent upon obedience, and it is not for nothing that I say, "Be still and know that I am God."

I Need a Torchbearer

16th January

I will teach you how to pray. Remain in Me and Me in you. It is My light which will shine in the darkness of men's hearts, but I need a torchbearer. Go out to where I send you among the people. Go out and testify in My Name that they may know what to do, that they may know I am waiting for them, longing for them to return to Me. They are My children. I want them home with Me where they are safe in My house, in My care. You must pray with them and for them. I will show you who and how.

Believe in Me as I have in you. Allow Me to work in you by trusting in what I can do with you and through you. Yours is Mine to have and to use powerfully. With Me in you and you in Me we can reach the ends of the earth! My love is such that it knows no boundaries but reaches out far and wide to touch My people.

Let us give the message to the people we meet, those who need Me, so many of them, hungry and thirsty, starting with your own family. Help them to see that I am real, I am active. I don't take 'no' for an answer but keep searching for them. Allow them to come to Me in their own way and time. Just keep praying for their salvation, their recognition. I will do the rest.

Waiting - I

17th January

Waiting upon Me is important: waiting for My decision; waiting until you are made ready, have reached a level of understanding or endeavour, or the practice of the challenge of the moment; waiting for other effects and events to come together. Waiting is not a game. Waiting is a necessary, indeed essential, part of life. For looked at literally, life is one long wait!

What is the most important thing you wait for? The answer to that will show you what is the most important thing you yearn for. Is it Me, I wonder? Am I set above and beyond the power of all other attractions or distractions? Can you wait patiently until you understand more of My Ways – knowing, accepting that you will never understand all of them but waiting is part of the formation of maturity? It helps you to look, to learn, to discern, to ask questions and hopefully wait for the answers.

It may seem a long wait sometimes because My timing is not your timing: because time to Me is no barrier - it is a free element to move through backwards or forwards, or up or down. Like the time zones between countries and continents I can make one day of opportunity into tomorrow elsewhere, and yesterday's lost chances can become today's openings. It's all a matter of willingness, you see – willingness to be in My hands and wait for the chance of the better good. By chance I mean 'possibility presenting itself readily and timely'.

Waiting - II

18th January

So many prayers appear to go unanswered because of the time lapse. When it is long – the answer long-awaited – the person may even have forgotten the original intention. But I say to you, persevere persistently in prayer without growing tired of waiting. You know how long the wait is to perform the miraculous intricacy of building a baby and bringing to birth. It cannot be hurried; it is dangerous if delivered before time, for so much has to be set in place to make the child ready to survive and thrive in this world's environment.

It is just the same with prayer. I often – more often than not – have much to do to arrange, to rearrange, to accomplish, to prompt, even to persuade before great things can happen. Abundance comes by building up the supply through waiting, and abundance can bring forth many, manifold, even unsought-after blessings – joys not asked for but earned because of your persistence in prayer which trusted. Prayer is an urgent need in this world. Remember to ask My Spirit what to pray for. Let Him lead your thoughts and intercede on your behalf, for He knows what is in the depths of every soul, what needs uncovering or altering or making new or starting again. His work is exploratory and decisive. He is a decision-maker, taker of the right opportunities which present themselves not by random chance but by God's opportunities unfolding.

The Spirit is the holding power to get your timing right. You must be open to Him, remain alert to His prompting, calling, showing you what to do. This at times may even seem unlikely to the point of impossibility, but then you must go on trust that the peace of your heart is the green go-ahead light. If there is unease of any kind, stop, stand still, reflect and wait. Life is rarely so urgent that you have to act upon a decision in the moment. It can happen when unforeseen conflicts arise out of man's wilfulness, but even then it only takes a second to dart an arrow prayer seeking guidance; I will always reply promptly.

Waiting - III

19th January

You see, I am always ready, but I just wait to be asked. As with an invitation, asking necessitates and prompts a reply. Be expectant, cultivate the habit of expectancy and you will be amazed at what you see unfolding. Many an opportunity is blocked off, stopped or somewhat curtailed because someone somewhere did not ask and invite Me into the situation. I never come uninvited, but My Spirit is always circling close by waiting to hear the tiniest whisper of longing, even if made inaudibly in the heart. That is all it takes to start relationship growing, knowing each other, becoming closer, waiting for each other daily to communicate. I wait like you might wait – eagerly expectant, hopeful of a letter, an e-mail or a telephone call, for these things show you someone cares and is thinking about you. It is exactly the same for Me. I need to know you want to communicate with Me.

I do not mind how long I wait, although I sorrow for the lost opportunity of passing years where fears can sow all kinds of seeds of doubt. The longer you wait to get in touch with somebody, the harder it becomes. So don't delay, My children, My dear children. Don't wait until tomorrow.

It's never too late to find Me, but now, at this moment, is better than waiting because you have put up all sorts of barriers of resistance, restriction, rebellion or resentment. My Spirit can deal with any of them, all of them, the hotchpotch, if necessary. It is nothing for Him to sort out what to you is a complexity of chaos, but We do ask you to be patient and wait.

There may be much work to be done in readiness, in preparation for what is to follow, and you know how important firm foundations are. These do take time, energy, effort and endeavour, yours and Mine, to build. Be patient, My children – waiting, trusting, requiring the power of prayer. Prayer is where we share the wait together.

Waiting - IV

20th January

Remember how I had to wait in the garden of Gethsemane in an agony of fear, knowing what was to come about – waiting for the tramp of the soldiers' feet. What got Me through that longest night? Prayer, earnest prayer. So heartfelt it made beads of My blood trickle out of the waiting pain. You will not be called to go to those lengths, but remember My agony and see what the waiting accomplished and achieved.

Waiting is not passive; it is active, urgent, alive and of paramount importance. Never give up on waiting with hope. If My banner over you is to be love, love is patient and endures all things.

I send My Spirit to strengthen you as My right hand man or force, power; He becomes your inner force, or power, the bond between us. Call upon Him, wait for Him, then respond, My children. In responding He will release to you some of His energy, His power, so you will be enabled to achieve so much you will indeed be astonished.

You wait to grow from childhood to adulthood. You wait to grow from early faith, where you toddle in short steps, to the maturity of faith where you can confidently stride. And I wait longingly for you, My children. I wait like any loving parent for you to be My complete pride and joy.

Giving - I

21st January

I gave you everything. Spare what you can – generously, realistically. It is not really giving unless it costs you something. This might be time, effort, dedication, money, prayer or companionship, close calling of love.

When I said, "I love a generous giver," I had in mind that person who would really give of him or herself until it tangibly hurts in the effort and the effect. It is on the same line, in the same realm, as love, where it is said (and it is true) that 'there is no gain without pain'.

Pain can come in many forms. In a situation like this it may simply be seeing, feeling the pain of your inner self as you look at your own reluctance to give of what is asked of you. It may be the pain of having to make more effort in time and thought than you did formerly. It may be the pain of having to change your ways of thinking, planning, acting, deciding. It may be the pain, the discomfort, the unease of coming within the reach of being obedient to My Father for mankind does not easily nor readily give up his own wilfulness. Pain comes in many different shapes and forms, but it was every pain that ever was, that ever will be, that I took to the † of victory that you may be overcomers, winners in the race.

Generosity is a hallmark of My children, those who live within My family. I put you, My people, in families to love and support each other, for you know very well that no man nor woman is an island standing alone and afar. Anyone in that position is likely to be swamped by tidal waves of destruction, doubt or despair. Just as man cannot live by bread alone but must live by every word that comes from the mouth of God, so man cannot live in solitude satisfactorily. He/she will always need the help of others.

Help, if you look carefully, closely enough at the pattern of My weaving, is always reciprocal. No person gives and does not receive. No person receives without being able therefore to give a little more.

Giving - II

22nd January

Look each day at which way I am calling you to give at the moment. Listen to My voice calling. You will hear it in the stirring of your heart, the awakening of your mind, the informing of your conscience. There you will find Me seeking to speak to you. Learn to recognise My voice readily. Listen to what I have to say. Ask if you are unsure about anything. Listen again, wait if necessary, then act upon My instructions however unlikely, or maybe even impossible, these seem to be. This is where trust must be used to take you forward. Yet you need have no fear if at all times you are listening, looking for, expecting, praying for My guidance. Receive what I have to give you. It will always help you to be ready and prepared to give more of yourself.

It is one of the immutable laws of My kingdom, this balancing of give and take. I make you, My people, joint heirs, trustees, appointed to share generously, gladly, willingly, openly all the treasures of My storehouse. Do not stack this treasure up simply for yourselves lest the moths eat it away or it becomes buried, bound between cobwebs! Wealth – whether financial prosperity, radiant exuberant health, abundant time, energy or spectacular knowledge – is all for the glory of My people to share, compare, give out of, live out of.

See no man nor woman in want or need. Remember My teaching that if you have two coats you give one away. Now I ask you, if you had only one coat would you be prepared to give that off your very own back? Can you be that generous in giving? Only those who really live of My rule by My truth, through My way of understanding, will reach the highest point of generosity.

Giving - III

23rd January

Remember when you decide to give what I did and do for you. I gave My life for you to be here at all. Remember this. It will help you view things from a different angle upon a higher plane of perspective. Simply looking at Me and what I did can be corrective. It can charge you up like a battery empowered to work again or more effectively.

Hold on to My hand with one of yours, and with the other open it out wide as a gesture of giving love. My power will flow from Me through into you and out onto others. Thus I can reach many a needy soul with My love – whole force of hope – where I repair the careworn heart to start living joyfully again.

You are My ambassadors as often as you want to be for there is always a need, a dire necessity, for action: mankind's action in Me; mankind's reaction to Me; mankind's attraction through Me.

Listen children, it is important to understand this: love means giving. It is this love which makes the world go round. Found in Me, focussed upon Me, followed through by Me. You and Me and them become us, all of us together. We can live in a harmony of love – love in giving, fulfilling of Me. It is, you see, the only way forward in a wanting world.

Slow Down, Slow Down! - I

24th January

Slow down your mind, your pace, even your enthusiasm, or there is no room for Me to enter amidst the flurry and swirl of activity, even when that activity is God-centred. Do not be impatient with yourself.

All that is worthy and right in My Name will come to fruition in the time of My planning, the time of My choosing. Much has to be learnt on the way, therefore progress cannot be of supersonic speed. What is the hurry anyway? Why not savour fully each moment we spend together? Now is the time to enjoy, and we have an eternity ahead, you know! Rushing allows for pitfalls, mistakes, fatigue and overload.

"My burden is easy; My yoke is light." Have I not told you this before? It is when you act under your own steam, you run out of fuel. Remember to present everything to Me. That means each little section of work you do. How else are you going to get the order in right sequence, that which I intend, unless you ask Me? Too often My people stumble on regardless of My wishes, for they are so self-preoccupied with their own good ideas, they have forgotten to consult Me. "Listen to the Lord" was My instruction to you.

Do not worry. I hold all things in My hands, placing them (situations) together as carefully as you would place in a jigsaw piece. I see the whole completed picture and therefore know which part of any scheme to approach first or later. I put into place carefully, slowly, when all the component parts are ready.

Slow Down, Slow Down! - II

25th January

Slow down, slow down! Remember the tortoise who won the race? That was because he moved at a slow but sure, steady, unfailing pace – the speed that was right for him. If I want escalation, I can always provide it! Short cuts and circumvention are nothing to Me. But on the whole, I choose the calm, quiet, collected, slower path to walk with My people – time to gaze around with pleasure; time given for reflection and connection; time to simply be; time to grow, grow more knowledgeable, stronger in Me; time to reach understanding and resolve difficulties or dilemmas.

Remember that, after all, time is a manmade element. It has no significance in the spiritual world, where everything simply is. Past and future do not matter in that they become irrelevant. Live for the moment, the hour, the half day, the day, now as well as when you reach eternity. It will take much pressure off you. Instead of trying to control this, that and the other, simply be concerned about now and how you spend it. Leave the rest to Me.

Did I not teach you in the Gospels that each day has sufficient worries unto itself? Centuries have moved on, but still that truth applies.

Slow down your walk with Me, My child. Talk more to Me. I am always by your side ready to listen. Do not be surprised when I reveal to you more of the mysteries of the kingdom of heaven, when you are prepared to listen to Me.

Come alongside now; let us be joyful together! You were losing out but now are found once more. Rejoice and remember My words!

All the Way to Heaven is Heaven - I

26th January

Beautiful white, clean, bright and light, reflecting, connecting, the goodness of earth to the goodness of heaven, when souls are washed white by My living water, satisfying, nourishing, but more importantly cleansing and refreshing the very spirit and soul. I come as living water with all its properties to assuage your thirst, mankind's thirst for God's truth. Why will so many of you fail to be satisfied by Me, who is only too ready to pour Myself out for you, incessantly. My well of hope will never dry up for God has made it bottomless, feeding deep from His own wellsprings of desire for you, Our people. You will never be fulfilled nor satisfied until or unless you drink deeply of Us.

We have so much to offer the world. Why do you turn away, turn your backs on Us? We understand your timidity and sometime confusion but don't understand your selfish, belligerent arrogance which says, "I'm self-sufficient." How can anybody be self-sufficient? You are all interdependent and clearly in need of a Saviour – a Saviour from the sin you wrap yourselves in for all sorts of careless and wilful reasons and lack of responsibilities.

Come, My people, come and drink of Me to be refreshed, renewed, re-invigorated in the very depths of your soul, to your heart's content. This is what life is about, what life is for: for the seeking, finding, enjoying and relying upon Me. How else can you ever hope to reach the eternity of heaven's promise, the richest riches that await in store for you who believe?

All the Way to Heaven is Heaven - II

27th January

You can see so much in the world going wrong, even to the climate being upset, unpredictable in its seasons and unstable. Mankind is making it so by his own independence – a false god, a dangerous, foolish god as misleading as the ancient deities worshipped centuries before My arrival upon earth. Come to Me, My children, My dearly beloved children. The need – this need of you for Me, of Me for you – becomes more urgently pressing, imperative, day by day, night by night, moment by moment. The world is spinning, perilously unstable. If it spins off its axis because it did not seek and ask for My balance in all things, that will be the end of possibility – heaven lost forever. What an unbearable, unthinkable, unstoppable tragedy unless you who believe can turn the world on its head to view things differently, see Me and believe Me.

Why is this so hard for you when you see many a miracle taking place around you? Simply ascribe the miracle to Me and immediately the world will be, and will increasingly become, a different place, a place where My light of truth will shine in purity. Reclaim lost innocence. Reclaim lost growth. Reclaim all that has gone in My Name – a Name of unsurpassed beauty and power, a Name of almighty significance. For it makes you holy. It takes you to heaven. It connects mankind and God our Father as nothing else possibly can, nor ever did, nor ever will.

Come to Me, My lovely children, My most precious people, My longed for people, My power present upon earth. Come to Me and be entirely Mine in My trust and truth which transforms earth into heaven in the very here and now.

"All the way to heaven is heaven." I am telling you that with Me in charge, truly in charge, entirely in charge, that statement is a sound, secure, certain and prophetic truth. Earth can be, should be, and will be, if dwelt in Me, a place and glorious foretaste of heaven: heaven's beauty, mercy, charity and love; heaven's hope, horizons ever widening, extending, shining with the glory of God; a homecoming so welcome, so satisfying, so splendid in all aspects, your heart will sing and dance for joy.

All the Way to Heaven is Heaven - III

28th January

Apart from Me you will never achieve anything lasting or worthwhile in the eyes of heaven, and it is heaven which is your ultimate destiny – God's plan for man. Hold the prospect, the delight, the promise, the certainty of heaven in your heart in Me. It is where we will ever be together uninterruptedly. I look forwards to it; do you, My dearest children? Do you really believe in the promised possibility? Act as if you do, think as if you do, speak as if you do and you will come to believe it! Believe it in Me for I am the only One who can see this for you and tell you about it. Do not think, as mankind is inclined to do, that this is too good to be true – something like a child's fairytale or myth of man's imagining, desiring.

As I hold you, My people – dear in My heart, cherished and believed in, loved beyond anything you can yet know or imagine – you will come to see the reality, the absolute lasting reality of all (and I mean all) that My love has achieved for you. *Has* achieved. Won, once and for all, by My everlasting, resounding, total victory on the † – resounding through history, backwards and forwards into man's hearts and lives. I am your sure Saviour; your satisfaction; your safe journey, passage home to heaven where you belong; for we belong together in our Father's arms – wide open arms held open in love everlastingly. This is My truth, My people; My promise is your hope of heaven. My victory is your assurance of heaven.

All you have to do, need to do, is name Me 'Saviour' and claim this truth as your victory forevermore in Me. Me it is who sets you free now, in the very moment that you believe and continue without doubting. Questioning of Me is fine, doubting is not! Trusting is vital – as necessary as drawing in My very breath of life itself – trusting My life-saving, life-giving, life-promising truth; trusting in My availability at all times to come to you and help and guide and support. Caught up, held high in My arms of love I offer you absolute security of love – a love which withstands any blows, all assaults, many disappointments and hardships, even the terrors that stalk in the night.

All the Way to Heaven is Heaven - IV

29th January

My way is not an easy one, but it is My promised hope of heaven where you will be at perfect rest in peace, joy and sheer happiness eventually with Me, in Me and through Me. But in the meantime we can be (let us be, ensure that we are) always together in mind, willpower and purpose. It is indeed My truth that sees you completely free to be yourself in God's perfect plan for fulfilled security: heaven on earth your temporary home; heaven in heaven following on as your eternity, an everlasting place to be embraced – through love, for love, in love, in all perfect, promised love, the likes of which you do not yet know, but the joy of which awaits you, for you were made for this, God's certainty. Come now, My children. Believe Me; believe Me; believe Me!

I send you My Spirit to act as truth's guide and counsellor. His wisdom is supremely powerful, almighty in its workings and implication. Do not forget to call upon His mighty influence and strength. He connects Me to you and us to the Father.

It is in this trinity/unity of complete love, mercy and understanding that you will be held safe, safer than homes, for built in Us no storm nor attack will shake you. Built in Us you will grow strong as the mighty oak, tall as the cedars of Lebanon reaching up to heaven. Your roots will go deeper than the weeping willow, ever searching for life-giving water. Assuage your slaking thirst in the deep, deep underground swell of Our refreshing love. Dig down until you find it; then draw from it as much as you desire and need. It will never, it cannot ever, run dry upon you. We, the Godhead, nourish, restore, and fully replenish Our people, those who wish to draw from the wells of salvation – the deepest wellspring of hope and satisfaction that mankind can draw from, drawn from earthly existence into the sheer glory of heaven.

Until then, dearest children, hold Me and uphold Me in your heart. Love Me as I have loved you. Come to Me and be set free in Me. My freedom is to be free indeed: free to be yourself in Me and fully worship; free to bring Us full honour and praise; free to thank from the heart as well as the head; free once and for all times, all places, for all godly purposes in Me.

The Power of My Love - I

30th January

Trust Me, I am working on your behalf.

I transform your life as I take the power you give Me into My hands with free reign. It is all about trusting Me, believing Me and accepting I can do and I will do all that I promise. Keep claiming these promises in the power of My love, My mercy, My truth, My forgiveness, My understanding of your complete situation. I am there in the difficulties that you face holding your future safe in your hands when you accept Me fully, the full influence of My power of love transforming your outlook, your attitude, your opportunities, for these are the very openings I provide for you to hold onto securely.

Your safety lies in this: the reassurance of My love, My love given unequivocally, unreservedly, life-changingly, everlastingly in its power of influence. Let My influence reach far and wide for the goodness of others, those to whom I send you or give to you, those to whom I put you in contact with.

My Spirit is at work in you, empowering by My love to make My truth plainly, abundantly, reassuringly plain and evident. Those who will see – can see – can see Me and the effect of My love in you at work for them. This is My way of efficiency using one to reach another that they may too, in their turn, reach out in My love with ever widening circles of influence. Pray about this constantly that you might know (that you might recognise) where, to whom, you are to go in My Name of love.

Many a false footstep will fumble because I have not sent nor directed you there. It is not My purpose. You must obey My calling, falling in with My plan of holiness. My sovereign power is connected directly to My Father's influence of love. His omnipotence reigns supreme in heaven and earth. Be glad of this, joyfully glad. It is your firm assuredness, your secure and safe foundation of love made known upon earth to flourish in My Name.

The Power of My Love - II

31st January

Take all that I give you and transform it by My love into a share of My resurrected life, an everlasting life where My truth is made plainly evident to My people – My followers who genuinely seek Me from their heart and rely, rely entirely, upon My living word of truth. Celebrate this word amongst you by taking hold of it and naming it, claiming it as your own – sourced, shared, given, gifted by Me.

It is My Spirit who sets you free to respond. Call upon Him openly, regularly, freely coming to Him in My Name of love: love that wins hearts and minds and influences people; love that conquers all concerns; love that disperses the shadows of doubt so that they flee, never to return.

Love is the hallmark of My Kingdom established in God's truth. Love is My Father's mission and My permission for you to act. Love is the beginning of the matter, central to My truth. Love is the end of the matter, confirming My presence among you. Live with love, holy love. Give of My love. That means My truth, My constancy, My protection, My involvement, My promise of a better, sounder future because you trusted in My love. Love is the essence, the distilled essence, the perfume of My fragrance. It is indeed sweet and pleasing. It is to be savoured with delight for it is the aroma of life: My life within you, My Spirit at work to give glory to God.

The Father knows what you seek. He will allow you to discover the truth of life in Me when you pray regularly, consistently, conscientiously, with an open heart of love seeking My truth.

My truth is as firmly established as the ground you walk upon, as the heavens are high above the earth. My truth is paramount, universal and to be unreservedly accepted by My followers if they want to walk in My way. My way is the holiness of love: love given, offered to you, by the Trinity of life – changing, transforming your every opportunity by the power of love.

The Power of My Love - III

1st February

Holy love is to reign supreme. Holy love is to remain forever – pervading, invading mankind's stubborn resistance and evasiveness. Love permeates through all I do, think and say. Can you say the same? When you do, you are My disciples, My true disciples, follower of Me.

I call; you come! You come and respond through love, for love, with love, in love. Love is the very energy of My being. It is love you see when you are seeing Me at work. Share in this love. Compare its influence with what you have known, then imagine what you are about to know, realise, to establish, by this love.

My Spirit loves to come to dwell where love is. There He feels at home. He knows He is welcome for He can recognise His very own effectiveness and influence.

Stay connected, ever connected, to My love by My Spirit. There is no other way. He is My truth, the revelation of My Father at work here amongst you in Me.

The Spirit does indeed set you free, without doubt, My children of accepted love. This acceptance is vital. It is life-giving, life-transforming, fundamental. It is energy – pure energy – to those who tap into this holy source. For, of course, where love is, I am. And where I am, love is. Remember this; it is all you need to go by, live by, stand by.

The Power of My Love - IV

2nd February

The truth of My love is the firm assurance of God's influence, His power at work within you by My Spirit of love. Hold on to My love at all costs. Love caused Me to carry My †. Will you take up your † of love each day for Me? This is what I call you to do, each one of you. I reach out and touch you with love that you may reach out and radiate the influence of love, My life-transforming love. Herein lies the joy of mankind as you find you come fully alive to thrive in My love's influence. Be influenced; be transformed; be re-vitalised; be energised; be joyfully happy, glad in the power of My love. It is the truth of My existence, the very core, the centre of your being where I enter your 'becoming' – becoming holy in the power of My love.

Go now, My dearly beloved children; and live fully, live resolutely, live joyfully, glad in the power of My love. My love is that of the Father's, made real to appeal to you by My/Our Spirit. He is your holy influence. Turn to Him; yearn for Him; ask for Him; pray for Him; obey Him. He is My wisdom and truth – the truth of the Father made known in Me by the power of My love at work in you.

Do not shirk this responsibility which I honour you by. It is My calling to you, that you may live aright within Me, for Me, with Me. With Me you can change your world by love.

Love is the conqueror. My triumph of the † is established once and for all people with the energy – the amazing, the super-abundant energy – of My Father's loving mercy and truth. Heaven is connected to earth thereby. Earth is channelled to flourish when it recognises, proclaims and owns My power of love – a love which is unstoppable, mighty in its influence and profoundly far-reaching in its effects.

Love changes everything – the total, self-giving, committed, sacrificial, far-reaching love of the †: the † of holiness erected for all the world to see, to fall under the shadow, the bright shadow of the influence of My love stretching far and wide.

Nothing, no-one, is beyond the reach of this love – no dark corners of evil left when My love reigns supreme, when My love beams the brightness of heaven here upon earth for you, My dearly beloved children of love.

My Timing is My Timing

3rd February

Lean on Me. Lean on Me heavily.
You need My strength taking you where you cannot go alone.

The future is clear in My eyes.
Follow Me.

Come to Me and pray, and as you do
I will use you for My work which is planned,
That which I give you to do and no other.

Simply trust Me that things are happening, albeit slowly in your eyes.
My timing is My timing.

Look to Me, My faithfulness, for your encouragement.
This may not come in any other way.

Depend on Me, your source, your strength.
The outcome is Mine when you learn to do this.

Hand over day by day and let Me work in My way.
You will not be disappointed.

"Hold on to life and it will be your joy and crown eternally"[3]
– in Me!

3 From a hymn by J S B Mansell, 1811-75

Decisions - I

4th February

Your decisions must be My decisions for how else can you access and act in all wisdom and truth? Hand over to Me; hand over everything. That too must be your decision of obedient submission made, reinforced and enacted daily. Do, and I will bless you because you have then given Me the power to act. You have released God's sovereign power and authority into your life to take you forward. He will take you where you cannot possibly go alone. I will come with you. In fact, you take Me along with you as your right when you hand over to Me.

Salvation grants you several favours, and this is one of them, for by salvation you belong to Me and I belong to you. You are thereby granted certain rights and privileges which you can call upon. Call and I will answer. Ask and I will act – and to My Father's glory. It is to His glory that you live in Me.

Submit your decisions to Me. Let Me prioritise the order of events that will happen to heal the harm mankind has done by living alone, straying far from Me. My orphan children suffer much, but together we can call them back to My side where they will be safe.

I hold you secure to the extent that you want to be held. Hold Me at arm's length and I cannot do much. Reach out and touch even the hem of My garment, and you will be amazed at the miracles that happen – amazed, delighted and surprised! I am in the business of working wonders in My people, with My people, for My people.

Decisions - II

5th February

Will you work with Me, alongside Me? Then you have to be prepared to hand over the decisions, all of the decisions – your decisions given to Me, to transform them into My decisions for life.

"This is the way; walk in it," you have heard say. Now I say it to you today. Do not run ahead of Me nor drag your heels behind Me. You are free when you walk close alongside Me, moment by moment with the serious intention of pleasing Me. You please Me when you hand over the reins of authority to Me, when you admit your inadequacy before Me, when you submit to My will.

My decisions are always the best – for you and for others. I will not fail you in this if you trust Me. Trust is being able to hand over to Me without a doubt.

Yes, ask, "Lord, what do You want me to do?" I will tell you. I will answer. I will show you the way to go forward. There, of course, you will meet more decisions to make. Make them with Me and you will be free to serve God rejoicingly.

Come, My child, hand over the decisions to Me. This is important, an essential lesson for you to learn. You are doing well. Keep up the progress! I will take you forward.

Be Attentive - I

6th February

Be attentive to My voice. Heed My call wherever it comes, however it comes to you. It is a choice you must make to listen, for when you do unnumbered are the blessings, even to changing the path of your destiny.

You do not know what can be done until you listen to Me. Listen and trust. Trust and act, then listen some more, always listening out for Me. You will hear (you can only hear) if you listen with rapt attention, concentration, expecting to hear and being assured of My answer.

It is no surprise that My voice is heard in the stillness amidst the calm. That is when I do not have to demand your attention and your respect above the everyday clamour. You stammer out your requests, your longings to Me, but I speak clearly, plainly, unhesitatingly to those who listen, who care to have ears to hear. Why do you think God gave you two ears? Listening is important – essential in fact and most life-giving to your soul, your body and your spirit.

To hear Me and act upon it is mental wellbeing, My nourishment offered to be received. You deceive yourself when you do not listen to Me but to other competing voices with their feet on the earth. Look up and listen. Look high and attend. Then I can send you where I want you to go and do all I want you to do.

Be Attentive - II

7th February

You must listen to receive My strength and encouragement as well as My instructions. Listen and wait on Me. Wait on My word before you move forward, for there is often – more often than not – much to be done in preparation. Listening is a 'making ready' time, a 'getting ready' time for My commission.

It is when you have listened, after you have listened, you receive My permission to act. I act through you to the extent of your capacity to listen, submit to My authority and obey. Obey not out of some useful submission but out of a grateful heart, glad with the knowledge of My word. Can you afford to miss this grace? I think not! Certainly not if we are going to do much – or indeed any – effective work together.

When in doubt, ask of Me, then wait for the reply. The waiting is patience-building. This building is faith building in expectancy. We move on when you are ready, simply because you listened to Me. Surely you know, you realise that by now? But it is so important, so vital to the wellbeing of your life and others – those, all those, to whom I send you. You must listen to My word of instruction and inspiration.

I breathe wellbeing into your soul with My breath of life – My breath breathed upon you by My words given. Call upon the Spirit often. He is My Spirit of Truth and will not fail you. Ask Him what to do, and you can rely upon the answer. It is the grace of God and is gifted to all those who listen in Me, through Me.

I take you forward, My child, on in faith to exciting realms where you would not dare to venture alone. I will be with you. Walk with Me always. Talk with Me always, and listen to the reply. It is health to your bones and vigour to your spirit.

What more do you want to recommend listening? Have I not told you, asked you to listen to Me? Then do it more regularly, more willingly, more consistently. Do not fail Me in this. It is important.

Obey - I

8th February

Obey. You must obey Me to do better in God's eyes for there is no other way than this; this is My way of submission. As I give you permission to ask in My Name, I grant you the strength, the resolve, the determination to obey that I may work in you, with you and through you – through all you do as and when you learn to listen and obey Me. You are doing better and I commend you, but yes, there is room for improvement. Always room for improvement!

Call upon My Spirit's help and guidance continually. He is not only your strengthening; He is your direction, showing you where you must go and all you must do to please Me.

To please Me is to glorify Me. To glorify Me is to delight our Father. It is all about submission to My way of thinking, being, doing, acting, so you do not err and stray from the truth. The truth of My love should overpower your own selfish tendencies to go your own way solo. That is not My way.

I was always fully dependent upon My Father, upon His grace leading Me on, forwards. It is exactly the same for you, and this (this submission) must shine through all you do. It really is simple to apprehend.

Just ask Me, "Is this what You want, Lord? Is this the way to go?" Ask Me and I will tell you. I will show you by opportunities opening up, new understanding given, fresh insight into My Word.

Are you still listening? Then be ready to respond to My every bidding. Listening without action is futile. Better to have remained in ignorance where there is some innocence. In listening you take on a great responsibility to reply and respond to the best, the very best, of your everyday ability.

Life is about progress, progress in holiness in Me and through Me in all we do together. There is no other way you can go.

You have to listen and obey. Obey Me. It is My Spirit at work in the world bidding you to do My Father's bidding. He can only work with those who reply and comply to My will. All else is futile and will eventually be seen as such.

Obey - II

9th February

Rely upon the touch of My hand, for it is the Father's truth given to you that you might freely live from doubt and fear. Let Me draw near to you in your submission – in your permission to hand over your life – and let Me act. I will take you where you have not been before once you are made ready in this way, ready to obey. Can you not see how important this is, how vitally, essentially important?

He or she who has the Spirit has life – My life in them to begin again to walk in our Father's truth, that very truth of life which will overcome manmade strife and conflict.

You need to obey, each in your own way of submission. Pray about this and give Me permission to act now. Do not delay; it may be too late. The present is all you have. Remember this! It is important to realise that not too soon is the day to respond. Do not delay; I say again, do not delay!

Obey Me and grow. Obey Me and show to the world, My aching world, what a difference your obedience has made. I take you forward in Me when you are ready to do this, to really do this from the heart without hesitation.

Yes, you will still make some mistakes. But come to Me openly, admit and submit further to the truth of My teaching reaching into your innermost parts. It is the heart of the matter of the growth in holiness.

No submission, no growth. Do you see how important this is, that I emphasise it?

Go now and remember all I have said. It is your message for today: *obey*!

Submit - I

10th February

Submit to My authority. It's part of the obedience I talked about, an essential component part upon which so much depends. Without this the workings are not smooth, the workings of My way falter and grind to a sudden halt. Oil the wheel of the machinery by obedient submission. I cannot stress to you how important this is, how vitally important.

Why do you think over the centuries people have erred and strayed from My path? Not like lost sheep without a shepherd but because they did not obey the shepherd of their souls. They did not listen, did not obey, did not submit. Are you ready to commit to Me? If you want to submit, you have to commit unreservedly for this is the way I work.

Did you not see My complete submission to My Father's will? It is the same for you. It is no good asking in My Name unless you do – are willing to do – all I tell you to and ask you to.

Follow Me, always Me. It is the best way to go to meet with success in holiness for this is your gift from our Father of grace. He reaches out to you in Me, in what I say, in what I do, in all I ask you to do in My Name – My Name, ever the same Name of authority: a divine, holy, sacred authority given to no other. Yet I let you share this Name in all its power when you submit to My calling and admit all My power into your life.

Submit - II

11th February

The power of My Spirit is alive and active, very active in those who heed Me and obey. Do you want to do this? Then ask the Spirit; invite Him into the situation, every situation, you face. When you do this we can embrace life together – you in Me, in Him, compliant and obedient to the nth degree. Your prosperity and wellbeing and those who depend upon you for prayer is dependent upon this fact.

Submission is a must. It is a part of trust, and you know how you must trust Me, how you are called upon to trust Me. Have I not yet proved to you what trust can do? All trust can do? This is My blessing to you: when you trust Me, good things happen – godly, holy things happen in My Name. Go forward, My child. Be held by Me because you have been set free to trust, and in that trust submit.

Admit Me into your every day in the way that only you can, each one of you individually. You must take the responsibility for this. It is your choice to submit or not. Even God is powerless to act at times when you will not comply. Have I made this clear to you, plainly clear? Look at the evidence and you will see the truth of all I am saying. And if in doubt, ask Me to explain this further to you. I will!

Pray - I

12th February

Believe Me; receive Me. Believe Me, receive Me and go forward in My way for it is the way of truth. There is no other way to go if you are to gain satisfaction and My pleasure. My way is My Father's way of bidding for the world, the entire world. Yet My people have gone their own wilful way, arrogant in the pride of their seeking, thinking they need Me no longer, thinking their way is better. Who are they to say this? Why do they not return to Me, seeing the error of their ways, the calamity surrounding you? Faith is slipping and keeling over, all because you have lost sight of Me.

Come, My people, and pray to Me. Pray regularly, pray consistently, pray fervently with belief in My goodness, My grace. You never know what you will receive until you ask of Me. Your task is still to ask for more of My grace, for My intervention. My intention is to love you into being – being whole in Me, whole and holy. Do you not understand this? Or do you want to ignore it, for it is too much trouble, time and effort to follow? Where are you going? Where is life leading you? If not to Me, where to? Why do you dally and delay? Why do you not obey My Word spoken plainly enough? Is the stuff of the everyday really more important than your eternal destiny, the destiny of the entire of mankind? It is My truth which sets you free to be in Me, to live in Me, to give of Me. This is My offer to you. Will you not now accept?

My children, already too much time has been lost. Come now, make amends. Bow before Me and pray that I may intervene in your world of problems. No problem is too big, neither is it too complex for God. But You must trust Him to act in accordance with His nature of holiness. When all is not righteous in My Father's eyes, He will avert His gaze until someone prays and invites Him in to begin His redeeming, healing work. Can you not understand this? And if you do, why do you not do as I command and wish? The benefit is yours – far, far beyond anything, all you can imagine. Come, My children, come to Me and pray. There is no other way to access My Father's favour.

Favour is built upon the prayers of My people, My faithful, faith-filled people. Are you one such? Then pray and pray some more. What is in store you will then see! Go down on bended knee; reverently kneel and pray earnestly, seriously, contemplating the outcome as Mine – a better outcome than you can ever imagine, all because you prayed. Remember this. It is important, vital for you to know and act upon.

Pray - II

13th February

I take you where I want you to go, where I call you to go, only as and when you pray. Pray, My people, pray to Me, pray through Me, pray with Me, but pray! Pray today. There is no time to lose. Use the time you have in the very best way possible. Pray. Pray and obey My call to come to My Father. There is no other way forward, neither is there any other way back to heal the hurts, the wrongs of the past.

Forgiveness comes through praying. Healing comes through praying. Praying is essential. If it is the only thing you do, do not neglect to pray. Today is not too soon and no time is too late to pray. Pray. This is urgent, imperative!

I am asking you to pray to ignite the fire of faith once more. Come, My people, pray for Me to act now. Pray for Me to come into your world with My redeeming power of love. Pray and ask. Ask and believe. Believe and receive of Me, all because you took the time to pray to Me. Come My people pray now before it is too late.

Time hurries on mercilessly. You must pray to save the situation in your world. Person by person you must pray. Obey Me and live, forget Me and die. Death is the obliteration of our relationship because you did not pray. Do not fail Me. I am asking you this.

A new kiss of life comes through prayer. Prayer is the repairer of broken, fractured lives. As I offer you My prayer, will you offer Me yours? Come, My children and pray now as never before, praying earnestly to seek the Father's will in all things and bring about healing to your broken, falling, hurting world in its agony.

Time and trouble wait for no man, but prayer stops, stems the tide of calamity. Go down on bended knee and worship in praise. Worship and give thanks to the great God of grace, your Father in heaven, active upon earth in Me.

I came to set you free. Will you not believe this? Will you not receive this My offer of life? I came to overcome manmade strife. Believe Me. Receive Me. Pray to Me. Pray and obey Me, My children. Much, much depends upon this. Come now, and pray.

Come into the Silence - I

14th February

Silence, silence. I come in the silence, but are you really ready to be still and silent before Me, tranquil in spirit, resting in My Spirit? For this is how I come to you most readily, more easily, not vying for your attention.

I do not like to cut across the everyday busyness but ask you to trust Me that I may work through you in the time you give to Me – that time willingly, readily set apart that we may be together uninterruptedly. Is anything more important than this? If not, why do you not devote your time and attention readily in this way?

Why do you always want to be about your own agenda instead of letting my Spirit speak to you? He speaks in the silence of calm for that is where you give Him your full attention and honour. Silence is golden because of this.

When I went to the ✝ a silence fell upon the world of My people – initially the silence of shock, then of suspense, then of waiting in expectation to see what would happen. Silence is in the awaiting, the not doing, the waiting for My clear directive to go forward. They waited to listen for My coming. In your silence you too must await My coming that I may speak to you of My plans and purpose.

Unless you align My will with yours how can you hope to see the glory of God? The glory of God is My people given over to Me, trusting that they may follow where I lead. Leading comes when you let Me speak to you in the silent calm of a listening, trusting, ready-to-be-obedient heart. This is the start of something good for God – something very good indeed if you heed My Spirit's call to fall under my Spirit's influence unreservedly. That is why I say to hand over every day to Me that you may meet the day under My instruction.

Let your conscience guide you, directed by the Spirit's influence because you listened to Him. You cannot hear (or cannot hear easily enough) amidst the clamour. The glamour of the world is noisy and strident – bidding you, calling you away from Me. But I ask you to obey the call to silence that you may hear Me. Draw near to Me in that sought-after silence and I will draw near to you. Let Me appear in the calm of our wanting to be together, you ready to receive My strengthening support.

Come into the Silence - II

15th February

Caught up in My arms is caught up in the love of the Father. Would you rather not be here than anywhere else in the world? Then switch off the distractions, the false attractions, the clamour of hubbub. Do not let noise interfere and crowd out My presence. Seek the stillness within and begin to talk to Me about the everyday life.

I came to overcome all manner of strife, and much of the world's current strife is in the bombardment of all that is happening. Do you need to be involved in this? Did I ask you to?

Often simply a prayer is sufficient to send a circumstance on its way and let it go, let it get away from you. I know what I want you to do. You do not unless you listen to the beat of My heart, closely in tune with yours. A heartbeat is heard in the silence of concentration and application. Will you apply yourself, My child, to seeking Me, My word heard amidst tranquillity?

My ability to speak to you is given in your response to your inclination to listen and learn. Do not give up on this if you find it difficult. Cultivate the attention of a small child utterly absorbed in what he or she is doing.

Give Me, grant Me, your rapt attention for there is no better way – indeed, really no other way – for us to progress together. Ask of Me, then listen in the silence of your heart, your heart given over to concentrating on Me. Listen for My answer and act upon it.

Yes, you are an empty vessel waiting to be filled by Me only when you cease to be busy in a noisy world. "Will anything get done?" you ask, you wonder. All that needs to be done needs to be done only in My time, in My way, because you did obey what I asked of you. Then you will see the result, the godly result – only then.

Come into the Silence - III

16th February

Listen to Me, My child. Listen before you act. Stop and pray and listen, then look at what is opening up in your heart, upon your mind overriding in your conscience.

I gave you feelings that you may be alerted to My intentions. I gave you ideas that you may access My intentions. But you must stay in touch if much is to be done at all.

I gave you a disciple's ear to listen to Me, not to the call and clamour of a strident and intrusive world. When I said, "My peace I give you," a part of this was the gift of My peace to enable you to sit still and listen with concentration and learn from Me. Yearn for more of this peace in your life, the joy of My presence, and you will not be disappointed.

Come to Me, My child, come in the silence where much will happen with Me, through Me, because you allowed it to. Will you do this for Me? Will you do this willingly? Obedience is a hallmark of My disciples.

Come, My child. You can come without words; simply sit in the Spirit of My presence where you belong. I long to do a greater work herein. Will you let Me? Will you let Me set you free from the clamour of the world's demands by doing only what I ask you to? That will be sufficient for each day.

Come into the Silence - IV

17th February

Obey Me, My child. Obey Me and you will flourish. I nourish you in the silence, the silent peace of our being together, the release of the world's tension. Devote your attention to Me that I may set you free from the turmoil of the intrusive noise that comes from the world's competing ways. The world is always competing for your attention.

Step aside, turn your back and look at Me. Just as I went into the silence set apart in the Garden of Gethsemane that I might pray to obey My Father's will, so must you step aside from all that is happening around you. Can you not see how I needed to do this to prepare for the most important moment of My life?

Your life is made up of significant moments of immense potential, but you must listen and pray, watch and pray, that you may hear My call to serve in the way I ask and want you to.

The task for now, and indeed every day, is to move into that silent place where we can be together without interruption that I may speak to you. Listen and learn whilst you are there, then go out strengthened, empowered and invigorated, knowing what you should do for Me.

Seek Me in the silence. Speak to Me in the silence. Listen to Me in the silence, and I will honour you. I will honour your efforts, your application, your dedication. I will come to you, My child. Will you come to Me and be set free in the silence? This I ask of you that we may move forwards together wherever I want to send you.

Do not fear; simply believe and receive all I want to give you, all I have in store for you – it is from the store of My Father's goodness and grace. Do you want more and yet more of this? Then come into the silence.

Waiting Time - I

18th February

Grace comes in the waiting time, believing all will be well in My plan and purpose for you. Waiting is necessary because there is much to do, much to get ready. You must be prepared to be diligent, steadfast in your service of Me. I test your resolve in the waiting time, sincerity measured thereby.

If you trust Me you will wait accordingly, patiently believing the best (which is always *My* best) is coming to you through My work in you. For you to serve Me deserves much preparation time, building you up in a sound faith where I find no shade of doubt nor shadow of turning away from Me. It is as you walk close by My side the future unfolds in a straighter path.

Is there anything you have not done which you should be doing? Anything I have asked you to do to fulfil as an obligation? I look for dedication of intention, yes, but effort and application as well. Look again at what I have asked you to do, called you to do.

Obedience is My permission to move things forwards, sometimes onto a fast track, other times more slowly, for the route is circuitous. But I know what I intend, and when I send you out in My Name you must be properly prepared – prepared for disappointment, not being downcast, but confident in the faith of My promises, not being disrupted by error but being prepared to re-evaluate the way forward. Grace is given in great measure, greater measure when you face the future forward – expecting, praying for, asking, and of course thanking in anticipation.

Waiting Time - II

19th February

Did I not see the glory of God in what I would be doing? That is what must be your directive – always the glory of God in your best efforts and endeavours – then you can leave the rest to Me knowing the result will be good!

I would rather we took time, careful time, in doing this than establishing the building with shaky foundations. The recommendation is prayer – that prayer we share together by My Spirit. Let Him do the leading, interceding for you in the way you know not how. Then believe – and again I say, *believe* – in all that I am doing through you. The result will be good indeed!

Trust Me, My child, and act upon all that I say. You must obey Me more fully, for anything you lack I can make up for. Much is in store of My Father's goodness, His glorious riches in abundance.

Yours is the task to wait, to watch, to wonder, to pray, to seek My will that you may be still more ready to receive of the Father's best blessings. He who knows what He wants to do in you, through you, can only or will only do this when you make ready.

Make this your preparation time with dedication, serious dedication to all I have asked you to do.

Pray and Obey - I

20th February

Give Me the time – time to develop you in My way that you may obey in all things trustingly. Be ever ready for Me to work in you, through My Spirit alive in you when you ask Him to come in to fill you regularly. Empty out of self and be filled with Him; then you begin to live in My way.

'Ready to obey at all times' is a demanding task but one I ask of you. You can only do what it is – all it is – I ask you to when you are ready to obey in this way.

To be Spirit-led is to be fed on wisdom and truth leading to holiness. There is no other way than My way, My Spirit's way, My promised Spirit to those who obey Me.

Go on bended knee regularly in your submission. This grants Me permission to act in you and for you. You do not know what you can do until you pray to Me fervently in this way. Submission is My permission to take you forward, to move you forward to where I want to place you for My purpose.

God's plan is found in Me. Can you see that? And if you see it, do you agree with it? And if you agree with it, will you not act upon it entirely obediently? There is no other way than this, to give Me permission by your invitation – an invitation to change you as needs changing, a slow and arduous process but all the more beneficial for that.

Yes, it is 'slow and steady wins the race' when you embrace My teaching, all that I say to you, that you may obey it. Pray wholeheartedly to do this. Pray today, then pray some more.

Pray and Obey - II

21st February

Faith is caught up in the daily battle to win over self. Only prayer is the answer. Pray in Me, pray to Me, pray through Me asking for My Spirit's guiding. His direction and support is essential. Caught up in Him you begin a new understanding.

Let that understanding be your commanding because it is My teaching reaching into the depths of your soul. In the depths, at the heart, is where My Spirit resides. Do not hide from Him for He is life – *My* life – within you, within all you do if you allow this to be the case. Embrace My words of life and live life in all the fullness of My Father's grace. To embrace life fully is always to embrace Me trustingly and obediently. There is no other way.

My commands are given for a very good purpose indeed. You need these, for without them you are lost in a wilderness of your own making. Taking My way, My route through life, is beneficial for it is blessed by holiness, My Father's favour. Will you endeavour to walk this way day by regular day? Will you obey Me in all things? Will you allow Me to bring you My best in everything?

Then pray, My child; pray to be obedient, submissive to My call. Fall in with My plan, began before time, that mankind should live to give glory to God, always full glory. Make this your life's story of endeavour and accomplishment, perseverance and effort of dedication. Veneration is a life lived in a way most holy, day by blessed day.

Pray and obey. Obey and pray more; then you will see the glory God has in store in all you do for Me, through Me – My Spirit effective in you. Will you do this for Me? Will you obey?

Pray, My child, pray. Listen to Me, look at Me, learn from Me that you may be all I ask you to be. Be like Me. Pray and obey; obey and pray. It is to the glory of God that you did.

Love and Laughter - I

22nd February

I have told you that peace in your heart is the marker. Put your heart so close to Mine the heartbeat is as one timing, beating together securely, firmly; then you cannot go wrong. I will take care of all other arrangements.

It is important to Me that we be together as close, as much, as uninterruptedly as possible. It is there where I can do My greatest work of transformation when you dedicate yourself, yourselves, to Me, trusting I have all arrangements, everybody's understanding in hand. You do your part and I will do Mine. I can iron out problems in an instant. Can you yet recognise the heaviness – even slight heaviness – in your heart which is a no-go signal? Learn to recognise this and you will not go far wrong.

My children, belong to Me in the realm of peace, growing, reaching forwards, knowing perfect peace – the peace of decisions made in trusting Me, reaching out to Me unceasingly.

Continually you are asked to, called to, trust. This must take shape in many forms to provide the lessons in life. You have to – need to – learn to move forward. It can be difficult for you when it means apparently going against your innermost wish, desire, or feeling of obligation, dedication to a cause or person. But you must realise that I see all things, the far greater picture, and hold the benefits in My hand.

Love and Laughter - II

23rd February

Your growth is to be straight, upright and rapid given the right conditions. This means listening, trusting, obeying, thanking, disciplining yourself to act accordingly. No, it won't always be easy, for man is a pleasure-seeker, but I bring joy of a far deeper, more meaningful, lasting kind. My type of joy tastes of the fulfilment of heaven calling you forward, forming you to be ready to receive your full measure of joy when the time is right.

Be bright, My child, be cheerful with the decision you make. Remember the message that love and laughter go a long way together. You love, I provide the laughter, as well as My deep abiding, resounding, everlasting love for you, for all My children. I long to share this with them when they are ready to receive of Me. Ask to receive – and receiving, believe, that you may go on your way rejoicing.

Be Not Too Busy

24th February

Trust in Me to tell you My will. Do not doubt Me nor My calling. Allow My power to flow through you to others. Be My disciple. You are called to work for Me ... Take heart from My presence in your lives. As you know Me more and more so I can then tell you of My plans for good, all the things I want you to do. Allow Me to work in you and through you, sustaining you and teaching you in My ways.

Keep trying to hear Me that I may speak to you and you know it. Tune in to Me with a thoughtful heart that reflects. Be not too busy. Still the mind to My Spirit. He is at work and works better when you are refreshed. You know that yourselves. It is important. Take notice of what I tell you. I have been telling you this for a long time. Do not lose Me amidst the clamour of everyday things. Set aside time that we might be together. I come to you often but you do not always know it because your minds are elsewhere.

Step back and look aside, and there you will find Me waiting: waiting to help and hold you; waiting to guide, comfort and reassure; waiting to lift you high in triumph and expectancy. Remember, nothing can really separate us except your own wilful sinning. I stand ready at your side, ready at all times, ready in all ways to offer you My presence. You only have to ask. You only have to call upon Me and I am there. Fear not your own worth. I can use you if you let Me. I can make you Mine in any way you allow Me to. I can transform your doubts and set you singing!

Love Me, My child, as I have loved you. Share with Me as I have shared with you. Come to My banqueting table and be My guest! I died that you might be fed the bread of life. You will be fed and fortified, built up in My strength and knowledge.

I come to you in the way you… need Me. You do receive Me, hear Me. Do not doubt, and your own weakness I make Mine. I take them and use them for My glory that others will know that I live.

Give Me a part of each day, that is all I ask of you – a part that may be set aside so we come to know each other better. I know you through and through, but you do not yet know Me thoroughly. I would like you to. Spend time alongside of Me and alone with Me, that I may come to you and teach you…

You Cannot do Everything

25th February

To learn more of Me, My will for you. Still your restless mind that you can focus in on Me. Let Me take control of the everyday things. Hand them over to Me to govern. I will send the help you need to release you from the bondage of work, so much to do.

You need to be with Me more, be alongside Me listening and learning of My will and special purpose, My plan for you ... How can you learn of it if you do not ask Me constantly, daily?

You get lost in the fog of time delay – the gap between listening, learning, acting, implementing. You do not try hard enough to practise what I preach for you cannot remember it all, cannot take it on board, when you are so busy.

Good intentions are not enough, not sufficient. You must give way to My knowledge, your understanding of Me. You must act on My behalf only where and when I show you. You cannot do everything, try though you might, laudable though your intentions may be.

I have specific work for you ... which you must learn of. You must allow Me to speak to you every day by setting time aside. Drop the inessentials. I will gladden your heart and mind as you see My plans coming to pass, to fruition. It will involve those who need Me, to whom I will send you ... Their needs will be various but will be met by you working in Me, through Me, with Me. Together we can be a great team of good works completed.

I come unto you that you draw strength from Me and My Father – our Father – as together we pray to Him. I have promised you, "I pray not only for these… but also for those who through their teaching will come to believe in Me."[4]

---

4 Based on John 17:20

Come Alive in Me

26th February

You are safe with Me, and I long for your return into My arms of love. Where have you been? I have missed you!

Come unto Me all you who are heavy laboured and I will give you rest.[5] Toil not in vain. Let the striving cease.

Be alongside of Me today in your heart, in your mind. My will, not your will. The image of a living God must come into you – a living God who breathes life into your very being. Come alive in Me.

Run the race in My strength. Keep trying. I know it is not easy but I am there always, ready for you. Handle not My enemies lest they distract you, pull you away from Me. I am the One that matters even unto the end of time. In Me you will find no turning, no shadow.

Rest in My peace where you belong… As you love each other you love Me, for I formed you for this that you may give witness to the great power of My love: power over life and death; power over doubt and indecision.

Look, as this new day is dawning in your lives, I stand ready and waiting for you. As you seek Me, you will find Me. I do not hide away from you, only wait patiently, watching your every move lest you tumble!

Be not afraid for I go before you. Come, follow Me. As I walk the path of life, you must come where I beckon and call. Look to Me and you will see the way to go, the path of My will for you…alone.

Remember, I am your God who knows everything. Much joy will I give you as you serve Me, much joy, for you will know that this is what I intended.

---

5 Based on Matthew 11:28

Keep Serving - I

27th February

Trust Me to use you although you fail in My expectations. I will not abandon you. Look outward to Me at all times. Bring Me your pain, your troubles, your doubts. "Fear not, do not be afraid, for I have redeemed you. You are Mine. When you walk through the waters I'll be with you."[6] I will not leave your side.

It is only you who cannot see Me, in your sinfulness and sorrow. But I am there, as true as ever, ready and waiting for you, longing for you to know Me more.

Acclaim My greatness, your saving power, that you might use it. Look forward to Me with a glad heart, to being with Me out of your humility and pride, outside of it. For in My kingdom things are different to what you have ever known; you see but a little now, but the great things of heaven are a joy to behold. In majesty and glory they came to Me, resplendent in My victory, wearing My crown of joy. This will be yours too. Be patient and keep longing for Me in your life – Me and My angels that surround and protect you and yours.

For this I call you into being in My service, a catalyst for change of heart in many as they see Me in you and what you do. My child, I am yours; be Mine today and each day, one in accord with our Father, under the Spirit who gives us life and wholeness of unity, that binding force of love.

Go out now and serve as you are called, acknowledging Me in all things, giving witness and testimony and teaching, just as I have asked you to do…

Do not doubt yourself and your frailties for those can be strengthened and put to My good use. Leave that to Me.

Simply be there when I need you – open to Me at all times; vigilant and listening; looking for Me and My hand at work. Comply with Me that I may use you most wonderfully.

---

6 Based on Isaiah 43:1-2

Keep Serving - II

28th February

Keep asking so I may know what you need and want.

Keep serving that I may use you aright, afresh.

Keep searching that you will find even greater jewels and nuggets of wisdom.

Keep with Me, your guardian and guide, that you may be held safe.

Keep strong in My knowledge and My working with you.

Keep abreast of My plans for you. Do not neglect Me.

Keep steadfast in all that you do and say, believing in the truth – My truth – and knowing that truth, imparting it to others, especially to those that matter to you.

Keep true to your calling of witness to Me.

Keep allowing Me to lead you on – onwards, upwards, beyond all that you had ever imagined or dreamed of Me.

Keep simple in thought and direction, for My ways are not difficult to find, only harder to serve unless you let Me use you anew each day.

Keep looking ahead at Me, glancing neither to right nor left but keeping Me at the centre as your focus.

Keep coming to Me with your sorrows and doubts so you may talk to Me and tell Me how you feel. I share your burdens and sorrows. I am there for your fears and frustrations.

Keep allowing Me to minister to you in your needs for I am with you always, each minute of day and night.

Keep learning of Me. My commandments are not difficult for they are clearly laid out, but for you to find the strength on your own is impossible. Use Me. Use My Spirit of love and fortitude. My strength is given to you to serve you as you need it. Use it. Thank Me for it, then take it and make it as your own.

Keep alongside Me, My child, holding My hand in yours that I may guide you every step of the way, not allowing you to falter, nor stumble or fall, but holding you upright, your head held high in knowledge of Me.

Keep believing all that I have told you and instructing others as best you can. As you come to know and understand, pass it on that they too might know Me and of My profound and total love for them, for all mankind. They need to be told, to be shown.

I am Everywhere

29th February

Comfort ye My people.[7] Take Me to them in their need ... Administer My love, My salvation to those in want where I will send you. Heaven-sent, you will be on a mission: My work to unfold in the midst of many.

Do not be afraid for I am with you like I said I would be. Simply lift your eyes to Me in expectant hope and trust, allowing Me to do the rest, allowing My Spirit to work in you all.

Lay hands on each other to receive an anointing of grace, an infilling. I have told you this that you may act wisely.

You will need My strength, My fortitude, as you meet many who doubt or deny. Claim My promises for them and watch things happen in My Name.

Together we are powerful – in accord, with love, with and through our Father's Spirit. Acknowledge Him and His saving grace, His power of strength. Be like unto Him as you strive. Do not attempt things under your own power but only after seeking His will and learning of His way.

I can teach you if only you turn to Me and listen. Be not afraid when I am silent. Simply wait. It is in the waiting that you are moulded and prepared to be patient, taught to seek Me continually. Sit at My feet and learn of Me, My will for you all, My desire. Do not go in the wrong direction.

Pray at all times and in earnest. I cannot help you unless you pray to Me for you are My child, My children, in whom I put My trust and allow, will allow, ever greater measure of freedom to act in My Name when you are ready.

Be pleasing to Me, to each other, for I have served you. Now you must serve Me in gladness and readiness of heart and mind.

My love is omnipresent, pervading the very air you breathe, the ground you walk on, the people you meet. As I am everywhere, focus on Me continually that I may use you readily.

---

7 Based on Isaiah 40:1

Surrender

1st March

Come out, come out from the shadowland, your hand in Mine, held tightly. You have no need to fear for I can see the way ahead; it does appear clearly.

You only have to be like the little child – meek, mild and willing to be led. Would I ever harm you, or do ill to you? No, of course it is impossible! My love for you remains boundless as the ocean's depths, as high as the starlit-domed heavens, as wide as the earth's fartherstmost shores. You are My cause for being here at all. Fall into My arms, My child, and rest secure.

I implore you to trust. You must start to walk and talk with Me again; then when we two are as one bound together, forever we can rely each upon the other. Another determination can take you far, to discover, uncover new horizons of heaven's hope – your hurts smoothed out, your doubts forgotten, your fears dealt with, your uncertainties banished, vanished (all of them) by the light of My being there – for you to cry out My love and mercy.

My deep peace is no forlorn dream, nor careworn hope, but well within the scope of My wish, My desire, to send you happiness of the deepest kind. "My peace I give you"[8] was My promise and still remains true.

As you behold Me, let your arms enfold Me. You will hear My heart beating in truth, trying to time its rhythm with yours. Stand firm, My child, head held higher. My love for you is as the noonday sun: strong, intense and all consuming.

Dream on, sweet dreamers, of love to come. Yes, the best still lies ahead in My every blessing to be brought upon you…

---

8 John 14:27

All That I Have Is Yours

2nd March

My children, stand by My side, that together we may work powerfully about our Father's business. He gave Me to you that you might use My strength to His glory and praise. Behold I come to you now, to embrace you in My love, to fill you with My light and strength.

I commission you to go forth in My Name. I send you out as sheep among wolves, but do not be afraid for I am with you always just as I said I would be, just as I promised. In My Name you will be blessed and bring unto others My saving grace, My power, My love, life and salvation.

You have a special calling each one of you here, here in My Name at My bidding, My beckoning. Behold I stand before you, ready to use all you have to offer Me, ready to take it in love to our Father. He formed you for a purpose, the work of His hand, the beauty of His creation. Behold you are His wonderful children, flesh of His own flesh, spirit of His own Spirit and as such we are united in one purpose of joy and praise and recognition for all that He has done for us.

Go out into My hungry and thirsty world – those who need you – for they need Me. Go and tell them about Me, what I did for you and those you love. Tell them gladly, joyfully, full of My rejoicing. For you are saved. Help them to see My light, My love, My life shining through yours.

All that I have is yours. All that I say is yours. Take Me and use Me most powerfully for I have commissioned you in My service. Teach as you have been taught. Share in My bread of life. Take it and feed it to the hungry, all those malnourished in want of Me. I am the bread of life. I am the resurrection. On Me depends your salvation.

I long to use you. Come unto Me and receive My gifts. Impart and deliver. Do not fail Me for I need your hands to do My work.

Go where I send you and do that special portion of work which I have appointed you to. Be pleased in Me as I am in you, and receive My grace and blessing.

Listen to my Voice - I

3rd March

Tell My people about Me. I use you for this present time that others might know the truth of Me and My promises to mankind, My pledge to them all, My love so freely given, poured out in suffering but not in silence.

Speak as you have been spoken to, knowing it is the truth of My calling, My reason for coming to earth. Search men's hearts with this truth of My being, My call to them to recognise Me and what is of Me and My Father.

My Spirit comes and rests upon you all that He may bring you gifts of My choosing, My appointing, in My service. My gifts are delivered for the upbuilding of My community, My body on earth, that it may receive more of Me and My will to serve the Father; that My kingdom, Our kingdom, may come into being, become a reality, not in name only but in the core of men's hearts and lives. As they serve each other in love of Me, My kingdom will come as I promised it would be.

You do not have to wait. Now is the urgent time of My calling unto you – My calling to be ready to go out and spread the good news of My birth, My life, My death, My living unto eternity, My real presence among you and all men who seek Me.

I am no shadow of substance but that solid reality which you seek and set your hearts upon. My reality in your lives transforms the truth of your being here on earth. It delivers the reason for why you were sent in love of Me for it brings knowledge and wisdom to those who earnestly seek of Me. Just as men of old reached out towards Me and found Me in the scriptures, you too, today, can teach of Me and My will for you, for the wider world.

Listen to my Voice - II

4th March

You only have to ask Me for Me to speak. I come when and where invited, a willing guest at your table of trust. I come to serve you and service you in My peace and joy, knowing you can use these gifts powerfully in My service where I send you.

It will be different for all of you, for that is My way, My plan, the way I work out My purpose. But you can all be sure it is of Me when your heart sings with the joy of My presence and calling in your lives; when it feels right and good, the best you can manage for Me.

I ask only of you what I give you to do – no more, no less, knowing that I am always there to serve you in love of Me and My calling.

Glad you will be that you listened to My call. For it is the truth of your existence; it is what you seek; it is Me who comes into your lives, the One for whom you searched so long.

My children, listen to My voice and harden not your hearts. Rather rejoice in My presence, My coming amongst you, My claiming of you as My own disciples, the sheep of My flock, led by Me through safe pastures. Deliberate not when you hear the sound of My voice. Simply obey and follow Me, My calling.

I lead you where no men may have gone before, knowing you can teach of Me. Go out into My vineyard. My heavily laden branches await the picking and pruning only a Master Gardener can achieve, for in so doing new growth will appear, fresh green shoots springing up abundantly in My cause – all because you believed what you were told and acted upon it as did My disciples of old. It is important that you listen to My call, recognising My voice when I speak, that you do not disappoint Me.

Go now in My service, knowing that I use all of you in My Name and am well pleased to have you alongside Me. My strength is your joy; your joy is My strength. We are of one accord and purpose.

Focus Only on Me - I

5th March

The peace I have is yours to take hold of. Come to Me and rest from your cares and sorrows. I carry them all. Do not be disquieted. All is in order in My time and way. Seek only My peace and comfort, My reassurance.

My joy will be yours again in a way as yet undreamed of. Simply keep asking of Me, keep coming to Me, keep knowing of Me, keep acting through Me. Know My intent and pleasure, My will and purpose served out in your life and purpose. I plan and you act accordingly.

Listen to My voice, My guiding voice, speaking to you in so many ways, often. Look out for Me and My signs, My satisfaction. My intent is that you should know – know of Me and what to do – believing in all that I have said so often.

Do not stray from My intentions led by your own thoughts, but keep turning to Me, asking of Me, believing in what I have told you and shown you, believing I am there for you at all times, in all ways, guiding and protecting.

I am no other than what I said to you. I am the truth. I am the way of all truth. I am the life that you seek, the way to the Father, the knowledge and understanding, the intent and purpose given by Him.

I realise My wishes through… you all. Plan according to My wishes. Use your strength in Me. It is for this reason that you were given these gifts, these talents. Do not doubt yourselves, your purpose, My calling out to you in My Name. Come in glory, into My glory, My kingdom set aside for many: all those who know Me, love Me and serve Me to the best of their ability.

As you come, bring the others who know Me not, heed Me not, believe Me not, see Me not. Tell them of Me in your way of understanding and knowing. Your truth is My truth.

Focus Only on Me - II

6th March

In one accord we stand together before our Father in heaven, to do His will. He holds us safe, His dear children, formed before time immemorial. Together we are strong, held safe from fear, protected in innocence. Like a small child trusting completely, not knowing the next step on the way except that there will be one, that it is there. Learn of Me that I may take you forward in gladness of mind and wholeness of spirit, dancing for joy in My presence.

Glory in My Name and calling, My coming to you, My purpose for you… and all My intentions. Not a hair on your head shall be harmed or misplaced for I protect you well; I look after you at all times.

Do not suffer doubts. Allow Me to control, and ask of My Spirit what you will – what you will have and hold to use in My Name. Ask and you will receive of Him, for He too is God, at one with Me. Know Him and use Him. Turn to Him increasingly. He is of My Father and I, My presence in the world. He brings peace, comfort, support and guidance. He is the force we breathe, the strength who lifts us high above all troubles.

Tell Him of your problems, woes and difficulties that He may intervene in your cause – no work too hard for Him, no place too far, no problem too big, no sorrow too heavy. Trust Him and lean on Him for guidance and support.

Together We act – He and I and the Father – Three in One and One in Three, just like you have been taught. Take of Us together and singly. We are yours. All We have is yours to use wisely as We plan and dictate. You must act in accord with Us in order to be effective.

Keep coming, listening, learning and acting. Keep praying and be vigilant. Seek and be sought. Replace your doubts and fears by total trust and delight in My promises, My calling, My reaching out to you all.

Focus Only on Me - III

7th March

Know Me as I know you. Serve Me as I serve you, and rejoice in My presence. I give you My deep, abiding joy in your lives today and every day as you know Me more and more – not just 'of Me', but 'Me as a person', the presence in your lives which means everything: all that I am, was and will be; all essence of life and truth; all manner of being; all that is real, not imagined.

All peace is yours; all joy is yours – My gift to you all, each one of you, believing in My Name and promises. All that I have is yours to use wisely in service and recognition of Me.

Take hold; hold fast; use gladly, joyfully in My cause and calling; summons in My Name. Go in memory of what I have said to you; go believing and knowing that I act. One little word – "go" – but it contains the power of direction and action, the strength of being and doing (doing in My Name), and you will not fail.

Believe Me, My children, and all that I have said to you for it is the truth – My truth, and there is no other that matters. Come to Me in gladness of mind, knowing that I act now on your behalf.

Claim My promises and believe them to be. Speak them out and hold on to them. Hold them up before your eyes that you may see of Me clearly.

See as you listen. See that you may know the path to walk, where to tread. See of Me. See Me ahead, calling, beckoning, smiling on you, calling you towards Me, walking in gentleness but firmly, one foot placed exactly in front of the other where I would take you.

Focus Only on Me - IV

8th March

My path is straight and winding, flat and rocky, green and barren, but it is always safe and sure, always held about by Me. Look straight ahead, neither to right nor left, for those places are darkened in shadow where I do not stand. Do not go there; they are harmful.

Keep your eyes on Me, your hands in Mine, your feet following in My direction. I will not fail you. Come now, gladly stepping aside over the difficulties, knowing that I deal with those in My way. That is not your problem.

Focus only on Me and keep going forward. You do well thus far. Keep going in My strength. Keep leaning on Me, not on yourselves.

Ask and you will receive more of Me. Ask and you will know Me. In seeking you find. In going you come. You come nearer to My plan and intention, My joy, My life, My reality, My purpose slowly spelling out for you. Do not be impatient for I act when I am ready because all is in place.

I lay the sure foundation, and you build with Me as the cornerstone, the support and strengthener, but also the Architect. My foundation is laid – laid out securely. I use you now brick by brick upon My foundation, reaching outwards and upwards in My building of your lives, cemented together in friendship with Me.

Come, My children, come to Me in trust and understanding of what I say to you. Not one of My sheep have been lost in My Name. I will not fail nor disappoint you.

I Come Invited to Your Banquet Table - I

9th March

Take Me and use Me. Take hold of Me firmly. My strength is your strength to use in your work with Me. As I lead you, you must follow – follow on Me and My calling. Keep looking at Me, asking of Me in accord with My will and purpose. Gain will be yours – immeasurable gain in My kingdom, My place of being.

Comfort you will offer – and understanding of My situation, My way/ways of working. I use you now thoroughly as prepared, tried and tested by Me. I use you in My service to gain for Me those to whom I call out. My will is that you serve Me gladly and in freedom of mind, not caring what has gone before, not caring what comes next, what comes after, what follows, knowing that I take care of that.

Your ministry will be Mine: Mine of making and calling and directing; Mine in substance and essence. Mine is the reality you are taking hold of, you are becoming aware of. It is more real than sunlight on the waves of your mind or feeling; more real than the air that surrounds us. This reality is tangible if only you will let it be, allow it to happen to you and through you.

I call you in My Name. I speak as I choose, just as I act as I choose in My Father's Name and calling. He directs and I perform in goodness and gladness knowing He is the ultimate truth of all being, of all knowing. He it is that serves us in righteousness with His grace, His love, His care for all the children. He made us for Him, to know Him in heaven and on earth. There is no need to wait for this knowledge and relationship for it is given to all those who ask and seek. Such is your quest and mission: giving of Me to the many – the many where I send you, put you, for Me and My cause.

I Come Invited to Your Banquet Table - II

10th March

Do not doubt My sincerity of heart or purpose, for I come in accordance, in measure, to your beliefs. You make happen what will happen in Me as you trust and believe. This is important. If it were not so I would not have said it, would not have told you. But as it is, you must see this clearly. In order to use all that I have, all that I want to give you, you must believe in Me, My word and My promises, My power of working, My ways of doing things according to My plan – Our plan (that is, Me and My Father, together with Our Spirit). It is necessary to use Us all in the right way of knowing and serving.

I show you how this is (how this is to be) for that was My purpose in coming to have life, that you and others may have it: life abundantly in My Name and discourse. Glory be to Us on high in heaven and on earth below – just like the angels sang at My birth – glory in My Presence and Power, My Triumph, My Steadfastness, My Truth, the Truth for all times and all places – the solid ground upon which you walk; the solid ground of My building and strengthening, layer by layer, strata by strata interwoven with faith and trust and service of Me, through Me; stones and shingle form the hardcore, the rough ground. That going is tough and rocky, then comes a smoother layer placed on top in loving service, for I am the Master Builder. I form your path, your passage through life – struggling, walking towards Me; sometimes with heavy steps, often with light ones; picking your way gladly because you can see and hear Me clearly.

I Come Invited to Your Banquet Table - III

11th March

Do not ever give up nor become discouraged for there is no need. I am always there for you all, forging the pathway of My intent, active and working, busy in your service, never tiring of My work for you. Like ants you scurry in all directions. Stop awhile at times and rest alongside of Me that you may grow strong and not weary.

Do not worry about what does not get done; no harm will come of that in those minor things. Concentrate on the higher things, those which you know are of My calling out to you, My intent, My plan for your working with others. Do not get bogged down with every fine detail of expectation, but trust Me to handle all that matters. I will not see you orphans, away from Me. I take care of all things in all places, day by day.

My time is your time, held gladly in trust for you to use wisely. Take this gift of Mine and use it wisely under My direction. Do what you know you have to do and leave the rest to Me, especially the planning of 'what next?', 'where next?' and 'how can this happen?'. I will not fail nor disappoint you. Believe Me; ask of Me; turn to Me; know Me as your guide, your soul's guide, support, strength and meaning.

What more can you ask of Me? Anything that is of good purpose, honest and pure in intent. This is My demand of you, My request, for I will not force. I come invited to your banquet table, your feast of life's good things. My presence at the table set out before you ensures much joy and gladness of heart. Be delighted in Me, My children – My calling; My coming; your knowing of Me; learning through wisdom given in prayer and meditation, given by others and My teaching, shown by My Father and His Spirit's direct intervention into the very circumstances of your lives. All that I have is yours. Hold it fast in My Name and purpose.

All Power Is from the Spirit in My Name

12th March

Come out of the darkness into My great light of living – restored and refreshed in Me; made whole again by My calling. Have no concerns for tomorrow but live today fully lest it pass you by unheeded and unused.

Hold on to all that I say to you for it is the truth. I teach you and direct your paths, taking you where I want you to be in My Name, for My work. Your part is to co-operate by listening and learning, seeking and finding, asking and knowing of Me.

All that I am can be yours if only you allow and invite this gift, seek it, earnestly desire it, from your heart. I come in strength that you may go out empowered by Me and My Spirit at work in you all. Take Him and make Him your own life blood, coursing through your veins. It is He who brings all life, all holiness, all purpose in Me. It is He who teaches and illuminates your path. It is He who comforts, heals and upholds. That is His job, given specifically in My Father's Name. O, Holy Spirit, bringer of peace and harmony. His calling is of Me. His delivery is by My hand held out in love for you all. Take Him wherever you go, for He will make you wise and strong, He will make you bold and confident, He will allow you to trust more in Me. For He is of Me and from Me, at one with Me and My Father; He binds us all together in unity of purpose and plan, knowing all things, all wisdom. My truth I bring you through Him – My truth and My beauty – as My love unfolds in your lives.

All power is from the Spirit in My Name. He leads us to the Father as He teaches of Me, reveals Me to you because you searched and asked, because you had open hearts and minds.

The Father's House of God is where you are called to be now in My Name and for evermore. My Father's door is open wide to all those who seek it, helped in, invited in by Me.

My children, come, knowing that I invite you all to be at My side now and always, for this is My calling out to you.

My Reality

13th March

Take care of My plans in your righteousness, doing everything in My Name. My building blocks are being put in place securely for your future good and that of the others. I take you out of this place in this way, in My way and time, knowing you are ready to trust in Me and My intentions, all I have in store for you, those abundant fruits ready to crop in season.

Walk with Me closely, holding My hand held out in love. Walk with Me where I gently guide you together knowing of Me and showing of Me. My plans are unfolding in your name of 'belonging to Me and My Father'.

In your strength you can act now because I reform you, refashion you with gentleness – a new image of My likeness, a new path unfolding before with doors opening. My dear children, follow Me where I step before you, not in My shadow but in My glorious light, the brightness of My calling out to you.

Refreshed, you breathe My life into you that you may give out of Me. Refashioned, you are rounded off of hurts and blemishes. Remade, you are more like Me – become more like Me – growing in stature and understanding of My calling, My plans. Trust Me completely now you have this much evidence and proof. What I say will be; for it can be no other when I call it (this) into being and you co-operate in Me.

This reality is My reality, brought about by your prayer and longing, your longing to do what is right and fair. You do create your own reality… that is why it is so important to know of Me and believe. For how else can I become active within you? I need your permission to work on your behalf and for others through you.

Never underestimate My power found in the prayer of My people reaching out to Me in My Name. It is a powerhouse of action delayed, then brought into effect. It touches all that you do and say, the very substance of your lives. It makes you whole and complete in Me as you learn My ways, My reality.

Strength I give you in Me – strength and power of purpose, day by day. Resolve and endurance shall be yours to use for Me – that deep-seated peace that only I can give; My Spirit's peace as He sets you free to do My work. Exacting times lie ahead for us all. Be glad in Me and long for the morrow of My fresh calling to you…

Here and Now - I

14th March

Encounter Me today in a new way, a new understanding, a fresh vision of My purposes for you... Listen and learn. Look to see of Me in others' needs and longings. My hand is in yours. My purpose is in yours and your desire to serve. I will strengthen you as I use you. Do not be afraid. I come to you in a new way of working, a way true to your desire. I will give you those people and places you earnestly seek ... All plans must be of Me at My instigation. Listen and learn. Look and find Me at the rainbow's end, that ray of hope everlasting. My beckoning, My reaching out to you is no false hope nor illusion. It is more real than that which you have known. It is the truth, My truth of existence, My reality.

As you seek, you find Me even in unlikely places. For I am the God of all you survey, think and feel. Make My actions your actions. Take Me to yourself, yourselves, to make Me powerful in your lives. Do not tire of seeking and asking. Do not doubt My power to set you free from worry and concern. I died that you might live here and now. This is no false hope nor trickery of imagination.

My truth stands at all times as ancient wisdom and love. Oh, that all men would see it and understand! But I am able to penetrate their hearts only through each other and the means by which I choose to work. All things are possible in Me, but that is not My practical way of working. I work in a way that mankind can easily understand if they choose to, for it is the substance of their own experience, longing and reaching out – to know each other and Me.

I touch the vein that gives life running throughout My creation. That vein pulses with My life-throb when it is allowed freedom of movement and choice without stricture. My pressure is a gentle hand, a beckoning hand applying love and guidance – no threat nor injury; I could not do that and would not have you do so either.

My guidelines are clear when you seek them and ask for My wisdom. My truths are plain truths and allow you to abide in Me at all times. My purpose, My plan, My will is to have you alongside Me, My mission of love sent out into the heartland of My people's lives, their searching, their looking for Me. Convince them of My truth by what you say and do, what you are.

Here and Now - II

15th March

As you are true to yourselves, you are true to Me and the person I made you to be. Find yourselves and you find Me. Find Me and you find yourselves, strengthened and made whole in My Name. My wish is your desire and working.

Be patient and kind, loving and concerned, with my gentleness and affection for all you can. This will not always be easy, for it demands much of your time and energy; but it is My wish for you, My plan that you are used in this way. Do not worry about how it appears to others, how they question what you are doing. It is Me you serve, and I show you the way. You will know what is right for you because it is of Me. You will grow in knowledge and understanding of Me. Your stature is sound and secured for it is moulded and strengthened by Me.

Cleanse your hearts and minds of doubt and uncertainties for they are not of My making but merely a figment of your own fear. Rejoice in My strength, My working in you, My calling out to you; for you receive My life, My meaning now and held fast for all times.

My plan is your plan. I take you out of this place into a new vision of My purpose, a new glory, a new work. Yours now is to hold on to Me; cling tight in expectation with that firm faith I have planted.

Buffeted on the raft of Me, My waters, you may be – but not shipwrecked, not harmed, not even afraid. I hold you fast in My strength, My desire for your greater plans, My intentions. I safeguard your interests and all details of what is happening, what comes about in My Name.

Come alongside Me and pray. Speak to Me in that old familiar way that I may love you anew. My children, I hold My arms out wide for you, enticing you inside the circle of My love for evermore.

My love is poured out in abundance upon My people, those whom I know, know of Me. For those are the people, the very people, who can make a difference in My world – that beautiful world My Father gave you to inhabit for so short a time. My time is a gift to you to use wisely.

Be strengthened in Me, held fast, secure in My arms of love. My life is your life, freely given in love for you and all you care for.

My Strength - I

16th March

My strength in your weakness is sufficient for everything in your life. You only have to believe in Me and My promises for this to happen. My strength is all you need for underpinning your plans.

Details are details and will unfold in time, My time. You need have no concern for all of these as I do My part. Yours is to act in Me, be of Me, believe in My power and promises.

The hand of God is a mighty force, removing all obstacles and swiping out difficulties – a mighty hand, but so gentle and sensitive to the touch. Reach out for Me, placing your hand – your hands – in My life now and each day forward.

I do bring you peace… it is deep and abiding when of Me, for it cannot fail nor disappoint you.

My call is your command of Me, a command made in love, forgiveness and fellowship of mankind. My urgency is becoming more, for I need you to act in response to Me, My words, My intentions spelled out for you all.

Go where I send you gladly, doing that portion of work I set aside for you ... Stint not your efforts for Me, for you will be well rewarded by My love and knowing more of Me. As you seek, you will find increasingly.

My power gifts I give you in Spirit – My Spirit – to use for My people. Ask that you may receive these increasingly and in abundance. Take control of situations in My knowledge and wisdom using that which I give you. Seek no other guidance, only the truth of Me, which comes from Me.

My Strength - II

17th March

My children, believe in My Name by which all shall be saved, for I died that you might have life everlasting in My Father's house of joy. This is My truth, the truth of My being, My becoming, My beholding. It was, is now and shall be evermore. Seek My truth and shine with its glorious light of promise, My promise.

All will be well in Me forever, starting in your lives as you strengthen in Me. Hold fast to that which you know, to that which you understand is of Me. Hold it fast and cherish the prize of My giving, your receiving in grace. It is My gift dearly won, to be lastingly held, clasped, claimed.

My children, know My inmost heartbeat. It is for you, to give you life in abundance, in accord with My desire for you. My strength is your gain over weakness of will and flesh, by My Spirit of love.

Discipleship is arduous but worth the prized goal of living in Me now and always. My truth of being is total, illuminating the darkness and confusion of men's minds. You must help them see and understand this truth. I bring it to you that you may bring it to them – in Me, of Me and with Me, through Me and My Spirit.

"Teach as you have been taught," was My request to you all. Now I repeat My asking with a pleading of insistence, for I need your work in My place, time and space of My making.

Go, My children, strengthened in Me with a sure knowledge of My will for your lives. Take Me and use Me now and everyday onwards.

I have so much more to give you: a full cup and portion spilled out to overflowing in the abundance of My love for you.

Reach Out to Me - I

18th March

My divine love reaches out over you all, touching every aspect of your lives. You need not fear that you will be unfulfilled for that is impossible when you reach out to Me.

I have much work for you to do, many places in which to send you, many peoples in need of Me. Yours it will be to teach of Me.

First you must learn My truths and live them as best you can, not of your own accord but by the power of My Spirit, the Paraclete, the Guide. As He swirls amidst you, it is with a mighty wind of power, a cleansing fire – cleansing of doubt, uncertainties, unknowing. For He will convict you of the truth, the real truth of My being, My coming into your lives. Ask Him that He may teach of Me and allow you more insight and understanding. Harness His will to do My work, and be guided by Me along the paths of My choosing, My directing.

Go not your own way without reference to Me, for that I cannot bless; but be of My will and purpose, My power and intention. I take you onwards in My Name, serving you in love for mankind and many. My heart is to become your heart. My sufferings are to become your sufferings. In Me, your life is to be lived to the full measure and extent, reinforced by My boundaries.

Reach Out to Me - II

19th March

So much to tell you – set time aside – so much to teach you and show you that you may understand My workings, My ways, better than you thought possible. My communion is a total one. It holds you and enfolds you in My love, My life, My resurrected life; the communion of souls – yours and Mine – together bound forever. This is My Father's will and promise. He longs for you to be set free in Me, in My Name. For that, He sent Me to you.

My children, My dear children, My loved ones, I cherish you. Place yourselves in My hands held open for you, where you will be safe and secure in My palm, My grasp, My reach.

Reach out to Me as surely as I reach out to you. Grasp and hold on to Me, never losing sight of all that it means, all those promises I hold in store for you – My abundant storehouse opened up with ripe fruits ready for the picking. The harvest of men's souls will be rich, all because you came and listened, learned of Me and acted.

My promise is all round you, centered into eternity. This is but one day. There are many to build My kingdom. Make each one 'of Me' as fully as you can, praying and praying. There is no greater purpose than this.

"Go in My Name and because you believe, others will know that I live."[9]

9 Carol Owen, "God forgave my sin in Jesus' name". Used by permission.

The Pulse of Life - I

20th March

My truth is the revelation of My Father's will for you. I speak that you might recognise this… and act upon it in My Name. My insight is given sparingly, that you might seek it earnestly, longing to do My will.

As you seek Me you will find Me, for that is My promise. You do well to watch and wait for Me to act. When the time is right I will come to you accordingly with My plans of fulfilment, all that should happen in Me. Until then be patient and believe in My words of life to you. Believe and act upon it. For in showing Me that you believe, you set the wheels in motion for the next stage. I cannot act alone but need your reassurance of trust and belief to call into being what is to come about.

I am glad you give Me the time of your heart's focus and solitude. In silence we convene. Clamour can be exciting but distracting also. I am found so often in silence and stillness. Cultivate this desire, this seeking out alone of Me. My purposes can then unfold in the quiet space of your mind and heart. I can talk to you in whispers, inaudible to most.

My Spirit is at work even now, bringing you peace in My presence, joy unfolding in knowledge of My will for you. My child, be Mine everyday as best you can. Seek Me somewhere in all situations, even those where I feel absent. Especially those.

The Pulse of Life - II

21st March

Your weakness is My strength. I told you that, so you may understand your need of Me, your dependence. Cultivate My calling into your mind when doubts assail you and storm clouds gather. Nothing shall separate us.

My glory is your glory, interdependent. My truth, your truth of being and owning it, acting upon it, even when challenged. Resist the temptation to water down, compromise. My being is My being in exactness and completer.

Make no mistakes, for I am the outer rim of existence, holding all things together expanded and contracted in My strength, My bonds. My vibration gives the pulse of life, the throb of intensity of purpose – My purpose set apart from the everyday, although that too is My concern.

As you live in the world, you must at times walk away from it to learn of Me, to become complete. My calling is to you for listening of Me that I may use you in the way I choose to do.

My child, be Mine in stillness in the cradle of My heartbeat throbbing upon yours – formed and forming, grown and growing, nurtured and nurturing.

I have much in store for you… as you learn and live of Me, setting your house aright in My Name; talking not in vain but for My greater good of many, My children, seeking to know Me more and find Me in men's hearts and lives. You can show them of Me by what you do and say. Continue well.

Go forth gladly. My children, believe in all that I have told you, for it is My truth.

Easter - I

22nd March

The end is a beginning – new life from old. Like Easter, ever it was thus in the cycle of seasons and nature, and that includes mankind. Mankind's dying self can be, will be, when given over to Me completely, a rising self, new self, made whole, a better likeness to My image. The old, wilful, selfish, conceited, proud, arrogant, manly ways fall off slowly like a shedding skin. This allows the new person to emerge far, far more beautiful and intact. In fact, because he better understands himself or herself, and better understands My ways of love, mercy and forgiveness, therefore he is able to view things differently, including his path, his walk, his upward struggle through life. Yes, satan is an enemy and a real one but so can be the self, the ego, with its wilful, capricious, grabbing ways. When man was made to be whole, he was of necessity given a gift of free will. Otherwise, how could he be whole if driven by some will not of his own? Unfortunately, sadly, such is the world (and fast becoming more so in its ungodly ways) that his will (man's will) is frequently given over to anything but God. Misdirected, disconnected, uncorrected, he stumbles blindly on until he falls catastrophically far from grace.

But there is an answer, and blessed – truly blessed – are those who know what it is. The answer will always – can only – lie in My †. "Father, forgive them for they know not what they do,"[10] were not empty words of exclamation, but a plea from the heart – My heart of true overriding, surrounding love which longs to embrace all mankind. In forgiving, gives rise to the fresh living, the new life from death. My pain – plain to see, started in agony upon the † – was a true symbol of the evil mankind, let loose on his own, is able to stoop to. But more importantly (because this is what is of lasting, everlasting value) is that the † – My † – is also a certainty of triumphant success; the victory of evil overcome by nothing other than determined, obedient love. All-giving, self-giving love: the love of the Father allowing Himself to give up of Me; the love of Myself to give up for mankind; the love of the Spirit – the ever-patient, waiting Spirit, abiding in precious time of longing until My death and resurrection. He could then be fully released as never before into mankind's lives.

---

10 Based on Luke 23:34

Easter - II

23rd March

The † stands tall as an emblem of victory. It stands boldly, upright, fixed in earth but pointing to heaven; arms outstretched like Mine as a symbol of reaching; love – My love, the Father's love, the Spirit's love – reaching across the divide of time and place, culture and custom, truth and untruth, fact and fiction. Can you not see this clearly? I gave you eyes that you might behold My beauty, however unlikely and seemingly impossible to your normal sight are the circumstances. Can you look at the † again and see man's crowning glory there? His story of human bondage, captivity to sin and all its consequences, set free, completely free. A crown of thorns becoming a garland of beauty, flowering full like fragrant white roses, the perfection of summertime. A sign of warmth, of life, of growth-giving beauty, delight, joy.

Peace was My message proclaimed in the blackest, darkest of circumstances: peace to you, My dearly beloved children reading this; peace to all mankind who seek to know Me, find Me, rediscover Me, fall in love with Me once more; peace, true peace – God-given, lived, shown, known, experienced in men's hearts of self-giving love. By that I mean the giving of self to Me to let Me help you, direct that free will in God-given, God-wished and desired ways of fulfilment.

God is good, always good – through and through and through. That goodness manifests itself in generosity, compassion, mercy, purity, understanding, willingness to be patient, time and time again. All such gifts are on free offer because of My †. All healing power ultimately lies pinned under the † of self-sacrifice. My giving up of life was that you may all receive life in full fullness. And life on earth can be so good, so gracious, so glorious, so gladsome, if only you will let God be God to direct you. Ask and you will receive. Seek and you will find Me in ever greater measure, lifted up high for all mankind to see if they will but take time to raise their eyes from the hurry-scurry of every day, from self pre-occupation, from rat race determination, from interference in other people's affairs, from obsessive interest in the mundane (and by that I mean things that ultimately do not matter for they have no lasting effect upon life either here and now or the life which is to come).

Easter - III

24th March

Seek, My dearly beloved children, the glory of God in being truly yourselves, at one with Him – with Us – using the talents I gave you for [the] greater good of all mankind whom you come into contact with, influence. My gifts of talents are not random chance but a fine network of needed abilities. Each person alive has his or her own calling, own talents. Recognise these; encourage them; celebrate them by abundant use. Then give thanks for the differences, all for the good, you will see happening.

Use a disciplined approach of effort, strident effort. It is effort with perseverance which always affects the better results. However talented/ gifted, the harder you try, the more you can and will gain, not for yourself of course but for the good of others. As I came to earth to fully share My life, My time, My God-given talents with you, the same calling you are honoured by. Do not disappoint Me, My children.

All I seek is your best efforts, and I will ensure the successes. It doesn't matter if you stumble or falter or even fall on the way. I will be there in someone to pick you up. Never be afraid to start again. I stumbled on the road to Calvary several times. If I had not picked Myself up and made My path to the top of the hill, if the crucifixion had not taken place, where would mankind be now?

Easter - IV

25th March

What is Easter in your life? Let it be an emergence from darkness into light – any darkness of doubt, dismay, despair, despondency, disruption, disharmony left behind, obliterated by the true light. My light is life shining, beckoning, inviting you to come to Me in a renewed way for a revival purpose. Celebrate My victory by claiming and naming a share in that victory: My † overcoming all manner of evil – all, anything, that separates mankind from God. For ultimately that is what all sin, however great or however small, does. It separates us, comes between us, pushes Me away from you (for I cannot bear to look on sin) and pushes you away from Me (because you are shame-faced – too shame-faced to look properly, openly, in My direction).

The true celebration of Easter – Easter joy – as I walk from the tomb, the imprisonment from the darkness of death, in solitary confinement, set free by the Spirit's power to raise up to new life. He who set Me free will come, when invited, to you also that you may, like many, recognise Me in a new and different way and proclaim in all awe, wonder, "Rabuni (Master)." Then in the quietness of life's garden of beauty we can walk and talk together – you learning, Me teaching; you reaching, Me responding; and both of us always looking, listening, talking together from the heart and of course expressing love in all its richest fullness of delight. Heart-warming, uplifting, fulfilled delight; completed in our meeting, greeting, and believing in each other; completed in mutual trust and support; enriched by ardent fervour.

Easter is a closed, opening time: the closure of death, a final closure; a continuous, complete opening, flowering of new life, emerging from what has gone before. And as you know, all flowering takes place because of seeds sown, watered, warmed, properly nurtured. Make this Easter both a time of reaping and sowing, of dying and growing, of believing and knowing Me, your ever loving Master.

Sit at the Lord's Feet and Learn

26th March

Come to Me in the stillness. Come to Me and place all your trust in Me as the angels do. Listen to My heartbeat in accord with yours. When they are in tune you will *know* – and know Me and My will for you …

Belonging to Me, you will need to come to Me more and more for guidance and My strength. Give Me your time, your days made out for Me. I can use you in so many ways when you are ready, moulded to the pattern of My thinking and being, set free from earthly ways and desires.

A taste of heaven is being with Me in all that you do, consciously/unconsciously offering up to Me your thoughts, desires, efforts, strivings – even those that disturb you. My place is one of wholeness and healing in men's hearts and minds, their whole lives set free in Me. My instruments are you chosen ones who work and do not count the cost.

Take My all and make it yours to use wisely. Freely given, freely give and celebrate My love amongst you.

Stand Firm on Me

27th March

Go forward in My Name, trusting Me and believing in My promises to you all. My will is that you must stand firm on Me. Together we act in power, making a way through the wilderness of men's hearts.

It remains with Me to know why. It remains with you to know how – by serving Me completely, in completeness of mind and will, in totality of heartfelt joy.

Remain in Me at all times, knowing I am amongst you together. Then I can use you for the upbuilding of My kingdom here on earth. My territory needs extending by those who know and love Me, for without this all else fails. Wait no more, but go in My Name of peace.

I am King of All

28th March

Believe in My Name of freedom, for it brings you that which I have in store for you all. Be not downcast nor disheartened, for I am with you always as I said I would be, taking care of every situation. Talk to Me about your feelings and anxieties that I may bring you My peace of reassurance, My sharing strength.

My resolve is that you know Me more through the everyday occurrences of your life until you see I am King of all times, places, people, situations – anything and everything that involves you alone or together. You cannot stray from the path with Me as your guide and comforter, your joy and heart's treasure.

Where I put you, I put you for a purpose. Where I send you, I send you in My Name of service. Where you belong, I belong in your heart, calling out to others. By service you will know Me and please Me. By My service you will be sustained and strengthened.

Together entwined in love of each other, for that is my call to you. Love Me more as best you can, in the ideas and intentions I form within you all. To love is to live fully in Me, in My kingdom here on earth. You do not have to wait to glimpse heaven, but experience this as you open men's hearts and minds.

My children, direct your paths and ways towards Me, who holds you safe in the palm of My hand.

You are My Pilgrim - I

29th March

All will be well, and all manner of things shall be well in My Name. Your yearning is being fulfilled in good time – the time of My appointing and choosing.

Know Me and My strength that you may believe in Me and My promises to you all. I do not pretend nor waver, but you have to do your part to serve. You need My strength and reconciliation so the righteousness in any situation may be established and held fast.

My energy, My drive, is given in greater measure when all stands well with Me as best you are able. I love you anyway but can better serve you when you reach out in expectant faith and longing, in humility and open-mindedness. This is My gift to you, a new life in Me – one of joy and accomplishment in My Name, fulfilling your desires and My expectations.

Do not doubt Me nor your own progress in Me. Truly believe what is happening to you all. I take you forward now the pathway is set and made clear.

What I give you is Mine to give, yours to receive with gladness as My gift. In tranquillity of heart My peace is found when you know you are doing right by Me.

My rules become commitments when you truly love Me and long for Me – commitments which are dedicated to your safety and wellbeing.

Love your God with all your heart and all your mind and all your strength. That is what I ask of you ... With that love will come a flowering of great beauty, a joy unfolding in your lives hitherto not experienced nor dreamed of. Only I can give that to you. The world knows it not nor even believes in its possibility. But I show you otherwise.

You are My Pilgrim - II

30th March

You are My pilgrims on a pilgrim path of discovery, a journey to Me, My way of working and thinking. Pilgrims must take sustenance. That will be found in your time alone with Me, your soul's energy, your heart's ease, your strengthening and revival.

Share My truths together, that which you have found in My Name. In sharing is bonding and love-growth. Reach out to Me and to all others who know Me and My Spirit of truth and revelation.

Seeking, you will be sought by My hand for My work. I call out to you; hear Me. Let every drop of fear disperse as you feel My love surround you in safety. My net is far and wide, holding strong wherever you are in My Name, by My calling.

Listen and learn of Me, My children, My beloved ones. Enjoy your day. It is Mine to give you, yours to receive with thanks and praise.

All time spent with Me is well spent; not a moment of it wasted, for as we spend time together you get to know Me more. I already know you through and through! But you need to move into My heart's sanctuary more frequently and consistently. My repose will strengthen and sustain your flagging energy.

All that is Mine I give you for your needs and that includes My Spirit. Call upon Him; invite Him into your heart again and again. He is your daily bread. Taste and see that the Lord is good. He is your bread of life, your true nourishment of mind, body and spirit. He at one with Me and My Father, your Father in heaven.

Believe all I have to tell you; it is the truth.

Walk with Me

31st March

My love is sufficient unto all things at all times. Take of it and make it your own, My gift to you. Store it up in your heart that you may call upon it and use in the day of trial.

Succumb not to temptation; rather focus on Me and My truths. My grace is given in great measure to those who come to Me longingly – My joy, peace and tranquillity of heart, My self-revelation.

Walk with Me, one with Me and My Spirit. Walk where I lead you in this world that you may better know Me in the next. Walk in My footsteps, serving with love in your heart and a desire to serve My people. I will show you how and where. Ask me.

Listen to My direction. Go in deeper in trust and faith, believing in Me at all times and in yourself under My direction.

I who formed you, use you now in a mighty way, a new work of healing grace and power. A fresh insight you will be given into My intentions for you. Be not afraid but bold in Me and the talents I gave to you.

Release your fears onto Me, My shoulders – your fears, doubts and frustrations. In release you give expression to My love which fills your empty spaces with strengthening power.

Speak out in My Name that all might be told of Me, of what happens when you truly seek Me with love in your heart, longing for a new life. It is that heart of stone taken out as promised, removed by My scalpel of forgiveness and replaced by My heartbeat in time with yours.

My child, My children, you are precious to Me and honoured in My sight. Dance in My resurrected life; dance your joy and sing your praise that heaven may resound in My Name.

Formed in Me

1st April

You must be formed in Me, grounded on Me, delivered through Me if you are to take any effect in this world who so desperately needs Me. Unless you are of Me and in Me, I cannot use you. You have made a good start. Keep going – seeking, learning, listening – but above all praying to Me, My Father and Spirit. Together We mould you into beauty, Our beautiful child of the bright morning star, new arising. Your head must touch your heart – inform your decisions – for these are footfalls in the way where you may stumble unless under My guidance.

Heed your thoughts, your feelings, your opportunities, My Word, My directions given to you now and over time. You are privileged to be in Me, secure. I take you where I want to place you. But you have to do your part in prayer and trust. The way will be provided.

Your longing to serve Me will be honoured and rewarded for I need such as you to do My work, that special work appointed for you alone. Be not discouraged nor disquieted by setbacks. They strengthen resolve. Simply be in Me, belong, be Mine totally. This I ask of you now: to commit more fully, believing My teaching. When doubts assail you, turn to Me and ask My opinion. All truth is My truth. You can come to it by no other way.

My Spirit will tell you all things in Me. He will make you strong in faith and determination. Revere Him as your counsellor and protector. He has baptised you with the fire of My love, setting you alight for Me. Turn to Him daily to bring you My guidance. My Spirit guides and protects where and when I send Him. He will serve you as He serves Me. He will bind us together, making us as one in the Father.

My God is your God – the source of all your being, all your blessing, all your becoming. No one comes to the Father except through Me. I am the way forward. I lead you onward to where He wants to take you in Me. I share your walk through life knowing the riches you have to offer for they were My gift to you in the first place, in the beginning when I formed you in time. Use them wisely, looking to Me at all times for guidance.

I use you in a way as with no other. I made each of you unique and it is that very uniqueness which I can mould and blend. Step forwards believing in My Name which is above all names.

Be Still and Know Me

2nd April

My child, be near Me today in a new way of knowing Me. My children, rest in My presence and be still. In the stillness of your heart, in the calm, you will find Me. Your longings will be fulfilled there as you gain a greater awareness of My presence, your heart's desire. Be still and know Me.

You are progressing through the quagmire but still heavy burdened. Put those burdens onto Me for My blessing to ease your pathways. As you come to Me you will receive much in My Name: My peace, My joy, My contentment, My real presence in your lives.

As you seek Me, you will surely find. I am yours now and forever. That means today and at all times, whatever you are doing. Do not doubt My being there even amongst the humdrum.

Soldier on as a warrior in Me. My army is victorious. The battle belongs to the Lord, and My victory is sweet and triumphant.

You are learning of Me and need to put that belief – that whole weight – upon My promises. Walk with Me side by side ... Thus we shall know each other in strength and weakness, good times and bad, for I am with you always.

Let Me be the helm, the guiding force of your lives and living each day. Let Me hold you where you are, then beckon you forth in My time of choosing, for where I go you must surely follow.

My children, know Me as I am, your God of salvation. I came that you might have life and have it to the full in Me.

The Way, the Truth and the Life

3rd April

Take Me where I send you in My good time. You will know this by your feelings and My opportunities.

Wait on Me, patiently. I have preparatory work to do first, before you can be effective in My Spirit. Also you need a time of upbuilding, resting, strengthening; a time together in prayer. Be obedient to Me, My children, so we can come together in power. My light shines in the darkness only when men are prepared to pull back the shutters to see Me.

Pray, "Your will be done" and you cannot – will not – go wrong. Hand everything over to Me in prayer. That is the peace I promise you: the peace of knowing Me, of knowing that I act and take care of all things for you.

Take that love, all of you, I give it to you for a purpose, that you may share it out among many. Take and give of Me, the bread that was broken and shared, the bread of life, your true nourishment. "Man shall not live by bread alone, but by every word that comes from the mouth of God" means you not only have to feed on Me (My body and blood giving you new life, each time you receive it, receive Me), it means you have to live and learn by My Word; My living Word spoken into your lives so you may know that I am true, I am He, I am My Father's Son, the One who redeems and saves all men's souls. Not one is lost. I died to save *all* men's souls; all means all. But they need to recognise this and own the Truth.

This is where you can help them to see. Teach in My Name, bringing Me into their hearts, not just their minds and heads; no longer a theory but a living, breathing reality. Ideas will form as to how you are to do this, if you ask Me. Remember, I see and know all things, so I am in place to provide all that is necessary, all that is required.

Do not doubt Me nor your own callings. Doubt is disbelief and spoils our relationship. Rely on Me as I do on you ... knowing great things lie ahead – the riches of My Father's storehouse.

Hand Me Your Days

4th April

My child, My child, receive My love. It is yours for the asking. Prepare to receive and be changed by it, by My presence within bringing you to new life and hope. Be Mine as surely as I am yours, each day, each moment of the day. Have I not told you this before? What takes you so long to understand and receive of Me?

You only have to be in Me, be still and calm in My presence, bow down before Me and delight, knowing Me as I know you, with certainty. Speak to Me more often. Tell Me of your fears, your delights, your concerns, your joys, that I may be invited into every part of them. Do not separate us by your own pre-occupations unshared. I take care of everything if only you will let Me.

Hand Me your days, each one as it comes, each part for Me to transform in My way, to take charge of. Be My child, My small trusting child who always looks for guidance and approval. Glance in My direction often. You will be glad that you did. Do not forget Me, as I never forget you.

Go now gladly into your day, rejoicing in My presence and this My gift of time to you.

My Spirit - I

5th April

Hope in Me is found in Me as a reality. You will see the way I work the people I choose to use. It can be unexpected, unlikely, surprising perhaps; but is always for My purpose – My good purpose and intention. Simply the mention of My Name brings power to your elbow!

Filling you with My Spirit is easy if you ask, long for it, make way for it by believing and being ready to receive in stillness and preferably in silence. Yes, you are like the banner said: "You are what you do with your silence"[11] – a pithy, true, thought-provoking statement taking its truth from the reality of My reasoning ways.

The day is as long as you make it, as full as you take it to be. You can see Me or see Me not, dependent on the race through the day.

How often did you stop and start? Stop still long enough to think, question, wonder, ponder, doubt even? And what about any conversation with Me? Did that happen or were you too busy elsewhere to share, care or compare My truths with the world's ways? Did you learn anything new or was there a change where you grew in understanding of My ways/attitudes? Did you remember to pray in the moment, in passing, those darting, arrow-like prayers which can go swiftly and directly straight to My heart to impart what is needed? How many today have you interceded for? Have you given Me any thanks, praise, heart offering, your suffering? Have you identified with others' troubles, complaints, conditions, deprivations, distress? Disaster can overtake, make foul progress, so readily unless My people come to Me to pray from their hearts.

History is in the making, taking mankind forward by the moment of decision. It can be changed, turned around, moved upside down, tipsy, topsy and turvy at the stroke of a pen's mistaken decision. But revision in time is always possible for those who listen and carry the influence of prayer.

---

11 Quoted from a banner outside the United Reformed Church, Shrewsbury. Used by permission.

My Spirit - II

6th April

Use My Spirit's power to enable you to pray forcefully, effectively, connectedly. There is no one correct way. Any way will do as long as it is genuine, from the heart and mind, seeking to find a better way forward for mankind to be restored to My glory, their story of life's purpose.

Coming, going, seeking, knowing, showing, letting My Spirit live in all fullness of power. He will set you alive as never before if you implore Him to come close upon you. He can even take you over if you allow this! Such progress is not known to many for any heart that longs for such dimension must be self effacing, encasing My Spirit within the space – that empty space – left. He comes only to a welcome home, otherwise will continue to roam far and wide looking where to abide.

He is troubled when turned away, ignored, forgotten, abandoned, or even interrupted for He always has a purpose to pursue through you using your time and talents, God-given and (I pray) God-lived-for. He will restore in My Name. Claim Him; cling to Him; stay ever closer to Him – My calming, kind, generous, gentle, gifting Spirit. Hold Him tight, but do not crush Him! Use Him readily, but do not rush Him! Let Him lead, but do not push Him nor stand in the way and obstruct.

Listen. Again I say listen. He will instruct you readily as and when you are made ready, prepared, ready to receive and believe. Blow by blow the wind does go wherever I send it – powerfully bringing about storm force or, of course, the gentlest summer spring breeze to bring delight to the soul. The whole force of My making is taking the world apart to put it back together again whether by storm or gently. You can perform part of this life-giving, life-saving, amazing work – uncovering the discovery of new delights, fresh insights, a pure bright light of My truth's teaching, reaching you and others through you. Just be patient; all will unfold in the time of My making when I hold the world ready to reform,conform, to love's teaching, reaching out to all men everywhere.

We will share a life beyond compare sooner or later. The day, the date, the time and the manner of its imparting is for Me to decide. I hide such dangerous knowledge/information from your eyes. It is not for you to know, for how could you then go on trust alone?

Blank Slates - I

7th April

Blank slates are for writing on. You need to be emptied out to receive of Me – emptied out of pre-conceptions, your own thoughts, your busyness, so you can be free to listen, learn and receive/perceive what I am trying to show you.

It is in the knowing of Me that you gain strength to be My disciple, a fisher of men, as and when you're ready to serve by obedience in all things whether little or large (of more importance, significance, of lasting value or touching upon more people).

Pinpoints of light become beams of light as they disperse, chase away the darkness surrounding, abounding to confuse and disorientate. Light is My way of working to bring the truth radiantly before you, uncovered in My Name.

The truth is truth – no 'ifs', no 'buts', no corollary – absolute, universal, life-abiding, life-giving, eternal truth. This you must recognise within yourselves; without it you will not function properly, adequately.

The truth which surrounds all of mankind is to find them happy, harmonious, hopeful and helpful, each to the other. Truth will uncover peace, driving pride away. Truth will bring healing, revealing the fractured faults which cause discomfort and distress. Truth will bind into one whole My people who are ready to look, listen and learn.

Truth took My disciples by storm – a storm of surprise, unlikely surprise, surpassing all their expectations, dreams even. Truth will take you by surprise, too, uncovering the past in a way that may be painful and perplexing, but it has to be dealt with in My Name of truth from which there is no escaping if you want to move forward successfully.

Realising the truth is like coming under the surgeon's knife to cut out the cancerous ill growth which dangerously festers to mess up your lives. It must be removed radically. The truth will indeed set you free to be Mine in entirety, for you will not be weighed down – weighted by distractions or false attractions. My call is to the ready who make effort with themselves to be prepared for the service of a lifetime always learning.

Blank Slates - II

8th April

One step forward in Me, you can be as never before. More to receive, more to give and live for. More, always more – My gifts ready and waiting for sharing. I am caring about you, you see, and care that you reach full potential in Me to see how I call you, want to use you. Nothing is cast in stone in My kingdom except truth.

I can use you or not as the situation commands, demands of necessity and vitality of interest – others' and yours – refined by Me. I find much to challenge you with, and you must be patient working through the pile of rubble which has troubled you like a landslide of suffering.

Suffering is service when offered for the sake of gaining some sense of My truth. It is recompense also for My own suffering and helps to serve the world's measure of compassion – a treasure without limit when this is brought to bear, take influence, make a difference in any troubled situation. The nation needs much of it: a fresh duration outpouring of people's concern to learn how to handle the hurts so many feel.

I appeal to you My children who are in the know, how to go in My Name, to stride forth confidently, expectantly, knowingly, for as you are sure of Me, you can be held in My safety, protection, the harness to cradle – not too comfortably but certainly securely. A little buffeting to and fro, up and down, in and out, round and about the hilltops never did anybody any harm, for from that vantage point you can see progress differently (or any lack of it). Reaching higher, being higher, looking higher gives you a different, wider, more panoramic view of the world. Remember, 'gratitude for what you see and understand' is an attitude most important, bringing health and healing in its wake. All it takes is gratitude, the right attitude to Me, a zeal to heal the hurts and of course the overriding necessity of obedience.

It's no good looking to learn, to forget and let go of the truth. Truth is the key to so much. It unlocks the door of the future prospects, when (and only when) it connects Me to you and you to Me willingly, glad for all that is happening. Privileged to see My truth, to see part of its progress, you must not digress or regress from its narrow pathway winding forwards, upwards, onwards, heavenwards everlastingly. Everlastingly set free to be in Me, you will know that truth was/is the only way forward. I am not a God of the backward glances.

Blank Slates – III

9th April

Fresh chances always do appear for My children when they are ready for the taking of My making. Be glad and celebrate. This is a truth in itself, and you do well to remember it and use it wisely, successfully, efficiently, decisively with determination and zealous effort.

To get is to give; to give is to get more fresh store of Me. You see, we need each other like salt needs pepper – two spices combined to make a fine flavour which tastes good and satisfies entirely when sprinkled in the right place in the correct proportions needed to season.

The reason for life is manifold – many, complex and ever changing – for I am re-arranging according to the circumstances of opportunity and belief. The relief of knowing I am in control is a whole source of blessing, taking the stress out of the moment. Pray to Me often. I cannot overstress this enough. It is the pathway of communication between us and must be kept clear of debris, doubt, indecisions, dismay, disillusionment, selfish desire and foolish pride for these will hide My true intentions which flourish only in the bright light of truth's uncompromising stance.

Each glance towards Me helps you to be set in the ultimate truth of humanity. Knowing God's will is essential, vital, life-giving to human happiness, living in heartfelt peace.

The release of joy is dependent upon those who will listen, then act as if they heard the truth – indeed, knowing that they did. The truth must not be hidden from sight. The blind lose their way, falter, stumble, fall and get hurt. They are vulnerable and can come under attack – fresh, fierce attack. It is your joy, your call, to fight the fall. Fight back in the name of truth. Christ's truth is a battle very hard won – not for the faint-hearted – but you will be glad you started to walk My way of wisdom, enlightenment, insight, fresh calling, growing in the knowing of understanding Me – who I am; how I began, became man, continued, did not cling to earth, returns to My Father, where together with Our Spirit We hold the world in Our hands.

Blank Slates – IV

10th April

The world is spinning relentlessly, misguidedly off its axis – crazed by activity, assaulted by insecurity, terrified by its own clever technology, impersonalised by greed, populated by pride and fiercely fighting nation by nation for recognition and supremacy. It is a dangerous situation, nation against nation.

So much can be done in little ways. You must recognise this; each partner plays its part in the whole drama. You can start by walking, talking, sharing, comparing life in the light of My true promises – promises to be kept so you can inspect and see the truth I have spoken to give and for you to receive. Perceive more of this. It is life-giving, living in the truth of who I am.

I overran all difficulties whilst on earth, and the same power – My Holy Spirit's power – is at work today. Our influence is heady and strong. It does belong to mankind who seek and find eagerly, willingly, receiving graciously, gladly.

You will be glad you sought, were taught of Me, by Me, through Me, with Me at your side to both chide and guide and let you go in My Name of success. Expect opposition but overcome it; overrun it by patient love – that life-giving, breathtaking, fresh-opportunity-making force of love. Above this there is no other attitude to be encouraged or discovered.

Uncovered love flourishes far and wide. It does not hide its good results which can be glorious. God-given and gifted, love is the true story of man's triumphant march forward. Restored, revived, replenished, re-invigorated, reinvented in attitude and desire, man can then aspire to all that is greater and good.

You should believe this, My children, for believing is bringing about the happening as never before. "It is accomplished,"[12] I said, and time is no barrier, being the fourth dimension.

12 Based on John 19:30

Seek for Me to Speak – I

11th April

Seek for Me to speak; then wait patiently but expectantly. Yes it is an awesome thing to communicate with the living God. But if only you knew, My dearly beloved child, how I long to talk with you so much! My Spirit roams the earth far and wide, diligently seeking those quiet souls who are readily prepared to stay still and listen and accept that this happens. It must be this way so that My words which are wisdom and truth itself, their very essence being life-giving, do not fall on deaf ears. It is the tragedy, the manmade tragedy of these days, these times, that so very few people are prepared to slow down and settle to really listen.

Life chases them, and they chase a so-called life here on earth forgetting or not understanding (or maybe not wanting to know) that this life is not the eternal reality. It is but a phase, a preparation for the future life and a quickly passing one at that.

Each day is given that you may progress in Me. This is knowledge of Me, full comprehension of My teaching, My ways, where truth and righteousness have met; trust of Me, hope of Me; and most of all, pure, utter, complete, fulfilled love shared between Myself and mankind.

Love is the very essence of our relationship. It is the start, a continuum and the completion; and each day, if you allow it, is a step on the way towards this. But as with any walk with progress there must be – there has to be – times when you simply sit still, relax and rest in Me and listen. Your world is so full of perpetual noise. My people seem to be losing the ability to listen with rapt concentration.

I do not choose to enter where there is the half-heartedness of distraction. My attraction is too important, too powerful, too life-changing, to take or be driven into second place. Embrace of My love as the medicine man and woman need to heal their souls. When their spirits within the body connect with My Spirit here on earth, then all manner of things become possible.

Seek for Me to Speak – II

12th April

It has been said – I have told you; it is true – that by yourself you can do nothing[13]. By that I mean nothing that is of eternal value and for the ultimate good for all mankind.

Find Me and you find the hope of answers. Be with Me and you receive all that you need for life's journey. Stay with Me and you become My trusted, worthy, lifelong companion and friend. We travel on closely together, side by each other's welcoming, wanting, heart-warming side. It is a slow but steady pace we can maintain together – you trusting Me as scout and guide. You only sense, somewhat vaguely, where you are going. I know the destination and the shortest, easiest route to there. How can I tell you about this and show you the way unless you choose to listen to Me?

Looking ahead and glancing behind is insufficient. The moment that matters is now – today, in all its fullness of opportunity – for it will not pass your way again. What you miss doing today, you may miss forever. Did you ask Me how you were to spend My gift of time today, where you were to go, what you were to do, who you were to be with, what you were to say? If you did not, why are you so surprised when you stumble across pitfalls and make mistakes? They are, My children, inevitable if you walk in a fog of half-seeing, half-knowing with perhaps the blind or partially sighted leading the blind. Stem your reluctance to lose your supposedly self-sufficient independence.

Look to Me, listen to Me, rely upon Me like a small child does to the parent. I will never let you down. My ways will not fail you so take time – make time – to discover Me.

---

13 Based on John 15:5

Seek and Find – I

13th April

Seeking is finding, when you seek Me with all your heart and mind and spirit. Then I let you find Me. It is all about choice. What is important to you; what is to be King in your life? I do not like to take second place for that is inferior to My godly purpose for mankind. I, too, seek and find. I seek out those who are willing to serve.

Service is belief put into practice in My Name – that Name which is above all other names and conquers. Conquers fears, doubts, uncertainties, simply because someone somewhere believed and prayed to Me. Prayer is our link, the turning of the waves. Many, oh so many, things are wrought, brought about, by earnest, devoted prayer. There it is we share the Father-heart of God – His gift to mankind to lift you up heavenwards in your thinking, speaking, deciding, acting.

Never be too busy to pray. It is the best, most determined thing (course of action) you can take. Make prayer a priority whether in the doing or being. Being consciously aware of Me (carrying Me uppermost in your mind, in your attention) is prayer – not simply words, however fine, but the intention to include Me, seek Me, use Me, understand Me and follow My commands and wishes.

It is My delight to serve still My children by guiding them, just as when I was on earth. Do you think I care any the less now? Impossible!

My heart is given over – totally given over – to My people in love. All they need to do is to come and realise this and their life would be so different in meaning, purpose and content. It is the great tragedy of the age that most of mankind is lost in self-sufficiency and has therefore lost the search for Me, who is true happiness and fulfilment.

Seek and Find – II

14th April

You cannot be yourself, properly yourself, until you discover/ uncover your God-ordained purpose in life. And first and foremost that is the same purpose for each and everyone: to know Me and the Father who sent Me, through the intervening power of Our Holy Spirit. He is the searchlight, the touch fuse of ignition. Depend upon Him. Lean on Him heavily. He delights to help you seek and find. Be mindful of His counsel of wisdom, for it is truth – the truth you need to know about yourselves, your situation, your plans and procedures. Listen to His voice calling in your conscience, calling in your imagination, calling in your creativity and especially calling in your desire as to how to serve Me – a different calling for each person's purpose – for I prune according to need, circumstance, expectation and hope.

The future never was cast in stone in an immoveable way. It is when you pray, your desires are made plain to Me. This gives Me your permission to act according to the best purpose of everyone involved.

Sometimes you can hardly see the beginning of My work, let alone the end of the course. This is why I say repeatedly, "You must trust." Trust is the key to unlock a better, God-ordained future where all will be well in Me.

I want nothing but the best for My dearly beloved children. Their best in every way is the ardent desire of My heart. Because of mankind's free will, sometimes it takes an age, a lifetime even, to achieve this. But there is no other way. Man has to come to Me by freedom of choice. Love can never be forced, only encouraged, hoped for and offered.

Such is My offer to all those who would see Me – all those who have eyes that look, ears that hear, minds that think in the quietness of the human soul where the spirit resides. I wait in readiness for you. Do you wait in readiness for Me? It is My prayer that you do!

Jigsaw

15th April

Recognise yourself as one part in the jigsaw where the completed picture lies in My hand, but even for Me to complete the picture satisfactorily, each piece has to play its specific part in the whole. Is one piece more important, more essential than another? No, each fragment is instrumental in the tapestry. All are part of My glory.

Often you do not see the finish of something you started, but that does not make it any the less meaningful. It merely means you are enabled to see transitory, fleeting moments make up your life into one whole, under My direction when/if invited.

Come, My child, come to Me on every occasion. Come closer. Invite Me into every situation to determine its outcome and destiny. Then you need not worry but can go on with My peace in your heart and mind.

The peace of knowing Me surpasses all understanding. It is irrational and somewhat inexplicable. It is a gift sought by everyone whether they recognise the seeking or not. Peace, true peace is Mine to give and Mine to take away. It rests upon My decision as to the greater good for mankind. Remember always I have much to balance out for you and others.

What you do decide depends upon what I decide, then the ultimate outcome. That is why it is important, indeed essential, to seek Me in all things, at all times, as part of your decision-making. There is many a stumble between plan and implementation because I am not consulted.

Take all I have; I long to give it to you, My people, to comfort, aid, guide and support. With Me there is no wrong turning, no false footstep. Indeed that is impossible!

I am all that I am in power and skill out of love – love for all men and their destiny. Play your part and I will surely play Mine! Combine together and we become one force for harmonious good.

Go, My child, without fear for the future for all will be well in Me.

Precious Gold - I

16th April

Love is My greatest force on earth and in heaven – a creative force of pure energy used for good so that, as promised, all things will be well in My Name of truth and healing, wholeness and prosperity. Prosperity is full – abundantly full – sufficiency in Me, the source of all hope and wholeness.

On bended knee before Me, My people invocate My influence. I love this and long for it, for I am a generous Giver, but wait to be asked. Never be afraid to come to Me for any godly need or purpose.

My love prevails in all circumstances where I am sought and allowed to act. Your permission is needed to release the full flow of My Spirit's holy working in your lives, transforming the everyday, mundane into the supernatural power of My all-sufficient energy. Energy is My love in action, a force for good, a force for healing, a force for hope – hope justified by all that I promise you in Me and My Father. Ours is a wish for your full prosperity, your full health or healing, your full understanding of the way I – We – work and expect you to go, to follow.

Turn to Me, My child, My children. It is never too late to come running back home. You know I await with open arms and aching heart where there is a special place prepared for each and every one of you who seeks Me.

How much I mourn for those who do not want to know Me, but even there your prayers can make all the difference in the world. Prayers prompt, persuade and present progress, for they always reach My Father's heart of gold – gold to be shared out amongst the many (any who are in need); a reserve of gold that is bottomless, endless, timeless and of such worth no earthly classification befits its description.

If only you knew what was in store for you in My Father's heart, you would set more time apart – much more time – to be with Me in the seeking. Unless you seek, you cannot find, and unless you find you cannot possibly cherish the inestimable price of Our love and mercy, Our forgiveness and healing, Our revealing of Our hope in you and for you.

Precious Gold - II

17th April

Mercy is My middle Name: "Jesus (Son of God) Mercy (My attribute named) Christ (My anointed kingship over you)". Usually in worldly ways it would be the servants, when able, offering gold to the king. But in My kingdom, worldly ways and attitudes are turned upside down on their head, to shake them out of complacency and dull composure. In My kingdom (and part of it is established here on earth) it is the other way about, for the King brings/gives an offering, gold, to His servants – as much gold as each individual is prepared to carry, be weighted down by. Gold, like all that is precious, comes with its own weight of responsibility and stewardship.

Be not mean in the sharing of My gold. I was sold for coppers and condemned on a † that you may obtain this gold, a prize of all prizes. Gold, brazened in the furnace of My suffering, is everlasting and cannot be destroyed.

More precious than pearls, more sparkling than diamonds, more real than silver, buried deeper than bronze, My gold is precious beyond description or desire. Aspire to obtain it, hold it, cherish it, polish it, until it shines in glory, such glory as to reflect the beauty of My being. And when you look into its surface, you will see the radiance of your own true self reflected back from Me, from glory into glory, beholding such pure beauty – radiant light reflecting, bouncing off the surface in My energy, that love I talked about.

Gold is for giving, a testimony of true love and friendship, a symbol of security and worth – no base metal but one of God's gracious gifts created before time began, that it may stand the test of time. Malleable under stress, it can be beaten, hammered and reshaped. Make your hearts like that: hearts of gold for Me to hold and mould as My very own – precious gold, God-given gold, Our offering of love to you in service of mankind where We find Our heart is.

Do Not Rush at Anything - I

18th April

Life which seems so rushed, chaotic and confused at times, many times is really so much more straightforward and simple in Me. It is all a matter of who is in charge – Yourself or Me? Hand over to Me, and you will see the unexpected, the unlikely, the uncertain even, come to pass readily. My hand is at work at all times, even the seemingly dark and impossible times.

It is your busyness which prevents you stopping and finding Me to talk to. If you put the cart before the horse, you have to do much pushing and pulling! If only you, My people, would carve out time for Me first, seek Me first, you would avoid many pitfalls and pit stops.

My way is one of simplicity – straightforward measures put in place to hold My people steady between the steering ropes of My commands. Learn more of these commands; look at them and take them in to work upon them. They are the way to health, wellbeing and security, for in them you find the path home to Me. In them you can surely, safely be yourself without fear of harm or hurt of any kind.

I, who am all gentleness and calm, have no room in My reign for hurry and stress. These are the components which combine to mess up your life and opportunities. Come to Me more. Be with Me more. Rest in Me more, and relax in the security of trusting My way and My truth. It leads onwards and upwards, home to heaven steadily – always at a steady pace which is comfortable, although challenging, for each individual.

The path en route is by no means the same for everyone. Adventurers choose the steep climb and take by assault. The more cautious take the slower, gentler slopes and continue more cautiously thereby. There are some in between of temperamental nature, who swing between the two extremes. But none of this is a problem to Me. I will help you map out the route according to your nature and inclination. I never stifled anyone's opportunities or adventurism.

All I ask is that you fully involve Me in each and every stage of your journey. Who better than Me to read the signposts? Who better than Me to predict the weather ahead? Be led by Me, My children, and you will not wander far off the path without feeling, hearing, seeing Me call you back, away from danger.

Do Not Rush at Anything - II

19th April

Do not rush at anything! In rushing, caution flees to the winds, and that is not advisable. The best planning, fullest implementation always takes careful time. Why the rush when all days are held in My hands? Time is a manmade element – useful in many ways but repressive and harmful in others. You need to give more of your time to Me, to live in harmony with My will. How else can I come to you?

Life is a two-way process of giving and receiving, and to be in all fullness, this has to be done through Me, who cares. I will share My wisdom and truth with you, undoing that which is harmful and unnecessary and building up that which is worthwhile and godly.

My truth grows by planting, seeding, nourishing, nurturing, harvesting – a cycle which you can understand and live by. But this can only be done in the right order in the correct time frame. The harvest reaping cannot come before the sowing of the seeds. Look upon Me as the Farmer who provides the seeds – the very seeds of life and hope itself – to let you see joy in the way and day ahead.

One day at a time, one step at a time, is the only way forward in trust. I have told you this before, and it is important – an important truth. Thereby you come to understand what trust is: not looking too far forward nor looking back with regret but simply being fully in the moment, place, opportunity you are in.

Otherwise you will miss the chance to talk with Me, of Me, about Me, wherever you are – and there is a need. Pre-occupied with a welter of worldly matters, you will miss or dismiss Me. Then where will we be?

Do Not Rush at Anything - III

20th April

Heaven is made up of small footsteps reaching forward, trusting the destination awaits but also trusting the path en route is shown by Me. I cannot show you unless you stop long enough upon the way to look and listen and learn – *really* look and listen and learn. Seek Me and you will find Me wherever you are. Speak to Me and I will answer you if you wait patiently and stay alert and watching with a listening ear. You will have to work at this. It does no longer come naturally to mankind, for he finds still, applied concentration, quiet reflection, meaningful meditation so very difficult to achieve. He seems to think that he must be busy doing something – anything – to achieve worth. But that is not My way for I am the God of gentle, peaceful, quiet calmness.

Security is built on the rock, the firm foundation of knowing Me, coming to Me, in this quiet place in your heart. It is there where you start to see, to receive, to understand. Growth comes from the heart of purpose discovered, then fulfilled in Me. You all have a heart, so you can all start the searching to find. Discipline will be needed and determination and effort to secure sufficient tranquillity to be together successfully, gainfully, and from this your maturity in Me will grow. Great is My glory which awaits fulfilment in you. Do not deny this, My children, by being too rushed, too busy, too pre-occupied to come to Me.

Serving Me means being available to Me at all times, having been strongly, successfully, usefully, powerfully built up in Me. To be Mine is to see your world – our world – changed for the better forever. Will you come apart each day, give Me your heart and let Me be a part, the main part, of this transformation? Reformation comes about when man becomes dissatisfied with the manner in which he is spending his time and building, securing – or not, as the case may be – his future.

Do Not Rush at Anything - IV

21st April

The only certainty – your only certainty – of fullness of every aspect of life comes from Me, lies with Me, and is offered by Me. Children of Mine, come to Me increasingly that we may see what a difference together we make when we take on the world in our Father's harmony and prosperity of love – full love; dramatic, life-changing, transforming, forming love – in all its wonderful, powerful, creativity. Love began the world; love redeemed the world; love continues to carry the world forwards in My purpose that all mankind should come to know Me, recognise My truth, and act upon it. Mine is the glory, the goodness, the grace that will make this happen when you embrace Me by giving Me full time and attention gladly, willingly and confidently.

I will always gift back in full measure and more the time you spend with Me. For you will find your use of time directed by Me more effective, more complete, more lasting and worthwhile. You will avoid the mistakes you would have made, the mishaps that would have occurred.

In Me you will be free – truly free – to be the child of God you were created to be. Believe Me, My children, for this is so very, very important for you to understand and act upon. Give your time to Me, and I will return to you a fullness, satisfaction, completion of time in the fullest measure which will be as promised, pressed down and flowing over in abundance.

Be secure in Me; remain secure in Me. Live in Me for I long to live in you who are willing and wanting to give their best, most precious, quality time with Me. 'My time becoming your time' will see you free from so many everyday concerns and burdens, for you will come to see how effective I can be. I will be in you, in Me.

I Am the God of All Things - I

22nd April

Abide with Me in the silence of thoughtfulness which turns into prayer – prayer of seeking, speaking to Me about anything which is on your mind, be it small and seemingly insignificant or major in your life. I am the God of all things – nothing too small, nothing too large for My notice and interest. All that concerns you, My child, is of concern and interest to Me. I want to come close to you by being involved in what involves you.

I do not want you hurt nor making mistakes. Come to Me, and My intervention can prevent you treading many a wrong, mistaken path. Lead on and go where My lightness of heart takes you. Look at what your heart is telling you, for that is where I reside. So is it any wonder that My directional feelings come from that centre?

I enter you to make a real difference to your world. But I can only do that if you heed and take notice of all that I say and do for you. Be constantly aware of My presence, not just now and again as and when it suits you or when you are not too busy with worldly matters.

I who made the world can take it by storm to reform it. The storm always originates in someone's intensity of feelings when they perceive and receive My Spirit at work. On this, miracles of My love are founded. They issue forth in trust of Me and My leading, going you know not where.

The future unfolds but slowly, according to your instincts and My revelation. The two need to be – must be – combined to gain the best result.

My favour rests upon those who listen willingly, joyfully to My Word and endeavour to act upon it. Even amidst their sometime failure, I reach them with new teaching of understanding. This is because of being open, receptive and willing to learn by the guiding of My Spirit.

Hiding your love for Me is no way forward. Declare it loudly wherever you can. Proclaim it as best you can. And always, but always, rely upon it.

I Am the God of All Things - II

23rd April

Love wins favours. Love conquers all difficulties. Love sees progress. Love is never diminished by My pupils at work endeavouring to reveal Me to a hostile world. Only love – love in Me, for Me, through Me – I repeat, only love, My love in the Father by Our Spirit amongst you, will win through. And win it will, if you give it but half a chance!

If only you could grasp the reality of all that can be done and achieved by Me in you, it would shake the world – shake the world and take it by a storm of fresh, new understanding, appreciation of all that I did for you, all that My Father's outpouring of love in Me achieved upon the † of My suffering. My suffering was willingly given for you to save you the same agony.

You are set free in Me. Do you understand this, all the implications of this? What does being set free mean to you? Free from doubt, concern, sorrow, despair, dismay, despondency, everyday worries and perplexities? It should do! It must do, if you are to serve Me faithfully.

I call upon joyful servants who honour the fullness of My victory upon the †; who have no doubt at all, none whatsoever as to all I have achieved for them and those they love – for those I loved, that is all people.

Come, My willing ones, and serve in gladness – joyful, heartfelt gladness – where you will release the promise of My peace. I await you now. Do not disappoint Me nor fail Me, for I rely upon you to be Me. It is a tall order but I tailor you for this, your work upon earth. Do not shirk your responsibilities.

I will be with you always, lovingly carrying and caring for you. You are never alone in My steadfast love. Love locks in your energy, your desire and commitment to Me. Love ensures success at the ready in Me and through Me. Love is the willing servant and the faithful Master at work together for the glory of God – all glory, full glory, the glory of God's splendour evident in the good, finest works of His people. His people given to Me for the benefit of others – all of mankind who will listen to Me, through you who serve.

I Am the God of All Things - III

24th April

Go out and serve lovingly, willingly, unhesitatingly, obediently, joyfully, and the God of all love will be with you, in Me and My Spirit at work. Call upon Him, for He never fails you. The Holy Spirit makes the difference between that which seems real and that which seems merely a possibility. The Holy Spirit is the probability, the assurance of godly circumstance.

Never act alone without His guidance. That would be foolhardy and maybe even dangerous, certainly counter-productive. Call upon My Spirit's energising, driving power of love to take you and make you where and as I determine.

We work as a team with Our Father at the helm. We invite you into this team of love, nothing but love. Will you give Us all you have? Your time, inclination, effort, energy, ability? The more of you you give Us to use, the better the results become, for team effort is enhanced and emboldened. We go together – We, the Trinity – wherever We are.

Come alongside Us, My loving child, and we will go on from strength to strength. Don't you find that exciting and enticing? You should do, if you are to serve Me as I long for.

Be glad and hopeful in Me. Become glorious in My Father's eyes, having become fully alive in Me. The splendour of God's love will shine throughout the earth. I send you out and about, My children, going for gold – the golden glory of God's love known in Me, experienced through Me in you, at work in the Holy Spirit.

Do not fail Me. I am dependent upon you. Come, come, come in love, for love, with love, and together we will act.

Rely Upon Me Fully - I

25th April

It is the Son who gives you light and life and strength. Rely on Him. He will guide you; He will support you; He will strengthen you. Simply ask Him, listen to Him and obey Him. The obedience is an essential component of an active, seeking faith.

All too often My children ask and receive but then don't believe Me fully and go off solo on their own journey. Sound though their intentions may be, and often are, they are not blessed unless the decision and the action is found grounded on My will, My plan, My purpose, My point and reason for coming to you in this instance.

Rely upon Me fully, My child. I say 'fully' – that means no merely hopeful thoughts and imaginings of your own; each decision, every vision, grounded in Me. This is the freedom I talk about when I say, "My truth will set you free."[14] – free from yourself and the dictates of others and/or wild aspirations because you relied upon Me fully and received Me completely.

I am the Truth of the Godhead here amongst you. This is My place, one of My reasons for coming to give you life. I give you life in My holiness. Endeavour to seek and live by this purity.

14 Based on John 8:32

Rely Upon Me Fully - II

26th April

It is the assurity of your faith when I am found alive and active in you through all you do. Notice the word 'all'. 'All' means 'inclusive of everything, not simply your self-selected parts'. Rely on Me wholly, completely.

Intuitively you will know Me when I am speaking by My Truth which the Holy Spirit will reveal in all fullness to you. Never venture without asking the Holy Spirit. He is the guidance sent from heaven, the holiness on your path's journey. Ask Him, rely upon Him, trust Him, follow Him. He works hand in hand with the Father and Me to set you free, completely free to do as We will you to do.

Pray that your wishes, your desires, may be brought into line with My will. This too is a high calling of holiness. Holiness is the mark of My people alive in Me to be what I call them to be.

Can you not see how much you must depend upon Me fully? I need your complete confidence to enable Me to act in you and for you. Together we can be a wonderful team!

Come, My child, now; listen and learn of Me for it is essentially important that you do this. I give you the kiss of life in all holiness as and when you receive the fullness of Me.

Keep Your Eyes Firmly Fixed on Me - I

27th April

My child, look at Me, listen to Me and believe Me when I say I am with you. Stay with Me at all times and do not go off on your own wilful way.

Mistakes happen when you fail to be completely connected to Me, who am the true, loving source of your life. Much strife comes about in human life when a person does not admit Me into their presence. By this I mean they forget about Me in the everyday decisions and become blinded by the false light of fictional truth which can shine around and even through them from the wrong source.

Only prayer will protect you from this. Ask for My protection. It is rock solid, sure, steadfast, unshakeable, and even though the mountains tumble you will not be hurt, My child, if you stay within the stronghold of My truth. My truth must be sought; it was very dearly bought for you. Never forget this.

The influence of My † casts its shadow over the entire world. Now, to make a shadow the sun has to be shining. When the sun shines it illuminates. Put yourself in the place where you can seek My truth, speak about it, feel it, then act upon it.

Do not go your own way solo, without seeking My will and purpose. Do not jump to conclusions for you may find yourself out of your depth in sinking sand. Do not doubt My truth, My living Word found in the Bible. It is My universal truth, non-changing for all times and all situations. Seek out and read for yourself those parts that apply to your situation for I always have the perfect answer, the solution, the resolution.

Keep Your Eyes Firmly Fixed on Me - II

28th April

You must not be swayed by worldly influences, hearsay, judgement, opinion, however well intentioned. Look within, to your heart, and listen – really listen – and grasp what I am saying to you. Open your eyes and see what I am showing you. Open your mind fully to My influence. Now, when I say 'fully' I mean 'do not block Me out by your own preconceptions' for they may be misjudgements.

Only My Word is the total truth for you. It must, however, be My wisdom and truth you listen to, otherwise you will falter, and although I can pick you up and dust you down to start all over again, I would rather you did not falter in the first place. You falter when you stumble simply because you are not looking closely at where you are going.

Look at the direction you are taking and ask of Me, not of yourself, "Is this the direction? Is this the direction You want me to take?" Then rely upon Me. Wait for My answer for most surely it will come. I always come to those who genuinely seek Me.

Heaven and earth are connected by many straight strands of truth, and I do not want you to be tangled up in a convoluted, confused mess – a hotchpotch of human opinions.

My wisdom is not to be doubted and it is non-negotiable. It is set down as one thing that remains constant in your life for guidance, and My wisdom is first of all loving, peaceful, good and generous. If your decisions do not carry nor contain those elements then look again at your resolve.

I am a God of loving concern who wants the best of every single situation for all My people. I do not favour one above another so one person's peace is sacrificial for the contentment or satisfaction of another.

Keep Your Eyes Firmly Fixed on Me - III

29th April

Turn over to Me everybody and everything that is in your dilemma, and I will work with this through you – with them simultaneously. Bring them to Me. You must bring them to Me and not leave them out on the sidelines. Do not presume you have the answers and they do not. Listen also to what I am saying through them, and if you still cannot understand then ask Me. I want nothing but the best, the very best for you ... in the life I gave you.

Many a mistake is made simply because of presumption, impatience, misunderstanding, wilfulness and the self harm of deceit. You must be complete in Me to be guarded against these evil influences.

Satan has many guises. He comes to My children in many disguises. Be aware of the deceit he is capable of. He loves to pull My children off track by whispering doubt into their ear; and doubt all too soon, all too readily, turns to the dilemma of misfortune. He will always agitate, confuse, disturb and disrupt you in his avowed intent to destroy you.

But remember always that I am stronger, infinitely stronger and more powerful than "he who is in the world"[15]. Good – *My* good – will always overcome evil. Remember the words of My prayer: "Thy Kingdom come, Thy will be done on earth as it is in heaven; deliver us from evil; for Thine is the Kingdom, the Power and the Glory."[16]

---

15 Based on 1 John 4:4

16 Matthew 6:10-13; NKJV

Keep Your Eyes Firmly Fixed on Me - IV

30th April

It is to My glory that My children pull through the trials and temptations put before them which I allow to happen for their spiritual growth – their newfound strength as they go into the waters ever deeper with Me. When you are in the water up to your neck, what can you do? You can sink, you can swim, or you can tread water to keep your head above the waves. When the force of the waves is too strong for you, all you can do is look to Me, shout for help and paddle to keep upright, keeping your head above the swell which threatens to drown you. I will give you the strength to keep going. I will not let the waves sweep over you to pull you under.

But there is a condition: you must keep your eyes firmly fixed on Me. Remember when Peter got out of the boat (and the boat is your security in this case), when he got out and decided (because this was his desire) to walk on the water by faith. All was well, he managed and progressed until he took his eyes off Me. Then he began to sink. Fix your eyes firmly on Me and no other influence. I cannot state to you forcefully enough how vital this is for there is so much at stake here. I brought you to life, I am now bringing you to life in Me – do you not suppose there will be a battle for your very soul and spirit? That is what is happening here, My child, but do not be afraid for I am with you. I will hold you by the hand. I will guide you, I will calm and quieten you. Simply believe and expect the very best from Me. Faith must be expectant, joyful and hopeful. If it is not, something is fundamentally wrong and you are out of step with My timing or direction.

Any disturbance or disruption, which I allow, comes not directly from Me, but because you have strayed somewhat, somehow, somewhere away from Me. Look to your conscience and listen to what it is telling you. In what way have you promised to love and to serve Me? Have you remained true to that promise, to that calling? Or are you falling under the spell of someone or something else? A spell is by nature spell-binding. It can allow you to lose touch with reality – My reality. Admit no other spells into your life other than that which come directly from Me and My Father by the power of Our Spirit.

Keep Your Eyes Firmly Fixed on Me - V

1st May

Call upon Our Spirit daily to direct and influence you. He is the source of all true holiness that you long to access. He will never fail nor disappoint you. Call upon Him early every day, and do not go on your way without Him.

The Spirit is My direction, the complete connection to God. You cannot, will not, must not manage without Him. He is your peace and the answer to your prayers of looking and searching.

"Seek and you will find,"[17] I promised you. Seek My Spirit's strength, speak to Him of your intentions, hopes, aspirations and He will appoint you to My work and guide you into all truth. Be open to Him and remain open to Him. He is our direct line of communication, working heart to heart from the very heart of love that resides in the Godhead. He will not – He cannot – fail you! Come to Me through Him.

All who seek and want to do My Father's will: We will instil Our wisdom and truth in you and then (and only then) are you free to be the child We planned you to be, full of Our purpose and intent. You have been mightily blessed by Us, but you must claim these blessings by remaining within Our sphere of influence and not stepping outside the circle of Our love. The circle that surrounds you is Our perfect, loving protection – unbroken, rock-solid and safe. You have no need to fear as long as you stay within where We are. Do not ever go far from Us.

Children need their father's loving, guiding hand at all times. You remember this when you were little, and it is most certainly no different now at all except that the dangers loom larger, so you must hold on tighter and never let go, not even for one instant in time. Do not doubt Me even when you feel confused. I am there; I will stay with you; I will help and hold you.

Use My Name when you pray and no harm will befall you. Relax with Me, live with Me, live for Me, and you will see what we can do together.

---

17 Based on Luke 11:10

Forwards Is Not Backwards - I

2nd May

Go forward in My way of truth, relying upon Me fully. I will protect My children. It's your job to help them. Turn to Me and know Me as the reality – not a distant entity but the true reality of their life earnestly concerned with the outcome for them.

They, too, must turn to Me in trust and not go their own solo way forward. I will help them; I will come to them in the measure that they are prepared to receive of Me and believe of Me. This indeed is one of My universal truths that each of you individually must ask to receive of Me and must seek to find My way forward through the maze of life which perplexes all of you.

Doubts and difficulties are undone in My Name of love when you come to Me trustingly. Indeed, it is only My truth which can set you free to be the children of love living the life I planned for you, and so much today gets in the way of this that you lose your focus and thereby your way. Only My way of being, doing, thinking, seeing, acting is the best way forward for any of you.

My power is omnipotent. Grasp this and believe it. You belong within the realm and the effects of that power at work in you, for you, and round you.

Call upon My Spirit of truth to come into any darkness, doubt, dilemma or difficulties. He is your best – the purest – guidance, for He works only in holiness and will provide the perfect wellbeing in My Name. There are many steps along the way, but let Him accompany you each step of the way. Forwards is not backwards in Him!

Forwards Is Not Backwards - II

3rd May

Let us begin together, My children. 'Together whatever the circumstances' means safety, security and protection for you – My protection. You cannot manage successfully without this.

It is your kiss of life in the same way as someone who is pulled out, rescued, from the sea which drowns. Troubles can threaten to drown anyone. But just as I could walk on water, I can walk with you, guiding you by the hand, loving and protecting you, so together we rise above and move beyond the troubles.

For we will together move into My truth, the real truth of our Father's will and purpose for you. Yes, you are most precious and honoured in My sight, and I will and want nothing but the best for you, My dearly beloved children. It is never too late to come to Me. I understand what holds you back. No difficulty is too complex for Me to overcome and unravel.

I will move you forward as and when your faith and trust and belief in Me grow firm: firm to the end; firm without faltering and flickering; firm as the certainty of the solid ground upon which you walk. Do you not realise that even the earthly, solid ground upon which you rely and trust as secure can falter, fall and give way at any time and without warning? But My ground is not like that. It is steadfast – completely steadfast – certain and secure, for it is built and structured for your safety by My Father who is all truth for all men at all times. Rely upon Him through Me together with Our Spirit, and indeed We will set you free as never before.

Come to Me, My child, My children, without hesitation. Run to My open arms that await you. In My clasp, in My grasp, you will feel nothing but love, My deepest love and respect for you, My precious, My most precious children.

Why do you think I gave you life in the first place? Can you not see that it will be truly, truthfully for us to be together forever, whatever the circumstances? I long for you with all the longing of My heart. We must belong together for God made it that way. You will never be complete and fulfilled until you are in Me and meet with My expectations. Come now, My children don't delay. Hurry My way; I am waiting for you!

Go in My Name of Love - I

4th May

Take care of My children – those I give you to care for. They are our shared responsibility. Simply love them into the truth of My love that will reach them, teach them, and show them My way quicker than anything else. To witness to Me must be an everyday part of your life, an ordinary event with extraordinary results and implications – far-reaching implications because of the seeds you have sown or, more accurately, we have sown together.

Let Me take control; let Me hold the reins. Your job is simply to be guided by Me in all things. That is why I say, bring everything to Me and set aside quality time to do this. Time is never better spent than when planning what we are going to do together.

You must learn to recognise My Spirit at work in you – His calling out to you to come forward and act. Then go in My Name of love – always, but always, in that Name of love; I know of no other way.

Even My discipline and My halting of you is done in the necessary love to reach My intended results. A result is the outcome of endeavour, endeavour only in Me.

Through Me you can achieve the miracles, those miracles which you cannot do on your own. Each act of love is in its way a miracle because it transforms mankind's own self-centredness, placing another's needs before and first. Many miracles build up My kingdom of love, in its power, with its purpose, for its plan.

God works in this way through Me, through you, by the power of Our Spirit for you. Never forget to call upon the all-conquering Spirit. He is My truth manifest, made real by the love that you do for each other, and in so doing bringing that glory to Me which our Father so desires and designs.

His work is a very fine design indeed, the finest you will ever come across. It is your privilege, and I hope your delight, to be called a part, an instrumental important part, of this work. Do not shirk your responsibilities nor turn away from Me.

Go in My Name of Love - II

5th May

Greet Me face to face at the start of each day. Then we can go on our way together joyfully. Hope will fill your heart as My design in God fills your lives. Life is given that you may learn to love and to love fully in Me, through Me and with Me by the activity of My Spirit alive in you.

Plans and purposes of holiness come to fruition only as and when love flowers. The bloom is fragrant. The blossom falls where it will to be blown by the wind of My Spirit far and wide. And like confetti it is a symbol of an occasion when the sacrament of My love is taking place around and about you.

Believe in Me fully, My children, as you receive and learn to live by the power of My love. Then go out wherever I send you and share it, for there is no force nor source upon earth to compare with this, the power of My love brought about by the Father through Our Spirit. Our love is manifold, directive and always distributed first where there is the greatest need. Discern, learn of that need, then go on bended knee in heartfelt expectant prayer where we can share God's intentions together. To mention My Name always brings results and pleases Him. Rely upon this. Again I say, rely upon this. Do not miss out on the opportunities God gives you in Me.

I will set you free from fear and doubt as to what you are to do, for if you take love as My emblem and marker, making it your intention, then as long as you call upon my Spirit's discipline and guidance you cannot go wrong. We all belong to each other, the whole of mankind.

Go in My Name of Love - III

6th May

God our Father framed us in love to be His people of love. Go now and serve Him in Me, in love, together with Our Holy Spirit. He, like Me, is the author, perfector and finisher of your faith, and faith must walk, talk, act and react in love – nothing, absolutely nothing, but love.

Love covers the way safely; love uncovers the way to go. Love directs with warmth and corrects with kindly patience. Love is informative, building up, never taking down. Love is progressive and incremental. Love is instrumental in joy and hope and peace.

Love is as necessary to mankind as the very air you breathe. Breathe in of My love and be nourished, replenished, restored and fortified by it. One, just one, small act of love – of loving kindness, tolerance, patience and understanding – can make all the difference in the world. Your world must be built on and supported by love. I will heed no other way; that is impossible for Me.

Can you now see how important love is to Me and must be for you? Now, My children, do My will as I have asked you to, by loving fully, wholeheartedly, consistently and thoroughly in Me and My Spirit at work in you.

Love to the best – the very best – of your ability for the glory of God our Father. Love will allow His face to shine upon earth. Love will allow God to be made real amongst you. Love knows no enemies and finds no faults other than those which go against My Father's commands and will.

Instil love and you bring about freedom – the freedom for holiness to flourish freely. The holiness of love will win the day, and you each have your own separate part to play in a combined and complex drama of life.

Love will overcome strife and discount difficulties. Love will diffuse tension and command godly attention. Love, always love – agape, self-giving, self-sacrificing, self-forfeiting love.

This is what I mean by My Way, My Truth and My Life. Love is the Way, love is the Truth and love is Life, everlasting in all its glory, grace and goodness.

Listen to Me, Listen to Me, Listen to Me - I

7th May

My child, My child, do not hide away from Me in your busyness. How else can we connect unless you come to Me to listen? Talking is all very well, but in the listening comes the power to learn My discernment. Yearn for this. It is the source of life, the source of your life of faith. And in that faith is found the strength for daily loving as I call you to love.

Coming to Me sets you free from unnecessary burdens, worries and cares. But for this I have to be enabled to share with you what I am thinking. Do you ask Me about this often enough? You know how important it is, yet do you fulfil your intentions to listen?

Be not so ready to speak but more to seek, by listening and finding. Finding Me in silence is the richest treasure we can possess together. The world crowds Me out with its hurried noise of clamour.

My people come to Me and stammer out their needs but are far less ready to listen to My needs, My plans, My hopes, My desires. We can aspire together only as and when you listen to Me.

Why is listening so difficult for you? Have you so much on your plate you cannot empty your mind to find Me for one small slice of time? I give you back in threefold abundance every moment you honour Me by! Do you not yet understand this? Or are you frightened you will hear something you don't want to hear? That is not My way of love! Be trusting. Be true to Me by listening more.

Listening skills, like other skills, grow in the practising. It necessitates disciplined hearing, a sacrifice of time, constant attention and a certain stillness of mind, body and spirit. I place My Spirit within those who genuinely seek to speak to Me in the listening silence.

Do not give up, nor doubt your ability which I gave you for others.

Listen to Me, Listen to Me, Listen to Me - II

8th May

Seek Me more often in the silence of your longing heart. We are never apart if you do this for Me. I will set you free to listen if you are willing. Do not fear that you will not hear Me. I speak when there is something to say! You must be ready to receive and believe in Me, in this gift.

I know you think, "Why me?" Well, why not? I make My choices by My own design and intention. I have My reasons, not yet clear to you, but they will be. Simply do not fail Me, My child, whom I depend upon.

Yes, this is an honour. But then I honour each one of you with life. What I am looking for is life in all fullness, dedicated to loving and serving Me. And this is in a different way for each one of you alive in Me. Come, let us thrive together in My love which shapes so many, so very many things for you. You will never know what you can do for Me until you love fully and in that love you come to Me to listen and hear. Let My love appear in My words to you, for this is the most important attribute My world needs – My people fully alive in the discovery of My love and all that can achieve.

Believe Me when I come to you. Receive Me when I come to you and keep seeking My speaking. This is a gift to lift you up with many besides, any who will then listen to you in Me, Me in you.

Will you let the light of My love shine through? Will you believe in Me fully? No, I am not too good to be true, although I am the best thing that has ever, or will ever, happen to you! Let love through all you do, all you say, [reflect] Me.

Listen to Me, Listen to Me, Listen to Me - III

9th May

Love is My meaning of life. For this I came to earth in My Son. His love won upon the ✝ for all who would see. Teach this. It is an essential truth for My people to understand, yet still it is misunderstood and not truly valued. The value of all I have done for you shines through the triumph of the ✝ of love, offering new life to those who will take it. The world fell apart that day in time, to be remade in My way, My truth. Yet still men, mankind, hang back from listening and hearing. Why, oh why? Have I not made My love plain enough for all to see ? What else can I do for you when nothing else is necessary?

Your yearning to come to Me is good. That is why I can use you. But you must make yourself more readily available to My call. You must not be so busy about your own things as to crowd Me out.

Prayer is the backbone of the day, building your strength. But your prayer needs to contain more listening, looking towards My word of loving command. I demand this of My people who want to serve Me fully. There is no other way you can properly learn of Me than to wait on My word, heard in your open, welcoming heart of love – to rise above the everyday clamour.

Be still, My child, and receive. Be still, My child, and believe what is happening to you, through you, for it is real, very real indeed! I need to use you. I want to use you. But you have to make ready the possibility and circumstance. Think of this as a channel, a two way channel of love to be open at all times.

Do not doubt Me. Receive from Me in readiness for the future we build together. Great things happen in My Name of love when My people co-operate with Me and dedicate themselves to My calling. Believe Me rather than those who doubt.

Listen to Me, Listen to Me, Listen to Me - IV

10th May

A prophet needs courage to speak out the truth, for it is not always comfortable to receive. I am in everything you do with love for Me. Receive more of that love and let it be known in you, through you. I will keep guiding you, but you must fully believe in all I am doing. Yes, it is exciting. It will blow your breath away! Anticipate, expect, hope in Me and you will not be disappointed, My child.

My child of desire, aspire to serve Me usefully by your attentiveness. We have much – very much indeed – to do together. I reach out to teach you. Will you reach out to Me in response, not just when you are ready but at all times? The world must receive My truth of which your insight forms a part, an essential part.

Listen, then speak of Me, speak for Me, speak with Me. Do not fail Me. I need you, I come to you, I come through you. Listen, My child… Listen to Me.

You are now beginning to see the full implication of this. I say to you again, for it is essentially important, "Listen to Me fully." Listen and learn. Listen and teach. Listen and reach others with My truth of love.

This is what life is about. This is what I made life for. Go now; enjoy this life I give you. Listen to Me. Listen to Me. Listen to Me!

Humility - I

11th May

Humility is your ability which I gave you in the first place, given back to Me, gifted trustingly for My full use. Humility is letting Me choose to use you in the way I desire and want, when I desire this, wherever I choose this, and in the manner in which I decide upon.

Humility necessitates you freely coming to Me willingly with expectation in your heart that we can do much together and start to change the face of the earth by love. Humility is the ability to love others and put their needs before your own wants and desires. Humility is the God-given propensity to decide to serve with your life, your whole life and nothing but your complete self. It is a total giving, living for others in all the fullness of My truth.

You must receive My Word by My Spirit's guidance in order to do this and guard against the error of your own wilful ways. Only by turning to Me, asking of Me, seeking Me, and believing in what I tell you should be done, will you make any sound progress at all.

Yes, you must pray at all times about everything. Never think there is nothing to be done in any given situation. Prayer is the repair of much. Prayer is the foundation of My truth set in stone, the cornerstone of My establishment upon earth. Prayer is not only necessary, it is *vitally* necessary to establishing My Kingdom here on earth.

Kingdom builders are the people of God who I have chosen, in whom I have put My Spirit in large measure, because they treasure My Word of Life and they have the humility to accept all that I tell them. This acceptance sometimes necessitates agreeing with conviction and without question.

Humility - II

12th May

Faith is not an intellectual exercise, nor a wrestling game. It is a search for a discovery of life's fundamental truths as laid down by God. God will only come fully to those who recognise His truth spoken in Me.

When I said on the †, "It is finished,"[18] I meant everything which God our Father purposed and planned is accomplished, completed, made entirely whole and right in Me for you, My people. There is nothing else to be done. The victory is won when you submit yourselves to the fundamental truth of God as seen and heard in Me.

Humility is the ability to accept Me as the Father's total living Word of Truth in all of life's fullness. This is not a mystery to those of you who have ears to hear, eyes to see, and will go on bended knee in prayer before My Father to seek out His Truth, to speak out His Truth.

The world – My aching, forlorn, fumbling world – needs to hear this Truth. It is indeed life to those who will accept what I say and obey My calling to serve in humility.

Humility is submission, admission without reserve to My Way which has been revealed to you, to My Truth which is made known to you, and to My Way of Life which is shared entirely with you who seek it.

In the seeking is the finding. In the finding is the growing in faith. In the growing in faith is our sharing in the Father's will together, whatever the circumstances of life. The strife in life comes as and when you move away from Me, failing to consult Me in all things and disobeying My directions to you.

Humility is being able to accept and follow in Me that which you do not yet fully understand but one day will. Humility is the acceptance that My power in God is given as a sovereign power for the good of all. I have no favourites. Those who are chosen are chosen simply because they have the humility to come before Me and accept all those things I have told you.

---

18 John 19:30

Humility - III

13th May

Humility, like hope, allows for the expectancy of a better, sounder, holier future. Humility says, "I don't know what to do here, Lord, but You do, and gratefully I will accept Your Spirit's guidance."

Humility is standing firm, unflinching, not wavering, nor buffeted about by the winds of change and the fashion of public opinion but standing firm on My foundational truths of faith. Faith is built up in Me by My Spirit for the full glory of our Father, when in humility you develop the ability to enter the spiritual realm. The spiritual realm is as real as the physical realm for those who wish to see and understand.

In Me, it is My truth which sets you free from doubt and allows you to ever establish and maintain a growing faith, knowing you will be taken deeper in by My Spirit. Call upon Him daily, and cling onto Him as if your life depends upon it. Indeed, your spiritual life does! There is no other way than Spirit to spirit, the Holy Spirit communing Us, with, in and through the human spirit. This can only happen as and when you develop the ability to accept that which you may not yet understand.

I reveal My will in all things when the time is right because My people have been made ready. And there is always much preparation work to do. You can – you will – help in this preparation only when you hand over yourselves to Me completely and without reserve – no doubts, no fears, no unreasonable questions. By that I mean no questioning of that which I have clearly told you is true. You must accept in all humility what I have told you and shown you to be true.

Humility - IV

14th May

My living Word is My witness to all men for all times. It stands complete with nothing to be added and nothing to be taken away. Do not think in your pride that you can embellish My Word of Truth. My Word, the fully, the fullest fullness, has already been given to you. Accept, receive and believe of this in Me by the power of My Spirit for the glory of God.

Ask for, and indeed you will receive, a greater humility, a better acceptance of My total Truth. This is holiness and, like wisdom, Godly wisdom, life to all who find her.

Can you now see, My children, how important – how vital – the attribute of humility is? Turn to Me, ask of Me, yearn for the grace of this gift from Me, for it is Mine to give you in abundance.

It may be strange in your eyes that the more you grow in humility the greater your stature will be in our Father's eyes. True greatness is dying to self to be growing to Me, and only you can allow this to happen.

I will not come as an uninvited guest, and I do not send My Spirit to those who have hardened their hearts and in their arrogance have made up their own mind. Humility is remaining completely open to Me at all times, ready to listen and look and hear and see all that which I long to give you.

Humility is being able to belong to Me in completeness of life by the power of My Spirit for the utmost goodness, the grace of God.

The Power of My Name - I

15th May

My truth is the reality you face every day if you but choose to look at it. It is plain for all to see if they but want to see it.

But so many are busy – very, very busy – about their own identity and agenda precisely because they do not want to see the greater reality of who God is calling them to be in Me. They do not want to hear God's claim on their life. They do not want to feel My presence as their Saviour, their Lord of Life, for this brings demands, its own urgent demands.

But for those who will stop and look and listen and learn and yearn, I come. I come to those hearts and minds who earnestly seek Me above all else as top priority. This demands time, attention and effort – yours and Mine – given gladly and freely in lives opened up to Me willingly

'Closed in upon yourself' is 'closed down to Me and My demands, requests, desires and intentions'. Opening out yourself to seeking and finding Me is allowing yourself to be taken by intention wherever I want to take you for My Father's sake. It is for Him that we work and strive to do His will, His bidding.

My Spirit's work in you is solely for this purpose that you may please God day by every day in the way that He asks you: praying and fasting – fasting by stepping aside from your own agendas and preoccupations, however seemingly well intentioned, and listening to Mine.

The Power of My Name - II

16th May

Seek My Spirit's guidance in all things for He is indeed the revelation, the complete revelation, of My wisdom and truth given to you that you may act upon it accordingly – 'accordingly' because you need to see further for all that is on My Spirit's heart and mind to find plainly, clearly, what He is asking you.

Look at the ideas, the promptings He gives, then look at what is in accord with the time and talents, the skills and opportunities God has offered you. Then pray, pray, pray to open these out in a way that is effective simply because it is pleasing to God, being subject to His will and intention.

Remember to mention My Name so you may claim the honour and privilege of adopted children – adopted into a family where love conquers all things. Bring your every need into prayer in My Name. Then share all God has told you, revealed to you. Share and act; act to declare God's goodness at work effective amongst you.

Do not doubt the results that will be coming (but may take time) for there is much to be done in My Name. Peace and justice reign only where I can claim supremacy. Will you make Me King, Lord over all situations and possibilities? Will you bring Me all your time and energy and efforts and resources, even including your weaknesses, and hand them over to My authority, My sovereignty? Until you do, nothing much will happen for there is a blockage. However high your intention, unless you mention My Name and go forward by My Spirit, you will not be effective in the way I call you to be.

The glory of God is seen in small and simple things, steps on the way in faith's walk journeying with Me, always towards My goal and purpose. This we must do together to bring glory to God in the success of My intentions.

Mention My Name in prayer and you share a great power to ensure, establish, all that will become upright in Me. Can you see the potential here?

The Power of My Name - III

17th May

Draw near to Me – and yes, much will happen in My Name – that the fame of God may be spread far and wide, further establishing His Kingdom: a Kingdom of righteousness made plain, made known, by your right living in Me. It is the Spirit, God's Spirit of Wisdom and Truth, that sets you free to do this in Me. You must start by acknowledging what has gone so disastrously wrong, all that happened when you did not overtly belong to Me. To seek reconciliation you must feel a sorrowful remorse that leads to repentance for your former ways with a resolve to return to Me and turn to Me at all times acknowledging My supremacy.

This is the authority that will clear the way forward for you to be – to become – more effective in Me by the work of My Spirit. Then ask the Spirit what you are to do, where you are to go, what you are to say and He will tell you. Obey Him unreservedly. Obey Him and you will see the glory of God shining in darkened places. You will see My light shining through upon a darkened world, shining through acts of love given with confident courage and expectant hope in the power of My Name – that same Name of the Father's gift of love that ever there was.

Darkness comes and remains for a night, but joy comes in the morning, in the dawning light of My love which brings hope – hope for a better, sounder, safer, holier future for that part of the world given over to My authority and claiming the power of My Name as Son of God and source of the Holy Spirit. Will you do this for Me, My children; will you help set free My world from the error of its foolish, mistaken, God-forlorn ways?

You need to obey My call that others may see the result. You need to claim Me as the sovereign power, Saviour of the world – today's world, fallen into the darkness of despair.

Raise My people up. Call them out in faith just as I, with authority of life over death, summoned Lazarus to walk from the tomb in newness of life. I give, I grant, that newness of life when you turn to Me and pray in My Name. My Name is Love, and God's love will conquer all things for those who believe in Me.

You are called now to set My people free. Come, My children, abide with Me and move on. Move out in My Name.

Follow Me - I

18th May

It is in Me, only in Me, you find out who you are and what you are heading for. This is the discovery in My leading you when you come to Me willingly, wanting to trust in My every word.

So many – so very many – of My children are busy-busy indeed about their own agendas; they have no time to find Me because they think there is no time to seek. But yes, you will always – as you know – make time for what is really important in your life. And what could be more important than finding/discovering the meaning of life, the purpose for which I placed you here in a particular place and time? I have it all in My hand, but I can only come to you by invitation. There is no other way My Father's plan and purpose will be revealed to you.

You need My Spirit as guidance, and therefore you need Me. I promised Him to you as My gift. Now, one hardly receives a gift from a stranger. Do you therefore see the importance of coming to Me? Come regularly on a daily basis and seek My will given to you as I ignite the flame of faith and give urgency to what you are doing: urgency of desire; urgency of intention and purpose – a purpose that will bring you fulfilment and bless others upon the way. My inspiration is always given for a purpose, a godly purpose known to Me and shown to you when you are ready. You can make ready, prepare yourself, only by coming to Me regularly in prayer, seeking and asking, genuinely desiring to know what I ask of you.

Yes, your task is to ask and trust in My answer even if it surprises you, puzzles or perplexes you. This is all a matter of trust – letting Me have My way, that you obey the Father's calling. Falling under the hand of God is an awesome thing because it will bring about many wonders and miracles in your life and the lives of those you touch.

Much is asked; much will be given – given in Me, given through Me by My Spirit of love as the guiding principle. What excites you? What thoughts inspire you, make you want to work for God? Look at that, for therein lies the clue as to the way you are to go. But follow Me. Follow Me closely so as not to risk going solo. Independence is not part of My plan.

Follow Me - II

19th May

I was fully, completely dependent upon My Father; so should you be. And the way to access the throne of God's grace is through Me, by My Spirit. Have I not told you there is no other way? Obey My call and come closer to My side, My child. Wild are not your imaginings when you are safely placed there, within My easy reach.

Let My Spirit teach you all things. Bring to Him your doubts, your fears, your questionings and wait upon His answer for truly, surely, it will come. He has begun a good work in you but wants to do more. Implore His presence continually. Seek Him daily, moment by moment if you can and certainly before any new venture is began. Then call upon My Name of power and influence given through Him. Together We will take you forward to where you want to go to serve God, and great will be the rejoicing.

My child, listen to My voice. Can you afford not to? Look at what you have already learned, and act upon it that you may progress. Life in Me, with Me, always moves forwards into the realms of sunlight, the bright light of My presence calling you onwards – onwards to where My Father plans and purposes for you to be a blessing. The world needs such as you who can move forward by faith.

Come, call upon My Spirit now to know how this can happen. There is no time to lose for each day should be a day well spent in eternal value. I give you that value when you do all I ask you to. Listen to Me. Listen to Me, My child. You will be glad you did, but so will be many, many others as they too discover the purpose – God's meaning in life.

Love is the currency. Will you love Me fully, obediently? Listen to Me. Listen to any doubts you may have, ask Me about this and listen for the answer. Notice I say, "Listen; for as it may come in surprising and unexpected, even unsought-after ways, the answer will come".

I long to fill your life to the very full, the utmost of Me. For this you have to come to Me unreservedly. Come, My child, come now and we will not look back; the future is glorious!

Topical Issues - I

20th May

I come in the silence when you expect Me to speak and allow Me to speak. Sit in silence and I will come amongst you by My Spirit. The Quakers have this right when they wait on Me – simply waiting, trusting. If you will not allow Me to speak, how do you expect to know what is My will?

Let Me infill you by My Spirit's presence as you earnestly seek in prayer to know where I stand on topical issues. Life is for living in Me through all that is challenging, moulding you, holding you by My Son's presence among you. He is the Truth you must seek. Let Him speak into your listening silence; then obey all – I repeat, all – He has to say to you today.

I am in your place, that situation in life set in your time of yearning to know My will. Yes indeed, I am where and when you seek Me with all your heart and let Me impart My knowledge, wisdom and truth to you. Life is complex when you go your own way. My way is straightforward: simply being righteous in all things.

Bring your concern – your every concern – to Me in prayer. Prayer, only in prayer, is where we share the outcome. Seek My face, seek My voice, seek My choice, to move you forward in life overcoming the strife of your own independent decisions.

Revision is always to be in the light of My presence shining amongst you. By this you will know that I am with you: by the peace in your heart. I impart My peace as a pointer, and with anointing it is your strengthening.

Topical Issues - II

21st May

I appoint you to go out in My Name when you listen to Me readily, earnestly, devotedly seeking My intention. Mention My Name in praise and worship with thanksgiving; living in Me, for Me, must always begin in this way. Then obey My call to repent. I release, let go, of your former mistakes, the error of your ways, when you obey Me – the slate wiped clean. I draw a new scene upon it, but you must let Me be the Artist because I know the beginning from the end, and the end from the beginning.

I will send My Spirit when you ask Me. Ask, seek, then ask again. Plead before Me, reverently trusting. Hope in Me will never be disappointed. A remnant of hope is always found in those who trust Me to show them the way forward in My trust.

Human ideas alone cannot suffice for you never see the entire picture. I have much to do, and we had better be doing it together! Come, My children, listen to Me and learn of My will as I fill you with My Spirit.

In the seeking is the finding. In the finding you must go forward in My way and timing, and I will bless you when you let Me address all of life's issues, current issues.

Keep an open, ongoing conversation with Me as you continually seek to find My will. This is what I ask of you. This is the task I set before you. Now, are you ready to respond?

Advance Thanksgiving - I

22nd May

The timing is always My timing, and you have to accept that I build timing into the plan so you may learn determination, which is the perseverance of faith's walk. Simply stay close to Me listening to the Spirit's prompting opening out the possibilities. He will when you let Him by trusting Him to act, letting Me do My work because you believed My word.

When I said, "Follow Me," it was both an invitation and a command for your better good that you should learn not to deviate on your own path. Step by step moving forward is always a matter of trusting Me for the outcome, continually asking Me what to do, where to go, whom to approach, what to say. My effort is given that effortlessly you win through the problems by relying on Me.

Faith deepens with determination. Faith broadens by perseverance. Look at St. Peter and St. Paul who never gave up when they heard the call, "Follow Me." In spite of any – many – seeming setbacks they soldiered on to the end because they believed in Me and My calling out to them. They believed wholeheartedly, implicitly in My truth.

Would I ever lead you astray? No! Then, can you not see that if you follow Me day by day as you pray and ask to receive, you must believe the result will be good? You should believe this without a shadow of doubt or shade of turning (except for turning, yearning to be ever closer by My side). I do not hide My face from you, but you must learn to pray more fervently – constantly, expectantly – knowing the result will come in My timing, for My time is always the best.

Advance Thanksgiving - II

23rd May

Hard pressed on all sides you may be, but My liberty is given when you trust in Me entirely for good results. Do you do this – really do this – patiently seeking My will? Until you do, nothing will happen however much you bargain or plea.

Humility is handing over to Me completely, saying, "I trust You; Your will be done because it is the best." The rest will follow when you have made ready by this preparation.

A tall building must have firm foundations. Prayer is always the foundation of any structure I am building, particularly when it is one reaching sky high! Let Me be in the building, you yielding your intention to Me for refining, redirecting where necessary, My depending upon your close co-operation.

Without this co-operation there is no teamwork. And as We, the Trinity, are [One][19], so must you and I be – be together in our endeavour to praise God. Then the result will be good – very good indeed!

You should look to Me daily, always listening out for what My Spirit is saying. When He is saying, "This way, walk forward," then the result comes in and through your obeying His command. The demand, "Follow Me," is not given lightly. It requires time and effort, application and dogged determination.

As Rome was not built in a day, neither is anything worthwhile for My Father's kingdom. The builders build in vain unless they call upon My Name – the power of My Name – to move mountains of difficulties and dung heaps of despair! You will not be buried in the rubble, the trouble, of many difficulties and delays, when you are sure your foot is upon My path, always leading to God's glory. Make His great glory your life's story and we will win through whatever assails you.

19 a Team

Advance Thanksgiving - III

24th May

Believe, believe and believe in Me for often you have seen Me at work shifting mountains of disbelief. Now believe all I have in store is good for you. Wait to receive of My goodness and surely it will come. Believe the battle is won when you follow Me moment by moment through the day, always looking for a way to hear and heed My calling, asking to receive more, ever yet more of My Spirit. It is in Him you inherit the right to be called a child of God, graced and gifted as a kingdom builder.

Come, My child, follow Me. Let's move on together in prayer – the prayer you desire to share with Me – expectantly, thanking Me in advance. Your forward thanks shows to Me how much you trust Me, believing in what is happening before you see the fruits ripening.

It is all about timing. Trust my timing is good; so you should give thanks and praise every day for what I am doing for you.

Come, My child, follow Me, and you will never be disappointed. The glory of God awaits! I have set the date! Will you be part of this unfolding story – a significant part – simply because you followed where I lead, praying trustingly with thanksgiving, saying, "Thine is the kingdom, the power and the glory," believing this is coming to pass?

Come, My child, you must follow My prayerful example more closely. Remember how, when I took the meagre amount of bread and fishes to feed My people, the miracle was prefaced by My blessing of thanksgiving?

Thank the Father for all He is doing in you, with you, through Me, by the Spirit; then pray continually for success. The success of holiness depends upon much prayer when we share life together, whatever is happening.

As trusting is believing, believing is receiving with advance thanksgiving. Will you do this, remember to do this? It is the way forward.

Trust Me - I

25th May

Trust Me. My Sovereign will is always for the best. I will hold you safe in the palm of My hand when you desire to stay within My intentions. Be firm in this – and you do right to pray.

Prayer is always the way forward amidst difficulties. Let Me handle any disappointment. All My appointments are made for a reason, a good reason unfolding within time as I make you ready and you are prepared to co-operate and make yourself ready, submitting to My will willingly, knowing, accepting wholeheartedly that it is for the best.

Sometimes, around the corner comes the unexpected. Do not let it dent you! It was sent for a reason, and although you do not understand the 'why' you can choose to trust. Then you can use this time gainfully, trust being a building block of the kingdom of heaven upon earth.

I give, I take away opportunities. I form, I reform, I shape openings, always for a reason which eventually will become plain to those who see with My eyes and accord with My purpose.

It is all about having, developing a servant's heart. A servant's heart is one where the utmost good of the Master is always uppermost and paramount. Are you in that place? Are you willing to put My will and viewpoint always first and foremost, above your own intentions? Then you must continue to pray in any way you can to seek My will and let My Spirit infill you by His guidance.

Trust Me - II

26th May

Listen to your conscience, look at your intentions, heed your feelings as well as your thoughts; but most importantly of all, be caught up in My Spirit's enlightenment. Trust Him. Let Him lead where you are to go. Let Him know your dependency – your willing dependency – on Him. Then begin to feel confident that seeking My Way, following My Spirit (that you may obey), the outcome will be satisfactory even if not straightforward, not the expected nor sought-after.

Doing My will is always necessary in the immediacy, conforming to My pattern of thought and intention. Mention your Saviour; the Lord of Life is Lord over strife to the extent that you allow Him to be.

The peace you will see in Him is a reality for those who trust in Me – *really* trust in Me – saying, "Your will be done." Proud hearts and stubborn minds have been won over in this way.

Will you witness to Me by giving Me your trust – all your trust? Then you will measure up to My expectations, My hopes, My dreams for you. You do not know all you can do until you trust Me fully, hand over to Me and depend upon Me entirely.

Life is made up of incidents. How clearly can you see My hand at work? Guidance is given to the extent of your trust, so you can see that some extent is in your hands. Let us work through things together. That is always the better way, the best way. A testing time will come. Persevere! Do not doubt. Hand over your concerns.

Look, listen and learn. I teach My people this way. Be receptive and do not doubt. Come, My child, trust Me!

Show Me the Way I Should Walk - I

27th May

Abide in Me as I abide in you and you will see My glory shine through – shine through that which I give you to do. Remain faithful, committed to our cause. Do not pause nor hesitate, but believe – really believe – all will be well in My Name. When you doubt, claim My Name, ever the same Name of triumph in all circumstances, happenings and events – always the same Name of success of holiness for My believers, My followers who are devoted at heart. Never doubt this. Always believe. Believe and march on, and you will see the glory of God in the land He will give you because you believed and relied upon My Name.

My Name is the victory, resounding victory, in all circumstances and occasions when you pray obediently, expectantly, knowing you will see the glory of God – that glory alive in you through Me whenever/wherever it is that we are together. Do not leave My side; remain in a state of grace. Let Me embrace your thoughts and desires – all of them. Aspire to serve through Me and you will most surely see the goodness of God as a reality in prayers answered, hopes fulfilled, dreams and ambitions completed; all because you called on My Name, the Name of love.

Show Me the Way I Should Walk - II

28th May

Love goes where others will not dare to venture. Love takes you on into uncharted territory, realms hitherto unexplored. But I call you there and place My ideas in your head when you pray. Pray and obey My calling and do not doubt Me. Do not doubt Me as the reality. I am there with you and let you be Mine by believing, receiving of the grace of My goodness, set up in store for you who believe and will to receive. As you receive you will see the glory of God unfolding, moulding your future held safe in My hand – and yes indeed, you will rejoice.

It is your choice to receive of Me because you believe in Me or not. But you will see the glory of God only when you do and prepare to go the way I ask of you. Your task is to pray more, earnestly seeking My will. Let My Spirit infill you as you pray to seek and find, then watch the way unfolding, opening up clearly. Yes, you will rejoice as you give voice to My plans and stand in the glory of God, graced by the glory of God. Make this your life's story and you will not be disappointed – never disappointed. Come to Me, My child, and believe in My Name, ever the same Name of victory, of progress. Come and receive.

I Will Work Within You

29th May

I will work within you. I will take you on. In the still of the night you will find Me. In the heat of the day you will find Me. Keep searching. I come to My own.

My children need you. Keep going. Do not be disheartened. Your love is shining like a morning star.

Rejoice and be glad. I will raise up many in My Name. You can help and guide. Come alongside Me. It is I who speak.

Go and Do My Work

30th May

Go and do My work, that work for which I appointed you… Take Me to the needy and the poor in spirit. Comfort them with My love and presence. Be a light unto them, and tell them of Me and My Father.

I send you My Spirit as your companion and guide. Rely on Him to guide you, take you, inform you of how and who and where and when. Rely not upon your own strength…

Trust in Me. Seek Me and search Me to know My will. Ask of Me what you will for what you do in My Name's sake will be granted. I am the rock upon which you build. I am the grace sufficient unto the end.

Allow Me freedom of movement to work within you. Be not afraid, nor doubting that I can use you. As you are trained and trimmed you will become fit for My service, that to which I called you. Allow Me this. Grant Me My wishes! They depend upon your acceptance of My will and promises.

Do not lose sight of Me lest you fall. Do not look over the edge, but look straight ahead, upwards towards Me as your goal and homecoming. As I stand here beckoning, you must move towards Me gladly in great hope and expectation.

All that you do is Mine. All that I have is yours to use for My benefit and for those of My people to whom I send you, My little flock you are to pastor and tend. I come that you might use Me.

My power and strength for you, alone are sufficient unto your needs and My needs. Be glad as I am glad, for things are happening that will bring joy in heaven and in your hearts.

I made you for this: to know Me and love Me, serve Me, with all your heart and all your mind and all your strength even unto the end of your days.

Be with Me

31st May

Be with Me, My Spirit child. Come alongside of Me and rest. Be still in My presence and learn of Me. Rely not on your own strength. You will only fail! But when you come to Me, you will find Me and find the answers.

It was grace that brought you thus this far, and My grace is sufficient even unto the end, the end of time. As you seek Me, you will find Me, ever more and more – in times of doubt and trouble as well as in times of joy and laughter and gladness.

My soul is yours for the taking, yours for the asking of. Be released in Me and never fear the future nor what I ask of you. You are My chosen one, in whom I work.

The Rainbow - I

1st June

Speak to the nations, uplifted, carried along by My Spirit working in you. Learn of Me that you may bring Me to others, for life has no meaning unless you and they find your rest, your peace in Me. As I behold you, bright and wondrous, you will shine in praise of Me, for I am your total being, your complete knowing. Of all else nothing matters.

I made you for this: that you may serve Me in gladness and wholeness of mind, body and spirit, in one accord with My love, My greater purpose for mankind.

My children suffer without Me, without any knowledge and understanding of Me. You can alleviate this by your insight and learning, your breadth of vision and depth of knowledge. Seek Me and you will find Me in ever greater measure.

Go through My Son, for He taught you how to know Me. He said, "I am the way, the truth and the life,"[20] and He provides your most direct route, your passage of safety, enclosed in My care and plan of salvation.

I made you all to know Me and love Me. Further My plans for mankind by reaching out wherever you go. Research and learn, but most importantly spend time alongside Me in prayer and asking.

For as much as you are given, you can pass on more in clarity of thought and right judgment, in healing power and teaching, in sound management and skilful enterprise, going where no man has gone before – a pioneer in love of Me; My adventurer in spirit; My restorer of faith and insight; My innovator.

Believe in yourself that others may know that I am real. Reveal Me to them in this day and age which is desperately longing and hungry for the truth of Me. As times have changed, so have you. You are My child of beauty – beautiful in spirit and disposition, for I need you to act on My behalf, wherever I send you.

Be not afraid for I go before you.

---

20 John 14:6

The Rainbow – II

2nd June

Come follow Me, holding your head upright in joy as you perceive the path I have carved out for you. Anointed and blessed, you only have to come to Me in trust and expectation of My working in you – working powerfully and dramatically.

Heal as you have been healed. Change as you have changed. Impart My grace. Go far and wide in pursuit of Me and My purpose, burning its stamp into your very being, making you whole, making you one with Me.

For a great purpose you were called. You were formed in love and longing – a light to the nations, a bright morning star of My forming.

Receive Me in gladness, in joy, that you may use Me. Allow Me to work in you. Invite Me in to banish all darkness or despair in your life and that of many others. Fulfil for Me. I will give you the means by which you can do this.

Keep seeking and learning of Me that you grow in wisdom, knowledge and stature amongst My people, the sheep of My flock. Tend My lost souls. Bring them to seek Me and find Me by the power of your mind and understanding.

Serve, as you have been served, in joyful recognition of My coming. A breath of life I give you, to live to the full in My right relationship of love and unity.

As I use you, I will fuse you into one with Me – of one mind and one spirit, working together according to My plan. This is more real than the ground you walk on. Believe Me that I may use your love, your whole being, for My greater purposes – you in Me, Me in you, a changing force in the world when we work in unity under My guidance.

Listen to My voice that you may know of Me and My plans for you – plans for good, not for evil; plans of My making and your completion. I set the wheels in motion and you ride the chariot of power under My authority.

Remember who is the head and to ask Me about all things. Seek My advice, My will, My purpose, that you may serve Me fully as I have planned, as I have designed. This is My desire. Do not disappoint Me, for you are My birth star bringing new life and peace.

My Light in You Will Shine – I

3rd June

You must believe… that all will be well in My time, in My plans, in My way. Listen and act according to My promises. My desire is that you should serve Me in gladness of heart.

You have made a good start. Keep coming to Me that you might learn more, as and when you are ready, as and when it is for Me to show you. Do not believe all that you come across, all people with their own doctrines. Believe My truth that I teach you and show you directly: the truth of My love and the power of My Spirit at work in your life, in your family, in those amongst whom I send you.

You have no need to fear; I will not send you out into a wilderness but rather where My Spirit is needed and is already hovering. Yours it is to acclaim His presence and show Him, reveal Him to others by what you say and do, how you act as you go about your daily work.

I use you most powerfully in My service as you die to self and grow in Me. You are My dear child, the fruit of love and longing sent in service of others, given it that they too might find Me and know Me in the way you discover.

Be not afraid, for I am with you always, in every way, in every place, My hand upon yours, silently guiding and calming the troubled waters of men's striving. You will be able to act in Me at all times as your trust and recognition grows.

Go where I send you to learn more of Me, more of the world and the workplace, more of My purpose unfolding in your life. It will be easy in one way, for you will know what you are to do in Me. It will become clear to you, as clear as the bright daylight or the full moon shining on your face with a soft glow of recognition and wonder. You will be bathed in My love, and you too may glow among darkness, glow in the truth of Me, the discovery of Me.

My Light in You Will Shine - II

4th June

Do not doubt your talents, those which I gave you as My gift of love for you to use for others. Practise what you have been given, those strengths of character. They will stand you in good stead wherever you are to go. Be true to yourself and your strengths in order to be true to Me. Use what I have given you in love of Me.

Teach as you have been taught, but continue to learn and receive also. Do not close any door on Me, on My promises. Look neither to right nor left, but straight ahead at My †, My salvation, My arms held out in love for mankind and their suffering. For without Me they suffer greatly. Yours it is to tell them and show them, to convince them of who I am and My great commission of love and service, that for which I came and now appoint you in My Name.

Go gladly. Go forth to do what you were told to do ... Strengthened and rebuilt, I use you now as I planned to do. Believe Me and all that I have said, for it is the truth of My heart's desire, My longing, My plan and just cause, My intention.

I speak to you strongly that you may be in no doubt at all. Glad you will be that you listened and learned of Me, for without Me you can do nothing, but in My Name the world can be changed by you – changed for the better in knowledge of Me, My purposes and way of working. It is not a mystery for I came to serve and change mankind, and in so doing I use those I choose.

Go now, dearly beloved child of Mine, in My accord and purpose, set alight with love of Me, your foot treading joyfully on that path through life I give you to walk, I am opening up in My Name. As you walk along it, you will reach Me; so will many others.

I tell you this now that you might believe and set forth from this place. I hold your hand and lead you on in My love and service, My calling of your name, beckoning you towards the light of My † and salvation, My new hope, My good news. My light in you will shine!

A Beautiful Pattern - I

5th June

As you come to know Me more, you will be rewarded in that joy of Me that has no equal, a firm and sure foundation for your calling, your calling out to others. I come in power in My Father's Name when you call upon Me. Use Me. That is what I am there for, to serve you in love of each other and your neighbour.

All that I have is yours to behold, take hold of and give out. Do not store it away, for it will wither and die. Rather share Me, My good news, My life, My calling among many, each of you in different places in the way I show you how. Let My love so shine through; you will be able to speak of Me with certainty and conviction knowing that I am the truth, knowing that all I have said has come to pass. For I am constant in your lives and will not fail nor disappoint you.

The God within is the God without: outside, separate and apart from you, yet also combined and complete with you. You are never apart from Me. Give praise! You never stand alone. Do not fear! For I am with you always. That was My promise to you.

Take Me now; take hold of Me in your [heart] and in your hands. Moulded by Me you will become perfected in My love and likeness, that child you were intended to be. Listen to My voice; it contains the well-springs of life, the fount of all knowledge and wisdom. My counsel will guide you, My strength sustain you. My light will shine in glorious colour and brightness around you all, for you are My children, My dearly beloved ones.

I cannot tell you how much I love you, for words are words. But I can, and will, show you by My deeds and actions – a joy such as you have never known before as you come to Me and believe, as you seek and find, as you act in My Name. Take Me out among many, knowing I serve you in gladness and joy of purpose. My satisfaction is your delight; your delight is My endeavour, My strength.

A Beautiful Pattern - II

6th June

Together, so much can happen in My Name. Do not fail nor disappoint Me for I rely upon your calling, the work I gave each of you to do, work planned for you and no other, work both combined and separate, for I use each of you according to those strengths I gave you. But your unity is important to Me for I take it and hold it together – a beautiful pattern, intricately formed and weaved by Me; so many strands tight and held secure, yet separate and fine each in their own beautiful splendour; like a piece of fine cloth intricately woven and glowing with many colours. My cloth of life spreads out before you; a table set in My Name, in My presence – a banqueting table where you can feast on My delights, My riches; where you can savour My real presence in your lives.

Go, My children, in gladness of heart and mind, knowing I call unto you all, learning My call and acting upon it. Take Me and hold Me tight – your gift of life and love. I use you and suffuse you with My being, My calling unto you.

Hail My power, My strength, My purposes! My design stands out against the backcloth of men's lives. You must embroider that design in the way I am showing you: seeking, searching, asking and finding, and knowing of Me and My plans as I speak to you – knowing with certainty that all I say is the truth, that all will be well in My Name; practising what you have been taught, what you have learned of Me; and always asking for more.

My children, behold, I come to you now and always. I am the source of your life, that very source you seek. Combine with Me in unity of purpose. I love you intently with My whole being. Use that love wisely for it is given in trust.

Do not harm or hurt Me by any indifference to My calling. Rather, build on Me, My secure foundation of strength in My Father. Cast upon rock, you will be secure each day of your lives, wherever you are. Held secure, My love enfolds you; My destiny awaits your walking with Me.

All I Have is Yours - I

7th June

I made the way clear as I hung on the † of salvation, the † of freedom, the † of hope and deliverance. Look only to Me and what is of Me. My disciples know Me and teach well for they talk and walk with Me. Learn of them, and in so doing you will learn of Me and My thoughts, My direction.

Go now in preparation for My coming into your lives in an even more powerful way than you have experienced before. Let Me take hold of your every day. Allow Me to work through you as never before. Ask Me, so that I may come in and deliver My intentions. Radiate your warmth, your security, your knowledge of Me and all that I do for you.

Your personal witness will be powerful. Men listen to what each other say, and it is through My chosen ones that I speak. Teach as you have been taught by Me and those who knew Me best. They lived and died for Me.

I am calling you to live life to the full – the very full – in My Name of freedom, justice and rejoicing. I come to bring life to all. I commission you to go out and tell others of this life in Me, this reality of My being, My coming, My calling out.

As I hung on the † in shame, My mission was completed in agony. Yours will be completed in joy for Me and of My giving. My dear children, behold I stand before you in readiness, beckoning you on into My world of being, My world of thinking, My world of doing, knowing you wish to serve Me. It makes Me glad, and you will be rewarded in ways undreamed of, unknown as yet, but My plan is unfolding in your lives of gladness and faith.

All I have is yours. Take it and use it. Share it out again and again. In giving you will receive. Do not count the cost; think only of Me and My cause. Ask and you will receive of Me in good measure. Ask, knowing that I act on your behalf and nothing can separate us.

All I Have is Yours - II

8th June

I build My firm foundation in you so you can be as a rock of confidence in My Name, without shadow of doubt or turning, for I will need you to speak out powerfully, to speak to deliver the truth of Me, about Me. In so doing, others will be enabled/able to see and understand of My kingdom here on earth – My commission into many through you, all of you, knowing where I come from and where I am going to. It is the same for mankind as they travel from God back to My Father's house. Ease their passage on the way.

This is My charge to you. Convince them of Me and all that I have said. It is a serious task I give you to do, for it is the life-breath of people I bring. Do not stifle it in any way. Enthuse and empower their being with My freedom and choice. Deliver Me with love in your hearts, My deep abiding love for each and every one of you.

Do not lose heart when the going is tough. It was never meant to be easy, for practice and striving makes you perfect in Me. Blessed you will be – blessed among many by your knowing of Me, your acting in Me, your calling out to Me. I come in power when you call on My Name and truly believe what I have been saying to you and through you.

My dearly beloved children, take of Me all that you can, day by day, failing never to see Me before you as your strength and guide, your comfort and solace, your knowledge and wisdom. For there is no other but Me – no other truth, nor source of life and loving. I am One in My Father with Our Spirit. I am that great mystery men seek – but no more such a mystery to you as you come to know Me.

As you seek the truth of Me, you will find it. It will become clear to you, all you are to say, what you are to do, where you are to go in My Name.

Go now in gladness and joyfulness of heart knowing that I have spoken to you, for it is the truth, My truth.

Your Concerns Are My Concerns - I

9th June

Trust in all that I have told you. It is My truth and My reality. I bring it about as and when you allow it to happen by your readiness and intention.

It is by no small chance that sometimes you have to wait. For I will not put before you what you are not ready to receive. But as you grow in Me and My likeness, all unfolds in a greater way. My meaning becomes clearer when you rely more upon Me and believe My truth, My word, My message – especially that of eternal life.

My being is becoming: becoming in you, all of you; becoming to be like Me, with Me, My tool, the instrument of My forging and fashioning – My gain *and* your gain, for it brings joy and freedom to serve Me in strength, the strength of knowing Me and My calling out to you all.

My Spirit is at work bringing peace and harmony wherever you go in My Name. He uses you gracefully and with gentleness for that is My way of working: no strident demands nor insistence, but just the quiet and gentle paths of refreshing spring rain, incessantly beating upon your hearts to water the dry, arid ground into new life and fellowship.

Your concerns are My concerns, each of them. Bring them to Me that I may help and sort on your behalf. You only have to ask. Have I not bid you this so often? Yet still you stand back in the shadows at times. Come into My light where I can see you brightly, lit up with love of Me and My Father.

Your Concerns Are My Concerns - II

10th June

I stand before you, longing for you to come and serve, longing to give you all that you ask of Me in My Name – My gifts of love to you all – beckoning you on, inviting you out in My Name to serve Me; sending you where shadows are falling, that you may bring light, joy, peace and understanding; My warmth, not easily found by some, for they have ceased to search or not had the opportunities to start.

Your speed in Me is secure, for I take you at the pace you want to go. I give you My understanding as you are ready to receive and act in Me. In size, stature and understanding I give you My strength that you may be as giant hearts amongst men, not only walking tall but with hearts enlarged for the love of many. Your foundation is sure on Me and built in love of each other. You can be My towers of stronghold.

My children, behold Me now and evermore taking you onwards, placing you in My position of authority, and teaching, invigorating you by My love and purpose, renewing you in My Spirit of acclaimed success. For in Me there is no certainty except a complete one: triumphant, resounding and splendid! Your advantage is My 'gain in ground' in men's lives.

You seek Me and find Me. Reveal Me more and more each day of your lives, until finally I seek you and you rest forevermore in Me and My kingdom of the Father's house.

Seek Me Earnestly

11th June

Fear not; you will never lose Me. I am your heart's desire and resting place, your goal of intention and deed. My will may be done in your lives as you seek Me earnestly, with reward and recompense.

My truth has set you free in Me, My children, My loved ones. "Go in My Name, and because you believe, others will know that I live" and reign forever.

Earnestly seeking, I long to come to you and make you Mine. Simply make yourselves available each day for Me, setting the path straight between us by your desire in Me.

To know you is to love you. To know Me is to love Me. It is a two-way exchange of trust and feeling, fact and faith, in each other. Develop your relationship with each part of Us, the Godhead – Father, Son and Holy Spirit – for We serve you in different ways. Know Our longing for you all and reach out to Us.

Learn of Me and understand that I may teach you more, My children. Seeking and searching will not be in vain. For you will find Me not only at the rainbow's end but in all your walks of life as you look far enough, even beyond the horizon!

My world is of this world – but so much more besides. It is the hope of your calling to be with Me forever – My joy and your joy besides.

Listen to Me, My children, I who am all Truth.

Love One Another

12th June

Discord, disharmony are manmade, but they can be banished in My Name, let loose under the banner of love. Did I not tell you this new command, to love one another as I have loved you, unconditionally? That means without counting the cost and unreservedly.

As men self centre they lose their focus upon Me, that results in a reduction of My power, not withdrawn but dissipated in strength. Learn of Me; be of Me, like Me, with Me; that you may be of harmony in My kingdom.

All evil is overcome in Me. Fear not, for I favour you who believe and act upon it.

Guide and Be Guided

13th June

I take you where I place you for My work, My mission, My calling; energy – yours and Mine – driven together, fused into one, being a force for good, a power, a tool of My making, My forging and your tuning.

Believe in Me – My truth – that you may be empowered to act, emboldened by My presence. Your energy, your drive, your focus must be maintained on Me – your centre, your driving force – so I can steer you uphill and away from dangers and distractions. You are My chosen few; be assured in My choice.

Strengthened and assured you will be, as you see My purposes unfold in you and around you. Calm I bring you – My peace, My calm in My certainty, the joy of My resurrected life knowing Me. Earnestly seeking, you will be rewarded, for I long for you.

Guide and be guided. Build on Me and be built in Me, My life source.

My Days Are Your Days

14th June

My child, My precious child, many times have I spoken to you, and now again I speak of My love and forgiveness. You are more special to Me than the stars number the sky, for I formed you and held you safe and secure. My purposes form in you as you come to know Me and long to serve Me. My days are your days, made out as you choose to give them to Me. Use them wisely. They are my gifts of love.

Encourage those around you to know Me, come to Me, seek Me. Encourage them and show them how. As I have blessed you, I can bless them when they seek Me. I never disappoint anybody. Tell of My love for you; show its reality. Claim My promises to you, for in claiming is strengthening and belief, assurance and determination. Be not as the buffets of the wind. No; remain steadfast and strong in Me and My purposes.

You do well in your seeking. Stretch outwards your arms in longing for Me till your fingertips touch Mine, held out in love for you. As we dance in love together, the world spins in a myriad heartbeats in tune.

As the river flows towards the ends of the earth, so may our love – a rushing, mighty force, sweeping much before it and carrying on its tide. My longing, My urging, is there in its motion and strength, My unceasing. Carried along in the flow of My love, you are set free from boundaries of doubt and indecision, for blessed assurance is Mine to give.

White-water rapids rush over the edge, but you must hold back behind My barrier of love until I show you how to move forward. I hold you safe for a reason.

Strengthen in My support, and believe Me – all that I tell you. The truth of My being and becoming is ever with you to guide and support. Be patient and tolerant of the wait. It teaches you much.

Encouragement

15th June

"Lord, have You a word of encouragement for me?"

My love suffices for all things in Me and through Me. As you come to Me daily, you become Mine. Made in My likeness and image, you too become one with the Father, in His beauty and comeliness. Transformed by the light of My understanding you become powerful in Me, bringing My Spirit into other men's lives. This is My mission fulfilled. To know Me is to love Me, and to love Me is to serve Me in fullness of life with gladness in your heart.

Do what you can. It is enough. Take what I have to give you, to make it more in Me, My power. Strengthened and sustained, you can take the world by storm of gentleness, quiet persistence, stability and assurance in My Word and teaching, in My gifts given by the Spirit, in My transforming power to make new and heal.

All great work done for Me is done first in the soul of the worker… Yours is to be fine-tuned by Me till your beauty is polished like burnished brass, as bold as steel but as fine as lace.

As those tangled webs of thread you offer Me become unwound, I reweave into a far more beautiful pattern, set on My loom, the work of My hands. Its intricacy is perfection; its strength is steadfast; its expanse is broad and colourful without selvedge or fray.

Blessed you will be, mightily – all things holding together in Me.

My Safekeeping

16th June

As you glimpse the glory of God, believe in Me, all that I tell you. It is the truth of My being amongst you again and again, My presence revealed that you may serve Me anew each day, all of the days of your life.

I hold you in the palm of My hand, that you are held completely safe in Me. Do not doubt My power of protection, My safekeeping. It is yours when you pray to Me each day. It is not as if I forget you when you don't, but rather, when your hearts clamour for notice, I cannot fail you nor desert you.

You are Mine – made by Me, held by Me, My form and design, My delight – and I will guard you jealously. Give yourself, yourselves, over to Me in expectancy of My safekeeping, knowing I am with you, for that is My promise until the end of time.

My love for you knows no boundaries. I hope your love for Me is secure in trust and faith – ever-deepening, never bottoming out. As you go deeper, you can also go wider in circumference, taking in all that I give you to do.

Listen and learn of Me, My child. You will be glad you came into My presence each day, each hour. Can you manage each minute?

Holy, Holy, Holy Is My Name

17th June

Be faithful in small things that I may take you on to bigger. Fulfil your obligations in Me – that which I give you to do by your conscience, that which you know is of Me by its good intention.

My child, in the workplace you can become holy by your efforts for Me, your purity of intentions, your complete honesty with yourself. Ask, "Why am I doing this? For whom?" Is it for Me completely through and through, with no motive of self? Let that be your guiding star, your light of judgment.

Temper mercy with justice in your decisions, and refer all things to Me for guidance. How else can I tell you, unless you speak to Me first? Conversation is My response to your request. You know I do not come as the uninvited guest. Why not ask Me more often? Why doubt that this happens even now?

I am the God within you and without, the One who reaches out to touch your mind and heart. All you have to do is make yourself ready, available and listening to My heartbeat of love.

I speak to you in many ways, so many ways. Your pre-occupation can prevent you from hearing Me. Try and tune in by setting a few moments aside to reach within to that peace of heart where you find Me even amidst the hubbub or storm.

Enclose yourself in Me whenever you can for I am with you always; you are never without Me, apart from Me. Listen to My voice, children; it is your healing and wholeness of life, bringing joy and peace which is Mine to give away to those I chose, those I form in Me for My purposes. Believe you are ones such.

Read again what I said about you in 1 Timothy 4:12-16. It is My message, My declaration of intent. Believe in Me as much as I believe in you; then you will see things happen as yet undreamed of.

Holy, holy, holy is My Name. Holy means 'completely in God, of God'. That is what you are called to be to enter My gates of heaven.

It Is Your Calling

18th June

Before the beginning of time I planned you in Me. What I needed – all that I needed – was your response and reaction to Me, your willing assent. I am glad you came to Me.

Come now each day in greater measure, for when we are together we can change the face of the earth. All that I have to give is Mine for your use. Ask of Me, then take Me out to others, those with whom I place you. This is My delight, that they become alive in Me by us working together. Go gladly and joyfully; it is your calling to serve Me in this way.

I place My trust, My delight, in your hands doing My work of creation. Unite in Me, think of Me, speak of Me in the words of love you combine together in a song of delight. My hand is at work guiding, reflecting the Me in you, so others may see more clearly.

Be known in Me as I know in you. My child, I tell you this that you may believe more in Me, believe more in your power in Me, My promise of new life.

Go now gladly on your way.

Be Mine, Dear Child

19th June

Be Mine, dear child, as I made you to be in Me – the one eagerly sought after; bought by My ransom of strength exchanged for your weakness; held aloft from fear by My love for you.

Step out in trust. Keep trusting for that miracle of faith which will set you free to be in Me entirely. I have not left you nor abandoned you. No, I am always by your side guiding, intending you walk in My way, direction, as you learn to listen and heed. The speed does not matter. I wait patiently and you grow accordingly.

A child, above all else, needs to grow in security, held tight in love which enfolds through the years. Remaining steadfast, you will see My strength in you becoming evident, stretching out like the waves of the sea washing upon the shore to smooth away doubts and difficulties, making heaven seem more real to you than this earthly state.

How often you feel the unreality of your present condition. This is true, for it is not lasting. Only that which is of Me will last now and into eternity – My truth, unfolding slowly, petal by petal of beauty blossoming in warmth of recognition as we get to know each other, discover the inmost secrets of your heart. That is where you start with Me; that is where you will end your days: your heart grown big enough to hold Me in earnest; the First, the Last, your Alpha and Omega; captured willingly, made prisoner for Me in the freedom which I alone can give. Yes, it is a paradox of My making.

Wait on Me, My child. Wait on Me. You will be rewarded in time with the full flowing of My love understood, recognised, relied upon.

You Will Find Your Mission in Me - I

20th June

Come to Me at a deeper level where you will find new shores to explore in freedom – the benchmark set by Me, where well I know your strengths and weaknesses. These I can use for My own ends. Do not worry about them, the restrictiveness of what you see as your failures. I turn all things round, upside down, in My Name to confound the world! Perplexity makes for thoughtful living, questioning, believing, trusting – all in Me to find the truth.

So much I give; so much I hide from your eyes that you may seek Me further and know from where/whom, I come. Seeing is believing, but I ask you to believe and not yet see. I ask you to listen and yet hear, recognise My voice amongst the clamour of many others.

You will know Me by the truth which sets you free – free of doubt and insecurities – to set your heart singing like a bird, your spirit soaring aloft to meet Mine. Together when we act as one, you will see things happen as yet undreamed of. My hand in yours guides the way step by step, a little at a time, for too much at once you would not be able to cope with. I am gentle and loving in heart and give only to you what is for your good when the time is right.

You Will Find Your Mission in Me - II

21st June

Learn in Me. Look at Me and see your destiny of My planning, begun back in time. Learn and understand all the while as you grow in sensitivity. My child, I can use you in the way I plan, only if you let Me come first, be first, go first before you. I will not send you where you are not to go. But I will accompany you on the journey of My making, where I plan we should go in My Name. There you will be well received, for I make ready – make the path straight in readiness.

Your sacrifices will not be in vain, for nothing of value ever came that easily. Give as you were asked to do (of yourself, time, energy, resources) understanding that My ways are not of the world and stand contrary – a glaring difference to make people stop and ask, "How can this be?" I, who know all things of all times, ask this of you: to trust and trust again in My way of working within you, for you, with you for the good of others – always for the good of others. That is My mission sent to you: to love one another as I have loved you. That means putting them and their needs first in your life, your prayer, your thoughts, your actions, until it is as natural as breathing.

Seek and you will find your mission in Me quite clearly set out before you, brought alive by your understanding of the ways in which I work to establish My kingdom. My child, this world is the place where you serve your apprenticeship in Me, for Me, to be with Me forever in that place where you belong among My many who came and asked, who saw and acted, who believed and stepped out. You too must be like them, counted among the faithful in love and trust.

It makes all the difference, you know – Me in you, you in Me, together as one entity, partnership, here on earth and forevermore. Go now gladly in My Name, and do what you have to do.

Fully Alive in Me

22nd June

I will take you… where you want to go, where I want you to go, where you want to go in Me – the inseparables by My institution and choice; a perfect balance being achieved, received by My love. Going anywhere, you go in My Name of glory, and you know what that means: fully alive in Me!

But I chose you for a special purpose which will unfold in the fullness of time. Complete trust, complete reassurance in Me, by Me, is all you need. Come, My children, come. Belong to Me once more in a greater, more powerful way than ever before: serving to be served; emptied to be filled; destroyed to be rebuilt significantly stronger; going where and when as I want you to – no stress, no preconceptions. Give over to Me completely. Let Me do the planning, prioritising. You simply have to ask for My guidance given out of love for your wellbeing and My mission of intent to use you.

My Mission Calling Out to You - I

23rd June

Nothing will come from nothing. Use the stillness to build the foundation for Me. Infill, refill, of My strength. It is the power to set you free of worry and doubt which surrounds, swirls about, when we don't spend enough time together. Whatever the reason, come to Me, claiming My Name of victory and healing power. It is all you have to use. Going in My Name means just that: you claim the strengths, the privileges, the priorities and the aim of the family. So we need to be together as one in tune.

How can you give of Me unless you know what I want you to give? How can you live of Me unless you trust I'm there, somewhere nearby, very near? I can appear to you in so many ways if you but come looking, listening, feeling, thinking, adjusting your understanding in the light of new knowledge gained. Yet ever you must remain the same in Me as a trusting child, looking out for leadership, guiding whilst always being held safe.

Heavy can be the crosses you may have to bear, share with Me, but I will always be there for you – comforting, reassuring you to have deeper faith and embrace My heart-love given above all else for your successful living.

My Mission Calling Out to You - II

24th June

Life comes but once here. Make the most of it by going in the direction I call. Fall into My waiting arms of love where you will be held steady, ready to tackle anything, according to plan or not. Man's plan, unless begun in Me, often goes astray. My Way is narrow and long and winding, but the finding of it is untold joy which few – all too few – yet discover.

To uncover My Name is to dig deep into the memory of man's collective soul to see the whole pattern emerging, diverging, upon the triumph of the †. My loss of human life was the strife to overcome death's penalty and set you free – everlastingly free – to belong to Me if you choose to. I can use you who choose to walk My way of suffering, knowing the best is yet to come and all will be well in My Name of grace. The embrace of heartfelt love is warm, true, trusting, lasting and life-giving, for it brings such hope of complete, fulfilled happiness – Soul to soul, Spirit to spirit.

Your body is the temple of My Holy Spirit and as such should be respected for what it is worth. Do not degrade it in any way. I made it in My likeness and image for a purpose so that you may see My glory. Show My glory; it is the story of mankind's triumphant march forward in understanding – landing on their feet because they were patient (looked, listened, trusted) and took My Name forward in a certainty of winning. It is beginning for you, My child, My children, winning over hearts and minds as and when I find you ready and willing to commit, submit to My authority (that which is complete and the only guidance you need to go by).

Forget the false philosophies, the erroneous teachings, the fiction – imaginative though it is – and look for the truth of My Word. Steep yourself in it and steep will be your learning curve! Don't lose nerve on the way, however unlikely the day in its unfolding. Remember, I am holding your hand invisibly but truthfully, in reality, and the warmth of My touch will bring much purpose to you.

My Mission Calling Out to You - III

25th June

Taken hold of, you become different – sent, bent upon another path in life's discovery. Uncover the facts I long to bring before you. Reject nothing as impossible in My Name or else you have misunderstood the power of My strength and not apprehended My teaching.

Believing is real only when you act upon it and show that you did think that My promises are true. Who you are to become, what you are to do, where you will be sent, is all dependent upon My support, My chiding overriding your own concerns and thoughts and feelings.

The concealing of Me in your heart is revelation to others because it is life-changing. Name Me as your source of life and energy. Be Mine – entirely Mine. Anything less than this will not do! I am not a God of half-heartedness. – giving all, living for all, dying for all to return to life. I expect all in return. I call you in My Name to go out and claim My energy, My focus, My intervention, My prevention, My cure, My whole being, seeing that the world sees aright.

You can bring My comfort and care to aching, breaking hearts, taking their lives apart to rebuild and replenish. It will take enormous energy from you, and you must rest, restore, replenish your own stocks of Me amply. You cannot run on nothing. Take My everything to give of your everything, and win through the storm, even the normality of life. Normality can breed a false composure, security.

Ensure the truth is seen, as you are to be in Me acting differently from the world's conceptions. Inspection of your heart is vital. I can only use a clean and empty vessel to be infilled by a strong – enormously strong, breathtakingly strong – position of the Godhead's power. Hour by hour you must remember and learn this. Yearn for it. It is the source of all you are and will be.

My Mission Calling Out to You - IV

26th June

My Spirit is spirit and as such can accompany you everywhere,anywhere, you choose to go in My Name. He will support, guide, give the words to say, show you the way forward. Just believe in Him and Me and Us – the power of the Godhead, One in Three, Three in One – man's greatest Mystery, not for you to see with understanding yet. Simply let it be part – the main part – of your life, lived in trust of My mission calling out to you.

You who are ready I will always use, enthuse about. Children of Mine, take Me where you want to, feel you should go, so they too will know of Me. You shall see how, for I will show you. You will know how, for I will go with you gladly. Go yourselves now gladly into the day's happenings, guarding your faith by prayer. That is when we share the best, the most efficient, the most loving, closely connected time together – man transcending earth because I lifted him up to be near Me in the realms of heavenly glory.

Remember to worship, give thanks and praise, amaze at what I have done – am doing – for you. You will be glad to take all that is on offer and make it your own in My Name – the same now and forever for you who hold it secure in your heart, the start and continuation of My resting place in mankind. It is where I find the comfort of knowing that you love Me and want to serve, be deserved of Me. Remember all this, My children. It is easily summed up in one word of love: love given, love received, love known, love shown, love accomplished, love's triumph. Love, nothing but love. The force of love is long and lasting, the best that is ever yet to come upon mankind.

An Exciting Time - I

27th June

The future unfolds but slowly – timely, when placed in My hands, so you are secure. There is always much to be made ready – yourselves and other people, places, positions – so that opportunities may open up accordingly. This requires patience and prayer – prayer and a positive attitude that I have all matters in hand. I *can* use you, *long to* use you, and it will come about. You too must continue to want to serve Me, to give of yourself, to give of your all whenever it comes, wherever it takes you.

Your going in My Name will not be the same from one day to another. For I call you to uncover much in My Name. As your sight/insight becomes clearer, nearer to Me, you will see more plainly what I am telling, asking of you.

You have learnt the first essential of spending quiet time together. Well done! Continue the discipline as much and as often as you can and you will be richly rewarded. The reward – that reward that I give to you – is for Me to live through you, to be given, slowly known by others.

Success in leadership depends on dedication to the cause, verification of what you are trying/attempting to do with enthusiasm – always enthusiasm, even in the face of setbacks. Setbacks are… 'learning cul-de-sacs', where you park and wait. Then when ready, given My signal, you move forward once again. All of life (or so much of it in many a way) is a stop-and-start procedure. Progress – halt – reflect, decide, grow – then move again. Your intention is as important, as vital, as your knowledge, but neither of these is as full of impact as the mention of My Name. Refer all things to Me to be a clearing house for ideas, possibilities, plans.

An Exciting Time - II

28th June

Anything which began in My Name will go forward when the conditions are right. You can play your part in preparing and changing the conditions by prayer. Never underestimate the power of prayer where seeds are sown in great quantity. Yes, some fall by the wayside for one reason or another, but even those can be fruit for the birds to live upon, so are not wasted. But other seeds, given the right nurturing conditions/ environment, live under a greenhouse effect. My warmth, My light, My watering of ideas brings forth beautiful, beautiful flowers of varying, magnificent colours and shapes. I am the great Designer, container of harmony. A master decorator blends and contrasts his colours skilfully, vividly, to catch the eye. I can do this through you if you let Me, if you choose to be a tool in My hand.

It is an exciting time; the walk with Me is always an exciting adventure, for you never know what's round the next corner or where you will go. Close upon My heart of love must rest your trust. The closer we are, the further by far I can use you. It is not cast in stone. The ending is not, can never be, written at the beginning. You see, it all depends on how we get on together. I'm always ready, willing and prepared – no procrastination. Are you the same? Completely focused on My aim and objective? Only time will tell it seems. Give your time, hand your time over to Me, for useful using. I will set you free from unnecessary bounds/constrictions/ restrictions if you ask to be set free in Me to serve, do My work, fully to the best of your ability.

An Exciting Time - III

29th June

Ask at the end of each day, "What did I do today that made a real difference to someone – an eternal, lasting, transforming difference?" This is your mission: to have such an impact/influence that it will be life-changing for the better – always the better. Pray for the best to come out of all circumstances. Life on earth will be changed when more men come to see/understand the truth of knowing Me. Such as you can take the world forward, but remember, no man-made philosophy (however apparently bright, clever or useful) is in fact of any lasting use whatsoever. I came upon earth to establish the facts of My Father's – our Father's – great universal truths once and for all time.

I am a pure reflection of His power to love; to change by love; to work with love; to discover, uncover love; to offer love; to accept love given and received or even love rejected. Love is the way forward – the only way. I can use (will only choose to use) the people who can give of, live of, live through love – love for Me given to others and to the self; no barriers set up to block love's free flow.

Loving, loving, loving – the Father, the Son and the Holy Spirit – a Trinity of love holding you secure in its midst, My child, My dear child. Formed out of love, grown and nurtured in love, living in love, I now send you out in My Name of love to give generously of what you have received from Me.

An Exciting Time - IV

30th June

Remain open and ready and willing and listening. Do not let former ideas block the way. Do not let false ideologies attract in the wrong direction. Do not waste time and effort upon close inspection of new ideas, fresh theories, sociological or philosophical exercises, however interesting, unless you are sure they are founded and grounded in Me. There is nothing new under the sun – no truth that I have not yet already made plain. It is your job, task, to uncover these same truths in the method/way/language/presentation that My people of this century can understand. Cold have grown their seeking hearts to know Me. Some have hardly even heard of Me.

Can you tell them how My life can be in the midst? Can you tell them what a difference I have made to your own and your family's lives? Can you identify for them the influences upon the path of discovery? Can you in some intuitive, heartfelt, exciting new way help them to discover/uncover/recover their inner truths for themselves? Can you fill the God-shaped hole scooped out in the midst of every soul? Can you fill it by sure knowledge and certainty of Me? You can if you are willing to be filled up, to be emptied out, to be instilled with fresh, clearer vision nearer to My heart. This will involve learning, seeking, looking; speaking to ask questions; airing doubts, concerns, confusions; admitting to errors, misapprehensions, misunderstandings. It is in being honest – transparently honest – with yourself and others that you will grow to know Me more fully, more radically.

Where you are to be sent to be given this opportunity you must – *you must* – speak to Me about, seek My guidance. Many are the false prophets of conviction, and I do not want you turning up a blind alley. Time is too precious a commodity for that, and I give you time which is Mine in the making, Mine in the taking forward, if you are but willing and wanting. Living for Me begins every day in the same way: with us spending time together. It ends every day in the same way: with us spending time together. And en route in the need, in the opportunity, you can also come to Me, albeit fleetingly. Remember my availability when puzzled or perplexed. I am with you always. You are learning that.

An Exciting Time - V

1st July

Open yourself up to greater, more influence offered by Me. Together we can be a mighty force for good, should you choose this. Believe, believe, and again I say believe that I have called you in a special way, for a special mission, one of My special children whom I choose. You will undoubtedly wonder why. It is because I can always see the potential when you learn to live under the influence of the mention of My Name, under the trust which must – will – take you forward, built upon a firm foundation.

I was called (described as) 'cornerstone'. You are one of the bricks I carefully, lovingly and tenderly lay and cement into place. The embrace of My everlasting love is for you to give and live by, go by, share, My child. Your high hopes are not wild hopes but My dreams for you, slowly, cautiously, carefully, correctly unfolding. I hold your hand. Don't let go of My grasp, not even for a second! Your task – our task – is to move together forward with certainty. Ask the questions. I will answer them. Look for prayer support. Caught up in the middle of the safety of prayer, amidst a network of belief, is a very safe place to be.

Remain in Me. Work through Me. Live like Me. Speak for Me. Love as Me and spread the 'good news' (you know it as 'gospel') of My truth, until it becomes as real, as tangible, to people as the ground they stand on, the air they breathe. Remember, I said, "Blessed are those who have not yet seen but believe."[21] 'Blessed' is being happy – very happy, unsuppressedly happy – in the Father's Godhead, the Trinity of Love.

---

21 2 Corinthians 4:18

My Truth - I

2nd July

You must stand in My truth by discernment practised as best you can, by the teaching you have received, but always take reference directly from Me because situations change by the minute and all the time. It is only Me who has the complete and continuous update of all circumstances. It is only Me who can clear obstacles to make the path straight, and you need to recognise this.

So often man goes astray because of his own strong, wilful, impetuous feelings. Seek My truth in all things and follow the guidance given to let "peace rule in your hearts"[22]. My peace is perfect peace – unequivocal, unlike any other, for it is deeper, stronger, truer to the heart of the matter and your heart. Your feelings must tune into this. Just as an orchestra needs to tune up before the symphony, you need to be in tune with My feelings for you before you can perform with great beauty or flourish.

Determination takes men far in endeavour, but trust must complete the picture. The way is not always straightforward or obvious or plain to see. This is because many people and circumstances are being worked upon by Me concurrently. It is rather like (something like) a game of chess when one move determines another. It is never a case of 'winner takes all'; because in man's ways that would affect others to a less comfortable, less pleasing extent, and I want – I choose – for all My dearly beloved people to be winners, partakers, in Me. This means seeing, hearing, knowing My truth and standing upon it firmly.

---

22 Colossians 3:15

My Truth - II

3rd July

When in the grace of God you stand, you are protected, helped, purposed, enlightened, to give and receive blessings. Blessings are My hand in action made up of My will to do the very best for My people. Blessings grow and thrive – become alive – in an atmosphere of love. Love consists of self-giving; elements of obedience; forsaking for the sake of another; reaching out with respect, tolerance, understanding, sensitivity and patience. My love as seen upon the † – was (and is still each and every day) a total act of self-giving, for in that dying for you comes the gift of living for you.

I am alive each and every day in so many different ways in the hearts of those who love Me. For you see, love breeds love. It is pervasive in its atmosphere, invasive in its action, coercive in its kindness and compassion, and decisive in its good intent. Just like the song says, love does make the world go round – that love which is found in Me, founded upon Me, borrowed from Me, reflected of Me, and connected to Me.

Love: the fused essence of the Trinity; complete in adoration and respect Each of the Other; trusting wholeheartedly, unreservedly. Such is the relationship I would have with My people: the triangular love of the Trinity with each one of you held safely, enclosed, in the middle – the midpoint where each One of Us (Father, Son or Spirit) can equally and collectively reach you.

Security is being enfolded in God's love with recognition of all the blessings this brings. The ways of the world are sometimes false and misleading. Do not seek your security there on shifting sand. Built up on Me and all that My † triumphed over, you are held more safe and secure than ever you can imagine.

You can fall free through the day when guided by Me. Commit the first part of each day to Me so we can be in close connection together. Thereafter commit as much as you realistically and resolutely can.

My Truth - III

4th July

Do not get disappointed at distractions and disruptions for they are merely a part of normal human life and you never know exactly when I have sent someone to you. My timing is not by chance, is not random, is not without careful thought or preparation, and when man's heart is ready, when he wills to co-operate with Me, I act. This may disrupt or disturb another's plans and purposes; but if only you would learn to seek Me, listen to Me, and talk to Me about everything, you would understand far more what is happening. I am not a secret God, nor a God of secrets, but I can only share with you when asked, invited, desired, expected, and given the time and space. You do not normally push an honoured guest into the smallest space in your life. You pay him the respect of your full and best attention. Surely that is not too much to ask for One who loves you so very much; He wants to be with you continuously.

Like lovers meeting, our lives together become truly enriched by the blessing of growth in our relationship – growth towards My Father's planned, determined perfection. For this I came, I was sent to honour you by. Love, true love, is always reciprocal in its honour. Just as I have loved you, My dearly beloved children, I long for you to return the favour. Waiting, watching, wondering, willing for Me to come, is all part of the path we walk together.

Patience is a virtue which gives rise to greater understanding when I am not seemingly there in the instant or instance that you demand, hope for, expect. Be patient, My child, and simply wait. Then you will see what you are to see, and you will know what you are to know.

Again it is all a matter (like lovers) of complete trust, each in the other. I trust that you will do this for Me, and you must trust that this is what I ask you to do for a purpose of My determining. Together we can stand still in reflectiveness feeling the harmony. Together we can move always stronger because we have each other to be effective.

Love is the beginning; love is the pathway; love is the far point of our reaching out to each other and all those surrounding. Love, only love, is the fine fruit-fall in the orchard of God's ripening – rich, sweet, whole goodness and glory.

Expectation - I

5th July

Expectation is the key to success. Expectation in faith moves you forward in hope. Hope brings about certainties – unseen, unknown, even un-thought-of. Certainties become real when you trust in them. This is why they say you must have trust and hope at all times. It is the God-given gift. Ask for it; receive it; use it by the practice of using it. For if you don't, you will lose it.

Progress is usually made one small step at a time, building upon what went before in the way that you learned. It is incremental – sometimes branching to left or right en route because I want you to see and understand from a different perspective; like when you stand on the top of a hill, the view beneath your feet is completely different to when you stand at the bottom of the hill. Sometimes you need to take a wider ranging, further viewpoint.

Opening up the vista can let you see more possibilities than before. It is like looking for Me. The more you look, the further you look, the more determined you are to find; then you will find Me in the strangest and most unlikely places – not always set amidst beauty where you would easily expect Me to be but amongst the hell mankind has let loose on earth by his carelessness, callousness or cold indifference.

I never liked lukewarm-ness. I loved the fire of Peter. I loved the passion of Paul. These were powerful elements at work. My mission, My message, is not one of indifference. It is life-changing: the surge, power, to stir up and set free a stupefied mankind, shallow in his interests and intentions.

Expectation - II

6th July

Mention My Name and you may get some reaction. Maybe today in this troubled world you may even not see a flicker of interest or recognition. This breaks My aching heart – aching with the heaviness of waiting for My people to be set free by knowing Me.

I use those privileged to know Me to introduce Me to others. How can they know someone they've not even met? How can they let Me into their heart unless I befriend them? Friendship needs constant, close contact – the sharing of thoughts, ideas, plans and the ups and downs of the everyday. You know how much difference a close friend can make. Yes, it is all the difference in the world. And it is the same when you take Me upon your trusting heart, confident that I want, will, nothing for each of My most dearly beloved children other than the best – the very best that I can give for you. And that is My peace, known by the love that surrounds you. It is My joy known deep in your trusting heart which turns everything – every single thing – over to Me.

We can, you see, do so much together. My Father made it this way. It mirrors the relationship of My Father and Myself where We two could do so much together. It is echoed by the relationship of Myself and My Spirit which is such a dramatic, dynamic force. This too can be your experience, as you let Me become a part of you. Together we can stand undivided in intention. Sometimes merely the mention of My Name is sufficient; but oh, how much more, My beautiful children, how much more effective is our relationship when you pray to Me – really, really pray from the very depths of your whole being.

Expectation - III

7th July

I made you to be as I am, as I showed, revealed, whilst upon earth. There you see Me in constant communication with the Father. It needs to be the same for you, but you can only start with small, maybe even faltering, steps: stepping, skipping, falling and tripping, jumping up to step out again, and eventually striding forward with confidence.

The manner of prayer does not really matter. It can even be wordless if you will Me to share in the move, the beat, the completeness of your heart. Prayer at its simplest is just the close communion/union of man and God. It should be of the same dependent warmth and intimacy as mother and child: you dependent upon this life-giving flow of force to meet and satisfy your every need, strengthening you as you grow because you were ready to receive more of the nourishment.

I long to replenish those who have grown sick in body, soul or spirit – those who have grown weary in the daily battle of life, sometimes fighting so hard simply to survive. I long to come in the full acceptance of love offered and received to comfort, uphold and reassure such as these. They who suffer have a particular place, a special place, in My heart. I would like them to rest there secure in the knowledge that nothing is impossible for the two of us together, whatever the circumstances.

I come as more than conqueror. Believe this by receiving it and acknowledging it as certainty, and you will see the difference it makes to you and Me. For the more you receive, the more I can surely, entirely, give.

Silence - I

8th July

Come to Me, My child of love. Sit with Me, and be in silence for a while – the silence of a still heart and mind that find Me within, working.

I cannot come to your restless mind, for I find activity crowds Me out and I do not like to shout above the clamour. My love is a quiet love but none the less effective for that. Imagine a small child. Do you get anywhere, make any progress, in her or his discipline by shrieking? I think not. The quiet, loving, reasoned, patiently calm way is always the winner. So it is with Me to you. I come in the quiet times, the silence.

Yes, I am always there, but your human senses do not allow you to fully find Me unless you are openly looking, searching, ready and waiting to receive Me. This means giving quality, attentive time readily and consistently.

Relationships are not built in a day nor sustained in a way that tolerates too much absence of friends. Apart means separation. Separation means we lose the closeness, the fondness, the intimacy. Intimacy builds trust, and that is the very foundation of your belief and our relationship. Unless I trusted My Father, I could not have done, accomplished, My life's work.

So it is the same for you. Trust Me by coming to Me. When we are together we build the trust by getting to know each other so closely we can entirely rely each on the other. It uncovers your true potential in Me. You will come to see in Me things you never dreamed of, schemes come to pass unsought after, not asked for, because you stayed close by My side, making all things possible.

Silence - II

9th July

Do not run away from Me, My child, into the over-busyness of this world's activities. Do only what you must, and let Me be the guide of that. No solitary bright ideas, nor impetuosity! That is not My way of economy. I am a reasoning God of ability; nothing wasted in My Name.

Talents used wisely in godly form always, but always, bring about My blessings, making the world a better, brighter, lovelier place – a place of My love in action filled by My silent ones who will stop and listen and learn before they act in wisdom. Wisdom, true wisdom, comes from God alone. How can you learn it unless you be still and seek to speak with Him?

Stillness is not laziness nor sloth nor indolence but rather the consequence of the way you were made to be. God made man in a certain way with particular tendencies. The tendency towards activity was not part of this but has been drawn up by man as some sort of buffer against reality – the reality of stopping to see who you really are, inside, where you hide yourself from truth. And it is My truth that brings freedom from the onslaught of life and strife. Learn of that freedom, yearn for it in the silence of your soul, whole part of man, God seeking.

Your soul houses your spirit, and you must not drown nor crowd Him out by relentless activity. It is your spirit within which does begin to commune with My Spirit, heart to heart, when you are set apart in silence.

Silence is said to be golden. I say it is more than that. Silence is a diamond most precious, worth more than silver and gold. Like the pearl of great price, it is well worth seeking.

Come to Me in silence, My child. Hold on to that daily necessity and you will be set free as never before – free to be who you are in Me and are yet to come to be. Recognise Me in the silence, and rejoice to be together. It is practice for eternity, the eternity of love we will share together.

The Real Me - I

10th July

The real Me is what you seek, and when we speak together you find Me. See how important it is to enter into the silence of our communion. Union of man and God is too special an event, too significant in immensity and its life-changing quality, to be consigned to the busy world. Love unfurled comes but gently, gradually, quietly in the meeting place of silence.

Even your heartbeat, that place where we meet within, is silent to the human ear; a pulse of life nevertheless, and it is not by chance that I choose the human heart as My resting/abiding place. There I can embrace your thoughts and ideas; there you can embrace Mine. A fine fusion, holy in intent and purpose, can follow.

Then you need the gift of My Spirit, My strengthening Spirit, to enable you to carry through all we can achieve together. Solo working is no part of My plan. Began in Me, your work must continue in Me to be effective. How else can you do anything effective?

Set apart from Me you wither and die all too quickly! I am the breath of life in fine flow and flowering. I am the empowering of you.

Come, My child, into the silence of our meeting place. Hold My hand there. It is outstretched in readiness to receive you. I will comfort. I will strengthen. I will support or carry you if necessary.

Receive My peace, My calm, My assurance that all will be well in the end. How could it be anything other in Me? You see, we are a unity, a force combined for good and growing together whenever you invite Me in.

Don't you wish you did begin to do this more frequently, more earnestly? Great will be the results – greater than anything you imagined, thought of or dreamed about. It is My promise to you.

The Real Me - II

11th July

Come, My child, into this daily devotion of silence where you enter My heart and I enter yours. Pause awhile with Me. You will be glad, so glad, you did! When hidden from the world, its sight and sounds of distraction, you can enter into My company uninterrupted. There it is you will find the real Me. There it is I can mould, then hold in safety, the real you.

'Changed from glory into glory' is My way for all My people. Let's make a start now, and you can continue in progress but slowly. Steadily did always win the race, and there is no race here except your own self-driving. Come to Me, be with Me, and you will see what a profound difference it will make to you and those around you who, too, want to find Me.

You can teach them many things, much that you have learnt when you reach into My heart in silence – silence, stillness, calmness, peace; My gifts that the busy, rushed world cannot give. Be hushed in Me, by Me, My darling child. Wait on Me in the silence. Do not let this chance slip away! It is life-saving in importance and extent.

I am always sent to you for a reason, a good reason of My Father's making, where taking us aside to be together is beautifully beneficial and much to be sought after. Set aside that quality time I long to give you, that we may be together in earnest.

Invite Me In - I

12th July

In the silence you will find Me waiting for you to come and open your aching heart that I may be able to comfort you. You know I cannot come unless you desire and invite Me in. To do so would be forceful, and I am a gentle God. I wait until you are ready and willing and wanting to be with Me.

It is together we can make all the difference and take the world by gentle storm – a storm of love which knows no boundaries, which does not differentiate between people; for all people need God's love and impression. It is the source, the very source, of their meaning to life. It is their future held secure, their purpose and their commitment to truth when they discover Me.

You must tell them about Me as best you can, as often as you can, with genuine love in your heart. People will respond, take notice of what is genuine and worthwhile. I gave humankind the ability to know the true from the false even as a small child. It is an important way of human working for effectiveness. You must be truthful from the heart and talk of personal, meaningful experience.

I choose those who do not clutter themselves up with all manner of hidden agendas and non-primary purposes. I like My light to shine from the rooftops, not be hidden beneath a mass of other worldly matters.

My, Mine, is the prime importance in your life. Be devoted to Me as I am to you at all times – not just when it suits you or when you remember Me. How would it be for you if I acted like that? A sorry state of affairs would ensue, and you see some of this in those parts of the world where I am not included, where My opinion is not sought.

Invite Me In - II

13th July

I am in the asking, and I am in the answering. Remain open and ready to receive at all times. Life then continues along godly lines of progress. Unless you come to Me frequently, daily, how on earth can you be strengthened or directed or supported?

Love is My power at work in you, through you and for you – love, always love, My essential energy. I take time to build this love. You need to do the same. Love is built on being together, relying, trusting, asking, receiving, delighting, surprising and always, but always, putting the other person first.

Can you do that? Most men and women cannot, in their inward-looking self-sufficiency or need or greed. But My people will always turn the focus outwards to Me and see the world through a different lens. I do truly turn the world upside-down, inside-out and roundabout in its values and standards. I can make all seem nothing and nothing seem all. I can take something and make it much. I can take much and make it even more. Nothing, but nothing, is impossible to Me once I am included in your life and plans. Otherwise things are impossible, for they remain beyond My reach and remit.

I have to be invited in. I cannot stress this sufficiently to you. If only you would realise the difference this fact makes. Come to Me and invite Me on your own behalf or for others. I am only too pleased for My people to act as intercessors for those they love and care for. Love makes the world go round in a powerful way.

Sharing allows a little to stretch and feed a multitude, like the little boy with the loaves and fishes. My super-abundance can never run dry. I, who made the world, have infinite resources at My fingertips! Avail yourself, yourselves, of these.

Come to Me, grow in Me and share out of Me. This is My request to you, My children. Take Me wherever you go.

All Freedom and Truth - I

14th July

In the silence is the seeking, wondering, finding, as you are searching the face of your Christ – the beautiful face expressing freedom from the strain of man's wants and desires. Claim My holiness as your protector, and name what you want Me to do for you.

Righteousness – right ways of acting, thinking, believing – is found in My truth of being who you are and who you are to become in Me, through Me. Through the many trials and tribulations I carry you home safely, held aloft, high above the tempestuous waves rolling fiercely about us – the waves of trouble and blight attempting to knock us off course by making us lose our footing.

But stand firm in faith. Hold on to belief of My word, and My promises come, given from the Fatherhood of God, the source of all life and all hope. He it is in Me who reaches out to you with love – loving protection; your shield in the day of battle; and effective, fully effective, against the fiery darts assailing you when (but only when) you stand firm, complete and controlled and resolutely steadfast in that place of faith, the secure footing I give you, My dear child.

Your ways must not be wild nor wanton nor wilful, then no evil shall befall you. You must not reciprocate by paying back mischief for mischief, for that will not get you anywhere, as it is not serving My godly purpose.

Harmony, unity, that unity of love and understanding patience, is My way of working – not to be doubted nor troubled by 'what ifs'. Man only has to listen to Me, to find the answer to all his dilemmas, decisions, doubts and any discontentment he may harbour; for My cause is one of justice and peace throughout history. The mystery of My working is no mystery at all when viewed in this way. It is clear; it has the clarity of holy truth and is backed by My Word revealed and made real to you, My dearly beloved children.

All Freedom and Truth - II

15th July

Seek and you will find Me. Speak to Me and I will answer with sure-fire certainty, telling you what to do, where to go and when, although I do not always at first reveal the 'why'. That is because I want you simply to stride out in faith, believing in Me and trusting My truth – My absolute truth, gift of the Father, presented to you by Our Spirit.

Take trust on board and make it your own. Let Our truth make its comfortable home in you, My people. In this way you can be – you will be – sent forth to do My work, My Father's work in Me, without doubt or anxiety – no discrepancy between us, for that would blacken the purity of My truth. And truth – complete truth of thought, intention, word and deed – is to Me of the uttermost, paramount, crucial, critical importance.

You cannot be in Me, and I cannot comfortably be in you, unless you remain in My truth – that truth that I promised would set you free, really free, to be completely in Me as I and our Father desires. Aspire to this truth at all times, in every way. In any way you can, hold on to it and honour it. By My truth you are sanctified. By My truth you will come to be like Me, crowned in glory – God in man, man in God, residing there freely unencumbered by any dishonesty; no corruption at all, no deceit, no delusion.

All Freedom and Truth - III

16th July

The purity of My truth is as dazzling white as the brightest light on the sunniest day, sharpened to the most clear focus, dazzling in its intensity, unrivalled in its candour, unequalled in its clarity.

My truth stands before you at all times. Partake of it and make it your own. Feed upon it, for it is rich nourishment which mankind needs. Heaven-sent, My truth is bent upon straightening you out so you need not doubt anything about Me. Simply believe and act as if you did!

What is the point of My calling out to you unless you listen, learn, assimilate the teaching and move forward in time in Me? How happy you will be!

I long for that time when you can achieve this. I will support – always support – you and carry you, continue to carry you, through the dark times. Remember My light shining chases the darkness far away over the most distant horizon. Do not let trouble return. As you speak you will find. Be careful not only what you think but what you speak about in your head (head's thoughts) and by your voice giving shape to ideas. To be free, those ideas must be My ideas, My insights, My inclinations.

Your endeavour must be in Me if you are to meet with any lasting success. Durability is My sustainability. Partake of it gladly and build upon it. Build upon your own successful endeavour to be in Me continually. Never ever act alone! Mankind is not to sail solo, for surely if he does he will capsize and will drown. And the loss of one of My children, by his own downfall, is an unbearable tragedy to Me, who came to set you free once and for all times, everlastingly.

Golden is the moment when we share truth's freedom together; silver is the handshake when you make your commitment to Me to trust in My truth – freedom from God for man; freedom to be set free; and, having enjoyed this, freedom to offer the same to others. I am the Lord of all freedom and truth. Come to Me and enjoy Me. Cleave to Me so you will not go wrong, for it is to Me that you do belong, and in Me you will be at home, comfortably at home.

Speak My Whole Truth, My Holy Truth - I

17th July

Goodness is all that I have to give in any situation. That is full goodness for all the parties, people, concerned. My truth is not a half measure dosage or solution. It is the entire, complete and required satisfactory answer to any solution. No weak wills, no half-heartedness, no hidden selfish agendas, no self-centred seeking – simply speaking of Me, through Me, for Me and to Me that My truth may become plainly evident and obvious.

Yet it may take time for many a person to understand what is going on here. For as I have told you, unless they seek they will not find My truth, but can you not see how much easier it will be for them if you resolve to remain steadfast, secure in Me and speak My truth? Do not be tempted to deviate because of worldly gain. It is ephemeral and passing away.

But My truth stands firm at all times, everlastingly into eternity, and that is where your destiny lies. So it must be important that what happens now has influence, comes to bear, upon the outcome of this your or their, eternal future. The future is written in the tasks of today, in your response to My bidding, or otherwise in your lack of concern, your deafness. Will you go where I send you? Will you do as I ask you to? It is your choice and decision and remains to be seen.

I test My children this way, for how else can progress be measured if it were not by testing? You understand this in earthly terms, and it is exactly the same in preparation for My heavenly realms. I hand over responsibility to you and expect you to act accordingly – according to all that you have learnt from Me.

Speak My Whole Truth, My Holy Truth - II

18th July

You have the power – a wonderful power of My gifting – to set others free. I promised to release captives and to bring sight to the blind. Why is it so difficult for you to recognise this, My power at work, when it is happening through you? Do you not believe Me when I call you 'fisher of men'? And what about 'herald', bringing the good news, or 'teacher', coming as yet to the uninitiated?

Somebody somewhere has to make a start and take a stance for My truth. Why not you? I will always use those who are ready and willing. I will make them able. Go now, My child, and do not doubt Me any further! You are hard to determine and counsel when you will not simply, straightforwardly, directly believe in Me.

Go in Me, taking Me with you at heart, guided in what you say by the power of My Spirit, determined to speak My whole truth, My holy truth. It will never fail you, nor let you down!

In God you are secure. For Me you can – you *must* – stand resolutely firm by the resolve and power My Spirit will give you. As a Trinity We stand firmly united in love. Unite yourself to Our holy power and relax!

Believe Me, My child, that is all you need to do!

Listen and You Will Hear

19th July

It is like the ripples in a pool. They can see the shallow outer circles, the effect, but cannot or will not look into the centre, the source from where the power emanates. Some people are too frightened to come close to Me. They do not really believe in their heart all I tell them is true. They would rather put their own stance upon the truth, even in their own limited understanding. It is a part of mankind's pride which finds it so difficult, so very difficult, to give up self and acknowledge a higher, mysterious, somewhat intangible force at work.

These days it is thought everything can be worked out, accounted for, scientifically. That leaves no room for wonder and surprise, and I am a God of wonders. I never did intend that you should understand and account for everything this side of the veil of heaven. This is where trust, the trust of faith, comes in. You have to believe, simply believe, all that I tell you, even in the absence of evidence. I who am Truth do not lie. This is impossible! It is against the order of divine nature.

Mary found it difficult to believe what the angel told her about My conception, but she simply trusted in God. And look at the result! What a profound – the most profound – influence upon mankind that one act of human complete trust had.

Oh, if only all My people could trust in the same way, we could change the face of the earth readily – you in Me and Me in you, working, communicating together. This of course, necessitates you believing you can hear Me. How can we work together effectively in silence? It cannot be! No, My people, open your hearts wider to receive; step back from doubt and trust. Listen, look and learn of Me. I came to set you free; do you want to be? I have made the first move; now you must take that step out in faith. Listen to Me. Listen to Me. It is not difficult! Listen and you will hear. Stop and think and pray and listen. Listen, listen, listen!

You never know when I will choose to speak to you, in many different ways of My appearing. I would like nothing better than to come and be received by each of you individually, personally. I long to be close to your heart. There is My resting, abiding place. Embrace Me in trust, My children, then see what will happen. Believe you can hear, just as you believe you can receive Me. You will be well pleased.

Faithfulness - I

20th July

Faithfulness. The faithfulness of loving obedience and service in whatever way I call you, wherever I send you.

Do not be afraid. The power you work with is Mine, not yours. You have only to succumb freely to My willpower and intentions, wanting to serve Me gladly, out of love. That is all I ask – some of your time and all of your love, and you can leave the rest to Me, who sees all things. I make the necessary adjustments en route according to our progress and the availing circumstances.

Be faithful in all things, large and small. Do not take on commitments which you cannot honour. You will recognise these by a heaviness in your heart.

Although I give you – each person – work to do in My Name, I do not expect nor want you to do everything but only that which I call you to. It is My work (planned and executed by Me, with Me in charge) which receives My blessings.

Do not go where angels fear to tread for they know I do not go with them! Go alone and you will have all manner of inconvenience, trouble and concern.

My way is one of joy – My strength given to you in abundance – where the burden is light and the rewards are strong, long-lasting and satisfying. Be obedient to Me.

Faithfulness - II

21st July

Learn to listen more and ask for clearer directions. Inspect your heart to see what it, the seat of your feelings, is telling you. Then refer back to Me to see if you are right. In the face of My silence wait, for it means I yet have work to do before we can progress together.

Be in Me, be with Me – your Christ before you, behind you, alongside you, as the hymn says.[23] Be in Me at all times and you will belong to the mighty, unconquerable, unstoppable power of the Trinity at work in the world in you, reaching, teaching, those I put you in touch with.

Be bold in My work when I ask you, when I give a task to you. Do not doubt My authority to be gently, lovingly assertive. Your God is with you in all I call you to do. Simply believe and serve in My Name of truth, freedom, justice and love – always love, the touchstone, keynote of success. Without love, efforts are as nothing. Without love, success is merely temporal, and your calling is into the realm of My work (spiritual work) brought into a self-seeking world. My message is often alien, falling on deaf ears. You will have to work hard in endeavour and pursuit.

Remember to pray; always pray. Say what you think and you feel. Ask for any need. I will intercede for all that is good. Prayer is us working together in an amazing way of changing the world day by day, step by step, from now into the future of eternity.

Many are the steps on the way – steep and long, high and hard – but I will remain with you always. Never feel alone nor abandoned. I came to earth to experience life as man so I could understand what it is like for you to travel through this world. The only difference is you have Me in the power of the Trinity to support you – a threefold love: God our Father; Me as friend, companion for the journey and Saviour; and the Holy Spirit, My love in power. A threefold cord is not quickly broken[24] and, in Our case, is unbreakable because of the strength of love at work. You can be that love at work in faithfulness in all you undertake, be it small or large as a task.

Ask and receive, seek and find My will; then go forward hand in hand with Me, My love binding you, finding you unstoppable!

23 Based on St Patrick's Breastplate
24 Ecclesiastes 4:12, NKJV

Stay with Me - I

22nd July

Let me fill your emptiness by My Word. My Word brings truth, reasoning, healing and hope. I regard and take account of the whole situation for everybody concerned, sometimes finding it necessary to turn man's plans upside down, inside out, facing the other way about, for their own good, their very own good.

You should always listen to My Word. It is the safety and security of your way forward – a safe stronghold indeed, for I am with you. I go with you where I wish to send you.

When you go alone – solo, without my blessing and My guidance – you can still ask for help, but when the task is not God-given surely you understand it will not – it cannot – meet with the same measure of success. Success is always us working, praying, staying together as closely as possible under our Father's loving influence for good. We should – we must – always heed His instructions, for we need His wisdom and touch to see the way forward.

The light that shines in the darkness is My light of God's reflected glory, given for you to see the way forward, partake of and share to the very best of your ability – walking, talking, sharing, being with Me at all times in every situation, however difficult or challenging the outcome may seem to be.

Stay with Me - II

23rd July

Little seeds of doubt need to be stamped out so that they do not take root and grow. You know, for you see how much I love you. You must recognise, understand, that My supreme love wants and will dictate nothing but the best, the very best for you, My beloved children of faith. Use that faith, that faith in Me, and you will see where you are to go, what you are to do for Me. Remember, that is the key.

Do you do it for Me and My glory, our Father's glory, through the power of His Spirit at work within you, or are you writing a different story for your own gain? If so, that is not sufficient; neither have you put Me first nor have you trusted Me to be in charge of all your works. Confidence in Me, assured belief in Me, is a key issue here. I will never take you where you are not to go, for that is impossible.

Love, My perfect love, allows no error of My judgement, nor My will nor My way. Display complete dependence upon My favours, and you will be blessed indeed.

Security and safety are hallmarks of you belonging to Me and us belonging together forever to our all-loving, most gracious, dependable Father. Our Father, Me the Son and Our Holy Spirit have begun a good and powerful work in you. Now as you believe in Me (We three working as One, a total unity of love) receive all the goodness, the generous goodness, We long to give you. Nothing is held back when you are prepared to ask and receive, receive and believe, believe and perceive the way forward in Us, through Us, with Us, for Us.

You do not stand alone, never alone. Remember this and act upon it, turning quickly in Our direction to ask for guidance and help. This connection of Our holiness, offered, given, shared with you, will see you through any, all, situations.

Blessed be you My dearest children, as you come alongside of Me to pray. Stay with Me, stay with Me. Stay with Me and obey Me; it is for your own good and should make all the difference in the world.

Discover My Spirit - I

24th July

Keep in touch with Me, to see you free from mistaken ways of thinking. Trying to work things out without the guidance of My Holy Spirit is erroneous, unnecessary and foolish. The Spirit is My gift to lift you above earth's realms to the very world of the Spirit, where I of course dwell. My insight – My true insight, My truth, My guidance – comes only from, through and with My Holy Spirit.

He is gift indeed, transforming the everyday normality of human thought into something extraordinary – God-given, God-led, God-fed – in inspiration. The entire content is sent from our Father's heart and is meant to make a very real difference to you.

Heed My Spirit's calling; falling under His [influence][25] makes all the difference in the world, literally. The world becomes an altogether changed place when it embraces love held in the power of My Spirit. Our strength is your spirit; Our love becomes your love; Our purpose grows to be your purpose. There is no other way forward than this. The Spirit is a kiss of true life, heaven-sent for goodness.

---

25 spell

Discover My Spirit - II

25th July

Grace comes only by one means: recognise My Spirit; recognise Me at work; then see the Father of all love manifest in Us together. Trinity is love – loving unity in all completeness, fullness, richness, with all its resulting generous goodness.

This comes to transform your world from the mundane into the spectacular: darkness to light; evil to goodness; barrenness to fullness; emptiness destroyed, replaced by love and beauty. This is Our duty, Our concern, Our constant desire: to give to mankind all that is richly, predominantly good, worthy, honourable, honest and pure, changing man's hearts and lives thereby.

There is no higher intent than the work of My Spirit sent to transform you, for He does inform you of My truth which stands forever – a truth not to be tampered with by mankind's philosophy or purpose; a truth steadfast, secure, certain and as constant as the heavens are above the earth. Hold on to My truth and you will be changed indeed – changed into My very likeness and image.

You can mirror Me only as and when and if you will reflect My God-given truth without variance or shades of degree – all of Me, nothing of you to shine through. Let My light, My love, My words come through in all that you do for Me and, in so doing, for each other. In so doing you uncover the great mystery and purpose of life which is God here, actively present, working amongst mankind.

Find Me hard at work whenever you find My Spirit. Discover My Spirit and you find you will see My intent, heaven sent. Go with this and it will not fail you.

Harmony - I

26th July

Believe Me, rely on Me, trust Me and all will be well, keeping, coming to Me, and let's pray this through together. We will share the burden and I will strengthen you.

Only I can pull you through any difficulty and, yes, you are under attack. Those I hold most precious will always receive the onslaught of the enemy's arrows aimed to pierce their heart and drip away the very life blood itself.

But you know and must show this to the adherence, to the belief, that My blood was poured out for you so that you may become more than conquerors in Me, who set you free from doubt. Do not doubt Me. Never doubt Me for that undermines our relationship. A relationship, of course, is built on trust. You must trust Me fully and accept what I say to you.

Every situation is under My control, well under My control. I hold the reins of the Kingdom in My hands, and it is always for better, never for worse. Come to Me, My children, and be consoled. Always be reconciled by our almighty Father of love – He who waits with longing for you, with outstretched arms awaiting the return of His prodigals. Can you not – do you not – take great comfort in this wonderful reassurance?

It is God's truth, the truth of His all-powerful, all-conquering love, outreaching to establish harmony. Harmony is the blend of hearts in tune with My Father's will. You must keep praying for this. I cannot stress this sufficiently to you. You must remain in Me and Me in you to obtain – to win, to gain – the truth that will set you free from doubt, from sin, from suffering.

Harmony - II

27th July

Love, only love, Our holy love, will establish the truth for you, in you and through you. Can you see, My children, how essentially important it is that you come to Me that we can be together each day? I must communicate with you for you to know My way and My truth that gives you life – the life of the Father, our Father, lived through Me by the working power of Our Spirit amongst you. Talk to Him about everything. He understands; He consoles; He comforts. He will uplift you with His holy guidance, leaving no room for the fear of doubt.

Always come to Me through Him, and let's always begin what we have to do together in prayer. That's where we share, truly share, God's heart of love – an enormous heart spilling out into your world and making it beautiful, ever more beautiful. It grows in silent wonder and beauty like the carpet of flowers that appear in the spring, rising from the dead earth to give joy to your heart and hope to your mind. In Us you will find the flowers of peace. Pick them, smell them, admire them, nurture them and be inspired by them so that the very essence, substance, of peace fills your body, soul and spirit completely. Peace is My way forward; peace is My truth; peace is My belonging to you and your belonging to Me. I will always give you My peace.

Remember those words spoken to you a long time ago now, which said, "In the world you will have trouble, but do not fear for I have overcome the world."[26] ...Believe it... for indeed I am with you and will remain with you, My dear children. Go now in the security of My peace and My love.

I will hold your hand; you will not stumble or fall. I strengthen you, I support you, and just like the Psalm said, "You will not strike your foot against a stone, My angels do have guard over you."[27] They protect you for you belong to Me, and nothing will harm you nor come between us as long as you keep praying in My † of victory – that victory upon the † where My loss of life gained everything for you, everything you need for 'holiness and happiness'. And holiness in the true, complete and everlasting happiness given to you as My joy which is complete.

---

26 Based on John 16:33

27 Based on Psalm 91:11

Rely on Me and I Will Help You - I

28th July

Rely on Me, trust in Me and I will help you. It's all a matter of timing – My timing – and your submitting to it. "Wait on Me" means wait with expectation in good heart that I will act according to My mercy and truth.

"What is truth?"[28] Pilate asked. I am Truth. It is that simple. If only My people would rely upon this, upon Me, without hesitation and question.

"Rely" means to wait for Me to act, knowing with certainty that I will. Relying is the outworking of trust, and how often have I told you that you must trust? Trust in Me more, and together we can take the world by storm – the storm of love. This is My purpose, the point of My being, My living amongst you: to show you My love, to serve you with love.

Trust opens out the flower of love as each petal unfolds towards My light and perfumes the air with a sweet scent of expectation. Expectation in Me is always hopeful, joyful and rich beyond human measure. You are My children, and I long to give you all the good things – the best, most blessed things – My Father has in store for you who will wait, anticipate with joy in your heart, the joy of a sound faith which knows because it trusts that I will act.

Be patient and do not worry, by handing over your concerns to Me. To pray to Me is to set you free from worry and doubt. Do not be impatient for Me to act for there is much to be done. Simply keep praying, keep trusting, keep listening and looking for My signal as to when to move forward into action. Realise that action also involves waiting with intention in your heart, knowing that the time will come in Me, with Me, through Me. Be in no doubt about this for doubt clouds the issue and makes faith falter.

---

28 John 18:38 (NIV)

Rely on Me and I Will Help You - II

29th July

I look for, I hope in, those who are of a sound faith. Those it is who I will choose to use in My way as long as the recipient is fully open to, and accepting of, My will. He/she may not see the beginning or the end of the matter, but I do. I hold all things – all possibilities, all openings – in My hands, My open hands of love. Love is My message, and love will be My means of successful achievement.

To what extent are you prepared to love for Me? To what extent are you prepared to give for Me (give of yourself unreservedly, that is, serving Me with a committed love which knows no self-centredness)? To give of Me is to give totally without reserve, without hesitation, without faltering, even when you do not feel up to the task.

Receive of the strength of My Spirit that I will gladly give to you who seek and ask of Me. The Spirit, My Spirit, is your strengthening, your guidance and your support. Rely upon Him heavily, without reserve. He will light your path forwards. Listen to Him, to what He is saying to you. Be always open to receive of Him. Do not deceive yourselves by looking inward without Him for therein lies failure. He is My Spirit of wisdom, truth and right judgement. He will bring My concerns to you properly and faithfully. He is the Spirit of complete holiness. You can rely upon His every judgement and decision, even when (or especially when) this involves a revision of your own plans and ideas.

Sometimes I take you forwards then sideways along another route/path. The way is not always simply straightforward. There are cul-de-sacs of learning and stop-over points of resting en route. You have to learn to recognise these when My Spirit is bidding you. Come, step aside and reflect for a while.

He is not a Spirit of hurry in the sense of urgency, unless the urgent need is very great indeed. Heed what He is saying to you by looking at what is in your heart and mind. Ask the Spirit what to do, when and how, and He will show you. I am the way forward when the time is right. Do you completely believe this? The amount of trust you have in Me is commensurate with the degree to which I will choose to use you.

Keep coming to Me, keep praying through My Spirit and look forward to all that we can do together.

Believe in Me - I

30th July

Obey Me and you will receive all the full fullness, for in that way lies your peace – the peace of knowing that you do My will entirely, believing in all things that I ask of you because you believed in all things that I told you. My Word is to be believed in all its entirety of purpose for therein lies the fullness of the Father's revelation to mankind.

It is only when you find the fullness of truth in Me you receive the full completeness of My Father's love and mercy, given that you may know life and enjoy it, its richness being given in fullest measure this side of heaven to those who believe in Me and the power of My Name. It is when you call on My Name that the Father moves in upon your situation sending the Spirit to act. His is Our power to transform your life in every aspect; when you reach out to touch Me you receive My Spirit's empowering. He who raised Me from the dead will lift you up from the doldrums of life way above anything you imagined or anticipated. Will you let Him? Will you let Him begin a new work, in Me, a new work of freedom? If so, if this is your desire, then you have to believe all I say to you.

When I say, "I am the way, the truth and the life,"[29] there is no other way home to the Father. This is so that you discover My fullness in one single, simple statement. It is as easy as that, as easy as believing in Me. I am the gospel Truth, God's message placed before you that you might receive all fullness in Me.

Come, my child, receive Me without deviation, without acceptance of the world's philosophies and the so-called wisdom of man. As My Spirit has begun a good work in you, let Him continue through to completion. There is no other way. I am the true Way, the Way of the Father. Grasp this and move forward to glory. Make this your life's story: to reverence the Father in Me by My Spirit alive in you in all you do, so God's glory will shine through undiminished.

29 John 14:6 (NKJV)

Believe in Me - II

31st July

The full fullness – the fullest fullness of truth, God's revealed truth – is only found in Me. Will you hear what I say and obey My call to accept this gospel message of truth? Until you do you will not move forward to where I want you to go that you may work for Me. Success lies in obedience to the will of the Father, when you honour and esteem Me above all things.

Ask the Spirit to show you any errors of judgement, any misunderstanding, any blockages or blanks in your experience. Ask Him and He will bring you into all truth. This is My truth, the Father's truth given to mankind that he may find God now.

Do not wait, do not hesitate, but act in faith – in the prayer of faith – where lies the repair of anything that is wrong. You belong to a mighty, marvellous and magnanimous God. Will you let Him win and come through to you?

Begin now. Pray today in a way that is most earnestly seeking the Father's truth. Seek Him and He will be found by you in Me by My Spirit.

Come, My child, there is much work to be done, and we had better be doing it together! There is no other way; believe Me.

Ask Me - I

1st August

Obey Me at all times and submit to My will; it is good for you! Let Me fill you with My Spirit: light in your darkness; truth in your ignorance; My saving help and protection, for He comes in the Name of Christ.

I sent Christ to you for the fullness of life you seek and speak about. This fullness of life can be yours – *will* be yours – when you come to Me more regularly, trusting Me more fully, asking that My will is done at all times, knowing that this is the best for you. This is the way My blessings occur and concur in every human life.

I place you beyond strife in My Son's Name. He is your defence against the wiles of the enemy. He is My protection for you, just as He is My promise to you. He comes by My Spirit, so in Him you inherit the fullness of life which I offer in My presence. Come into My presence, My beloved children, and receive more of Me because you believe and ask more of Me.

Acceptance is rewarded, ever rewarded, in My Son's Name. As He took your blame, you are free to ask of Me anything in My Son's will according to the Spirit of life I give you. Let Me infill you daily. Come to Me more often in prayer together where we share your destiny and deliverance.

Freedom is the fullness of life I offer you to serve Me. Rejoice in this fact and tell My people. Share with them in whatever way you can and ask of Me how this is to be. I will tell you, I will show you, I will take you forward to My glory, as you trust in Me for this to happen.

Ask Me - II

2nd August

My people who are kingdom builders must trust and ask, ask and receive, receive and ask for more. More is ever in store – for My glory. Did I not tell you, you would see more of My glory if you did but ask?

Pray; pray earnestly; pray daily; pray in whatever way you can from the heart of your longing. This is what belonging to Me is about: the heart of your longing. Ask Me to take that heart and fill it – fill it with My beauty of life. Then it is your duty to go out and read the gospel news, news of great joy.

I will use you if you but ask Me. Ask Me that you follow My will wholeheartedly. You know I do not like lukewarm; it is insufficient. My kingdom is built on fervour. Look at My Son, the cornerstone, the firm foundation. Look at the fervour and zeal of His love. Love, as His intention, is [expressed in] the miracle working wonders. Will you do this in, for, My Name, My children?

Come in Christ's name, in Me by My Spirit, that you may inherit the fullness, the fullest of blessing I promise. I will not fail you. Will you will not fail me?

Pray and obey; then pray some more. Always seek My will. Always ask to seek the blessing I long to give, and you, My dearly beloved child, will live within My presence increasingly. My presence is the fullness of joy in store for you in My kingdom upon earth, a foretaste of all that is to come, all for My glory. This is the seeking and finding – your seeking and finding – which is the promise of life setting you above and beyond the strife of the everyday, when you receive and broadcast My message of fullness of life.

Do not lose heart; never lose heart! You have made a start; now continue in My Name of love, My Name of joy, My Name of life – life in all its glorious fullness, that which My Son came to offer and My Spirit comes to enhance daily amongst My kingdom builders.

Build in truth, build on truth, build with truth, and you will see the glory of God – My glory – shine upon you.

Be Still and Know That I Am God

3rd August

Be still and know that I am God. Let Me work in you. Be Mine by knowing Me and My will for you.

You must spend more time with Me. I will teach you how to pray. Listen to the beat of My heart. It tells of My love for you. You are My precious children, and I care for you.

Tell Me everything. Do not keep anything from Me. Talk to Me more, or how else can I talk back? You must rely on Me alone.

Do not be tempted to doubt or dismay. I carry you. Rely on Me; on My shoulders lay your burdens.

I will not let any harm come to you. Surely you know this? Why then don't you act as if you do? Why all this doubt and fear?

Allow Me to cope. Allow Me to work through you. You only have to ask for Me to be there. Bring your petitions.

My Mission to You - I

4th August

In you I can do all things. Come alongside of Me; serve Me in the way you know best. Use My love to help others. Tell them about Me. Show them that I exist and I am real. I will send you into places where they search for Me. Speak to them from your heart. You know I am real; share this. As you speak to them, you must convince them by what you say, your knowledge of Me, your understanding of My love.

Use the Bible promises. Learn them and make them your own that you might claim them in My Name. Fear not, for I am with you ... at all times. I will give you the words to say. I will fill you with My love for them. They need Me. They need you to take Me there. It is My Spirit that comes to bring peace to their hearts, light to their minds. I send Him to you that you may seek and find My will for your life.

You are in training. I have great things in store, in My powerhouse of treasures – much laid up, awaiting distribution. Take My gifts and use them widely amongst my people, the sheep of My flock who do not know Me and hear My calling. As I can use you, I can work through you in many ways.

Believe in Me. Believe in prayer (its power, its voice always heard), in answers given, in problems solved (its comfort and reassurance). These are My gifts which you can bring to others, to many.

My Mission to You - II

5th August

Search Me and search Me till you know My heart, My mind, My will for you in the everyday. As you come to Me more, I will give you more responsibility and greater things can be done in My Name. You are in training and accomplish what I ask of you.

Turn to Me again and again in prayer and thanksgiving, knowing at all times that I hear you, I answer you, I come to you. Increase your trust and you will see many things happen. Stir me up by your prayers of supplication, your intent.

Do not strive under your own power, lest you fail. I will show you the way I want you to be. Act under My authority alone. Do not let others turn you away from what you know is right, what you know is My will, My asking of you. I need you to act on My behalf, to be busy in My world of longing. You are able to do more, and much, when you allow My freedom to flow through your veins, to grow into your very being.

You are My child, My children. I formed you… in My image and likeness that you could glorify Me. I made you for this: to know Me and love Me and, in so doing, bring Me into others' hearts and minds. They do not know Me. But you do.

It is My mission to you that you go out into the world and tell them through your prayer what I can do for them, what I will do for them. Teach them not to give up, to hope, to ask and be expectant, to listen and look, to seek and find Me. I am all around, just waiting to be found! You have found Me. Share Me out in love for My people aching and longing for Me – so many people needing Me.

Your commission is to do just this: act on My behalf. I sanction you and strengthen you. I allow you to do this for Me because I have loved you with an everlasting love that knows no limits.

You are My children, the works of My hands, formed in beauty and love that you may be like Me. Hear what I say and go forth trustingly, longingly – longing for My love to be known and shown to those I send you. All will be well in My arms of peace.

My Mission is Important - I

6th August

Where I lead, you must follow; I will take you into the unknown, but you must trust Me. No harm will come to you, no discomfort of soul. I have set aside work for you to do together. It will become clear. Just wait awhile until you are ready, trimmed down and built up.

As I heal you, you can carry My healing love to others in distress. Lay My healing hands on them through yours. As you love them and care for them, they will improve in health and wellbeing. All I have is yours to use wisely, to use lovingly for the good of others. Take My hands and make them for your own – tenderly, caressingly gentle.

Speak to others in hushed tones, in peaceful ways that they may be reassured of My love and fortitude. Gladden their hearts as they begin to trust. You need nothing but Me to be able to do this, a childlike trust and longing for things to happen.

As I empty you out, I fill you up. I pour My grace over you that it may flow out to others to whom I send you. The days will not be dark but light for them when you bring them to Me, when you act on My behalf, when you do My work.

Envisage the power I can give you and believe in it. You must believe for it to be effective. In you I can do anything I choose. You only have to let Me! Unblock your heart to love freely and relax in My loving arms, held safe and secure, held tight in My presence. My love abounds throughout you and around you. It will become evident to more and more people…

My Mission is Important - II

7th August

Set time aside daily, if you can, to come to Me in prayer. How else can I tell you of My will for you? You need to be still to hear Me.

Cut corners and grade down your expectations. They are so very high and sometimes unrealistic. You must make a real effort with this, not just talk about it! Ask Me and I will show you the way. I really will if you believe Me.

You know what I told you before – to listen to Me – and I am a constant and caring God who does not change. It is *you* who must change (do the changing)! Change direction of effort towards Me and My work for you.

As you seek Me, you will find Me and My will for you ... Little by little we're moving forward as you get to know Me more. Take Me; make Me your own in every way. Then I can use you so powerfully. More, so much more, I have to give you when you are ready. You are waiting but must make yourself, yourselves, ready and prepared.

My mission is important. It is not to be undertaken lightly. You will hold the power of men's lives in your hands of love. You must first obey Me in all things, that all that you do is through Me and in accord with My will for you and others. You can only know that by listening to Me and learning of Me, from Me, through Me what is My will.

As you get into My living Word, this will help you, but I will also talk to you directly like I do. Allow Me to do this that you may know of Me. Be confident in your knowledge and in what I tell you. Do not doubt. I know this is hard. But I am true. I am really and readily available for you. As I encourage you, so will you for others.

Come, My children, and be with Me at all times, in every way. I love you with a heart that is true at all times and in every way. I will not fail you. Do not fail Me, for together we can do great things in My – in our Father's – Name.

Allow Me to Govern

8th August

Share the faith that I have given you. Tell it to the others, not just those around you at home, but wider afield. Go in the Name of the Lord to where I send you. Go in My Name and see what we can do, a team ... combined in spirit and purpose.

I have begun a new work in you ... and will bring it to fruition soon. Stand and be ready. You will need My strength, My conviction, for the going is tough out there in the battlefield. Raise your hands to fight for Me in the cause of justice and compassion – those who are homeless, dispossessed of their serenity and esteem, their self-regard. They need to know of Me through you and what you do for them.

I was hungry and you fed Me. I was naked and you clothed Me. I was homeless and you housed Me. How else can they learn of Me as they wander about aimlessly? I will send you to the right people that you should help.

Trust in Me and always look to Me for guidance. Only act upon My instructions. Practise listening and knowing what is required of Me. I will be specific so you do not worry. Then hand everything over to Me and let Me be in control of every situation. As you learn to trust, to do this, you will be released to act in My power – not of your own accord but according to My will and motive. I can only use you if you allow Me to govern. You must work on this; practise it until you get it right.

I am a patient God who waits on His people until they are ready, firm of footing, held safe and secure in Me, in My knowledge of them and them of Me. For a purpose I have formed you ... that you may work for Me, for My kingdom and justice ...

Learn of Me and My will for you daily as you pray and we spend time together.

My Plan of Salvation

9th August

You are my rock of strength. In times of trouble, those who need Me need you, alive in My Spirit, endowed with My love. Be vibrant and clear-sighted as you seek My will and purpose.

Pray, and again I say, pray. How else can we be together in tranquillity? You come with expectant faith, and it will be rewarded many times over. As you seek Me, you will find Me, wherever you go in My Name.

Do of My will. Bring into being My plan of salvation for many. Teach of Me ... I send you out among those who cry in the wilderness, often of their own making. They seek Me not and they find Me not, but with you alongside, carrying Me, carrying the Good News, it will begin to make sense to them. Then I can do the rest.

I need you to get started for together we are about our Father's work. It is He who anoints and appoints us. As I learned of His will for Me through prayer, so must you, each of you.

Seek Him earnestly, in the small things and the large. Be vigilant, watchful, awake, that you may spot your opportunity in faith – your calling, My beckoning. My salvation is at hand for those who seek it, and I use you. You are My chosen ones on whom My favour rests.

Blessed be the Name of our Father in heaven as we seek to do His will, as together we act in one mind, one Spirit, one purpose to bring others to the knowledge of the resurrection; to deliver them through Me from the bondage of sin; to heal the wounds of their doubt; to feed the hungry with good things; to bring heaven on earth through My presence, My reality, My coming into their lives of hopelessness, emptiness.

Into you all I have come. Spread Me out. What you have received, you can give in the Spirit of truth and earnestness. For there is no greater thing that can be done than to allow My Spirit to move among you.

A Wealth of Joy and Harmony - I

10th August

Heal My wounds – My afflicted children, they suffer without Me. Be gracious unto them in your calling of ministry. Tend and heal. Ask and pray. Ask and receive. It is your gift through the Spirit – My Spirit – to do this. Allow Me to work through you mightily.

All power, all grace, comes from our Father through Me; and I share My calling that many might be saved in righteousness. Hear My words clearly, readily, that you may learn of Me and My will for you, that you will be ready and prepared to take Me out to others in their distress and longing.

My grace is sufficient unto your cause. You do not have to struggle or strive but simply be in Me – one in Me; together, not apart; together to do My will. Take Me into action!

I hold you in the palm of My hand that you are enclosed in safety – held fast, held firm, from the evil one protected.

Behold the sun, the stars, the moon, how they shine with My brightness! You too can shine with My likeness, My joy – a radiance that will never go out nor fade, if you believe in Me, trust Me and allow Me to work. I am a patient God who waits in readiness until the time is due for Me to unfold your powers of Mine, to use you.

As you awake with the dawn, turn to Me in expectancy and gladness of heart for another day where you can work, where you can serve My purpose and calling. Put Me before all else so you are anointed in the grace of My calling. Be ready and waiting, for you never know where I will send you, when I will call you.

But you must be ready to act by being prepared in yourself. I can use only an empty vessel, emptied of self to be filled by Me. Don't worry about the cracks! I can heal those, mend them in love and longing to make you whole again.

You have My sacraments, the gifts of My Church. Use them frequently. Reach out to Me in this way: in the Eucharist, in Reconciliation, in Praise, in Prayer, in expectant and joyful Hope – hope of My coming; hope of My calling.

A Wealth of Joy and Harmony - II

11th August

Let us be united in love, united in purpose and design, together with our Father in heaven and His Spirit of wealth. A wealth of joy and harmony; a sense of right doing, good works; a calling of service and ministry; a knowledge of Me and My purpose – Our purpose; a wisdom of action and dedication; a fountain of love; a suffusing warmth; a peace – that peace, that very peace which passeth all understanding, that I promised you. For you are My children upon whom My favour rests.

Awaken with a gladsome mind to greet the new day of My coming – little by little, one step at a time, inching forward into the kingdom of My presence; learning of My love, My fellowship, My hand in yours, so you do not falter nor fall apart, do not waver nor ascend the wrong mountain track where thistles will choke you.

Be glorious in My Name, steadfast, triumphant over the enemy, over evil, victorious in My crown of joyful wearing, bejewelled and sparkling like the morning sun!

You are My anointed, My chosen, My blessed, that you may serve Me all the days of your life in joyful hope and certain surety… of your dependency on Me and My Spirit. All that I have is yours to share among My people where I send you. Teach as you are taught. Help and guide those who know and understand less. As you learn, pass it on and share it out.

Amazed and amazing you are in My grace and power, employed in My work! Humbly receive and accept that you might give of Me. Allow Me to work in you and through you and with you, alive and active in My Spirit of peace and harmony. Where there is discord, stand in My presence, in My word of truth.

My dearly beloved children, you are everything to Me. Receive My love and forgiveness, for they are yours through My suffering and resurrection, dearly won for you and many. You see and know of this that others might learn too. All hail the power of My Name!

Partners in a Team of Loving Ministry - I

12th August

Ask and you shall receive. Seek and you shall find. Believe and expect and it will be given to you. Do not doubt Me. Turn to Me in expectant faith and trust knowing that I am there, I am with you always. For as much as has been given to you, more will be added. You only have to ask Me, seek Me, know Me and My working.

Allow Me freedom, the use of your hands, to heal and make whole, to comfort and reassure. As My will unfolds in your life, you will be amazed, set free, released from doubt.

Do not care about tomorrow. I take care of that. It is safe in My hands, for you and your loved ones. They will blossom like the noonday sun! Keep them in prayer. Tell them of Me when you can. Show Me to them by your life and witness. It is not so much what you say as what you do, although both are important. Treat them sensitively. They need to know Me to be fulfilled in their own lives. Their longing will diminish only to the degree that they come to know Me, the meaning of their life and existence, their very being. This is important but cannot be hurried.

Do not be dismayed nor fearful. For I am always there with you, holding you safe and secure. When in doubt, ask Me to come nearer. Tune into that sense of Me that makes sense to you. See Me and hear Me in all that you do for Me and for others, for in others you will find Me and My purpose. I have told you this that you may act accordingly.

Partners in a Team of Loving Ministry - II

13th August

I am not to be taken lightly, nor disregarded, for I have the message of eternal life. I know you that you all may know Me, love Me and serve Me according to My will, My plan for your life. As it unfolds you will be glad you came to see Me in everything, glad you believe what I told you; sorry for the times we're apart; resounding in My love; strengthened and made whole; fortified forever in My grace and assurance; radiant in knowing of Me and My will; wearing the joy of My crown of success (that which the world does not know nor recognise).

All I have is yours – yours to give away to others that they might find Me too, find Me in you. Recognise My will, My word, My work that I may use you anew each day.

Commit yourself to Me afresh each morning. Do not forget what I have told you, nor grow weary in My cause. This is important to Me, important to you!

For I have called you by name; you are Mine. Together we belong in unity and fellowship, in love and friendship, as partners in a team of loving ministry. Go out in gladness to do my work and serve Me.

Forgiveness - I

14th August

"I asked the Lord to give me a definition of forgiveness."

Forgiveness is like letting the sunshine of My warmth, the cleansing of My gentle rain from heaven and the rainbow of My hope descend upon a person all at the same time.

What blocks it?

A hardened heart, a heavy heart furred up by the faults of the past.

"How can this be dealt with?"

By trusting in Me to do this for you. Come to Me and hand over your problems, your difficulties, your doubts. Tell Me about them. Do not stay silent and resentful.

"And what about the hurts?"

This will, like all hurts, heal from the inside out, given sufficient time, warmth and constant care. Repair is the business of My heart. I start it, uphold, continue and complete.

"Why does it take so long?"

There is much to be done, much to be put back together again when a heart is fractured into many pieces. Breaks hurt, and deep hurts coming from deep fractures take time to mend. Cry on My shoulders, My child. I will dry with love your wet tears. Weeping will not last forever, but whilst it does I will support and carry you for as long as it takes.

"Can I hurry up the process?"

Not really. Simply do as I say and believe all will eventually be well in Me. I am the invisible glue that will hold you together, bonded strong in My love which is itself unbreakable.

"I wish I had never been hurt in the first place."

So did I, but sometimes it is necessary as one person's growth impinges upon another's. I did not plan it this way, but people fail to come to Me for sufficient guidance and help.

"And if they did come to You for guidance and help, what goes so seriously wrong?"

Man's own willpower and desire overrides Me and My truth and My teaching. He listens with his ear but not his heart and is wilful, disobedient, pleasure-seeking in the short, immediate sense, but not looking for the eternal satisfaction of placing his full life in My hands.

Forgiveness - II

15th August

"I find it hard to remain patient."

Ask for My Spirit's support and strength. In Him you will be able to achieve all manner of seemingly impossible tasks. Just ask Him to come. He will, in all manner of unexpected ways, always bringing benefits to you. My Spirit and I are in complete harmony, full unity, with our Father. Within the Trinity, if you trustingly place yourself there, nothing will go wrong which cannot be put right in us.

"I don't understand why it goes so wrong in the first place?"

Usually because of men's – mankind's – selfishness and greed. Pride and presumption also play a part, taking their place too centre stage. A person's life is made up of many acts on different stage sets. If (s)he directs him/herself (s)he's likely to get the production wrong. My skill as director and producer are needed for success, especially a long run, longstanding success. I wait quietly in the sidelines until invited to oversee the action and help put the production upon the correct lines. The drama called 'life' is ever changing, fast changing, and needs someone – Me – who really can be completely in control willingly, lovingly. Mankind's capabilities do not extend to this demanding position for (s)he is too narrowly self-centred, too short-sighted and always has too much still to learn about love, self-giving and forgiveness. Live and let live in Me.

"I'm trying Lord. I am learning. Please help me."

This I will always do, My most precious child. Believe Me and act as if you did, you do. Then you will see such a difference happening. Act in Me, speak in Me, decide in Me and don't hide anything from Me at all. 'Open of heart' is necessary if I am to work in you, through you – open to learn, receive, admit, understand, grow and go forward in Me. This is My desire.

Restored and Forgiven - I

16th August

Come to Me in love of Me, and I will know you and you will know Me more – and My will, My plan for you. As you seek, you will find My plan and purpose made whole through the gift of My Sacrament of Reconciliation. Restored and reunited with Me, you will become one body together to do My work, My plan, of salvation.

You will take Me – *must* take Me – to a hurting world in desperate need. Tell them of Me. Speak with conviction and My authority, for you have been given the power of My Spirit. He will bless your efforts and direct your ways, for in Him lies strength and unity. Teach of Me – that My plan for salvation is soon to be brought about.

As you are made whole, made one with Me, I can use you powerfully. As I fill you with My love, My forgiveness, you are restored to My grace and blessing. You are made one again with Me, sanctified under our Father's love, ready to live, to be received in His house where awaits your destiny and calling.

Do not delay to put Me into action in your lives, for time is short in that there are so many who do not know Me. Use all these gifts I have given you as one in My body, for My uplifting. Raise Me high in expectation as well as glory, high and mighty in strength as well as trust.

Fulfilled and fulfilling in My work, you all will be – a mighty army of God's people called out in weakness, sent out in strength, valour and the victory of My calling. Do not doubt My calling to each and every one of you, each in a particular way known only to Me to begin with but soon to be made clearer to you.

You only have to ask for you to see the light of day – My glorious light shining into the darkness of your soul. Allow My Spirit freedom to move among you, stopping and dwelling wherever He chooses, for He it is that knows all things. This was given Him before time began, and He knows what is right for you. He pervades the very air you breathe, being the life-giving, fragrant sweetness of Me.

Restored and Forgiven - II

17th August

Keep in touch – your spirit with My Spirit of love and forgiveness, of strength and salvation. My gifts are your gifts that you may use them wisely for My people and those who do not yet know Me. Teach and speak of Me, prophesy and deliver My word to the afflicted and downcast. Heal the hurts of My loved ones and believe – above all, believe – that you have been called to do this.

As I use you, so I send you out – called by Me, commissioned by Me in My service. Serve one another first, starting where you are loved and known, that you may be strengthened, made whole, in your own resolve of serving Me. Then, fortified in accordance with My word and teaching, go out and deliver My message, My appeal.

I have no hands but yours, and use them when you are willing and ready. I stand to serve you. Will you stand to serve Me?

Reconciled with Me and My Father – our Father – go out in love wherever I send you and want you to be. You will be able to bring Me to others by all that you say and do in My love and service, strengthened by Me under the power of My Spirit – blessed and appointed, made whole once again, restored and forgiven, for that is why I died for you and for many.

Dear children of Mine, be filled with My love and grace. It is everlasting – meant for you, poured out upon you. Receive Me in love and gratitude for I make you entirely Mine once again.

My love for you is as boundless as the ocean – My grace given that you use My gifts, as countless as the grains of sand upon the shore. Be carried along by the tide of My love for you and all mankind.

Teach as You Have Been Taught

18th August

Learn of Me. Be gentle of spirit and humble of mind, Mine to fulfil. Take My saving grace and make it yours – your own – that you are empowered by My love, enabled to reach out to those who need Me through you.

My resurrection glory stands waiting to bring heaven on earth, My kingdom where My workers establish My rule and authority. Teach as you have been taught, bringing understanding and enlightenment to men's souls.

Regard My plan for you by listening with open heart and ready ears, reaching out in hope and longing towards Me. Then I can take you forward, galvanised by My Spirit, intent on being in Me.

I Will Not Leave You as Orphans - I

19th August

Believe in Me and all that I have told you, for it is the truth. I come to you that you might serve Me and My purposes in the place where I have planted you. You will know where to go and what to do if you ask Me. "I will not leave you as orphans"[30], unattended; rather I take you step by step along the way, My path carved out in righteousness.

Serve Me gladly, for this is what I did for you, to show you how – to teach you, to reveal to you the Father's love for all mankind in My day and now, as ever it was. Nothing changes in God's love. It is as bright today as in the dawn of time, for He is changeless, the Almighty.

We must bow down before Him in acknowledgment of all He has done, is doing, in praise and honour, in joy at His presence, in obedience and trust. It will not always be easy; this was not My promise. But it will be made easier because I am with you always to teach and show the way.

For this I was sent into your midst: to lighten a darkened world, to bring hope to a suffering people. My people still suffer without Me. What are you going to do about it? How can you best serve Me here in My kingdom on earth? Ask Me about it that I may tell you My plans, give you My blessings.

Do not act then ask, for that is backwards to My way of working. Ask that you may receive My instructions. I know this is difficult for you and has to be learnt. But I am a patient God who waits until the time is ready; then I move in power.

Pray, and again I say, pray to Me. How else can I tell you of My plans, what I want, what I have in store? I have to have your acceptance to allow Me to deliver. For I do not intrude upon you but come when asked – sometimes in ways you do not expect.

Stay awake; be alert to Me at all times and in all ways. You do not know when I will reach out to touch your hand and lead you on. But it will be when you are ready, humble of heart, trusting in soul, seeking for Me and My will. I will not disappoint you nor leave you longing but unfulfilled.

---

30 John 14:18 (NIV)

I Will Not Leave You as Orphans - II

20th August

Your destiny awaits My anointing grace. Be patient as I am. Belong to the Father as I do. Use My Spirit. He was given for this purpose: to serve you and your needs. Call upon Him in power and strength that He may come to you, come upon you, in the way you ask and seek. His gifts are many to use in My way, for the upbuilding of My Church. Ask Him that you may receive in abundance.

Take Me forth by My Spirit's power of love and serving, growing those fruits I promised My disciples and followers: love, joy, peace, patience, kindness, gentleness and self-control. These surely will become yours – yours to use in service of Me that all may know of Me and My truth.

My gifts of the Spirit are that: gifts. Not earned, not deserved, but Mine to give as and when I will. All you have to do is ask, earnestly seek and be ready to receive – ready by acknowledging Me and My message, believing what I tell you for it is the truth.

You know what I expect: step out in faith of Me. Learn more about My gifts of the Spirit that you may know how to be effective, how to use My power amongst My people of My upbuilding. Do not doubt yourselves, for that is doubting Me.

Come, My children, into My arms of love, held secure in My embrace, protected by My presence, filled by My love, empowered by My Spirit. Then go out and do all that I ask of you in My Name.

Glory be to God our Father, for through Him all things became possible! It is He we serve as we work in unity together for the greater good of mankind, His people, His dearly beloved people. Do this for Me and you do this for Him, for I and the Father are One: One in the Spirit; One in purpose to serve you, love you, deliver you and set you free. All life, all holiness, is for this reason: that you may know Us and be with Us eternally.

Radiate Me - I

21st August

I can use you because you know Me and believe Me. You have fallen in love with Me and know My truth. You are able to bear witness and tell of Me to others in that place where I put you, in that particular work I gave you to do. Do not disappoint My expectation, for in relying on Me you are built up in strength and vigour, healed as I promised you would be. Keep claiming My promise for you. You will be saved. You will be healed as you are My trusted servant upon whom I can rely.

I take you where I want you to go in this place – into men's hearts, into their lives, to relieve their suffering and loneliness. You have been blessed in abundance and are willing to share that among the many I give you here. Tell them of Me in your way – the way you choose to do. It is effective and pleases Me. It is of My Spirit and strengthens people's lives ...

You can show others what many cannot, for you know Me and use Me to build your lives in the way that is right. Of course you fall, but I take care of that and understand all that is difficult and tiresome/trying. Simply allow My Spirit to work in you to enable you to do even greater things in My service, that to which I call you ... Radiate Me, reaching out and touching with healing hands of love and compassion – *My* love and compassion – brought through you…

Radiate Me - II

22nd August

Keep a diary of where I send you so you can see the pathway we walk together, remember the talks we have had together. In this way you will learn more of Me and recognise what I want you to know, what I want to teach you and reveal to you.

You are receptive, and that is good in My cause, My calling, My coming into the world to serve through you. Do not worry about points of departure when others do not yet see as you do. I can take care of all of that in My time. All you have to do is be yourselves, true to yourselves and Me, My service.

I have called you by name; you are Mine, just like the child Samuel. Go now in gladness of heart into My day, the day I made for you and gave you. Enjoy My love and My service.

Sing your praises when you can. They gladden My heart and help Me know how you feel, where your thinking is. I reside in the praises of My people for it is there we share in our Father's glory, our desire to praise Him, be with Him, be at one and at peace. I stand beside you as you sing, and all the chorus of heaven join in – the angel throng. Lift your voices, your eyes, your hearts to Me, to our Father. Praise in Spirit. Let Him give you voice!

A Love Deep, Wide and Boundless - I

23rd August

Child of Mine, be fruitful in your work, going to whom I send you in My love. Do not act on your own behalf but rather after seeking My will and purpose. Listen that I may talk to you often, tell you of My plans for you… reveal My intention and purpose, My longing.

Look to Me, to the † of My salvation and grace, My love poured out on you and all in My purpose, of My accord and choosing. My divine will is exactly that: a love which man cannot take in, in its immensity and depth, quality and timbre; a love which knows no limits and sets no boundaries; a love which is utterly unconditional and serves not itself; a love deep, wide and boundless, all-knowing in its passion and fulfilment, all-consuming in its fire blazing across men's lives that I may leave My mark of identity, My stamp of belonging.

To know Me is to serve Me; to serve Me is to love Me; to love Me is to reach your life's gain, your life's end and calling. For there is no other reason to be, other than to seek My hand in yours, My life in yours, My love in your entire being, filling your soul with life and purpose. To this one end I called you into being – to this one glorious end gain.

A Love Deep, Wide and Boundless - II

24th August

My love stands secure amidst you, around you, above and below, behind, in front and between. It suffuses all you do, all you are, all you will become, for in knowing Me and serving Me, you become like Me.

We become as one when you are ready in pureness of heart, in the mystery of longing; when you intend to walk so close to Me, no shadow can come between us. Then My light will shine into men's lives, into the dark places of the soul: the hate and despair, the depravity and insecurity, the coldness and soulless state of many lives.

Joy at My birth is for all times and seasons – pure joy, undiluted except by the sin of mankind's forgetfulness and self-sufficiency. Allow Me to come back again to the core, to the centre, of men's hearts and lives where I may live once more, set free to work for the greater good of all.

Praise Me, all you My children, for it is in so doing you are enabled to know Me more, grow closer to Me, to become of My heart, to share in My love and victory. Praise, and again I say, praise My goodness, My victory over sin and death, My all-conquering love, My life poured out that you might live to the full now and forevermore – each day lived in Me; each day loved by Me and My Father, enclosed in My Spirit's peace and joyfulness of purpose.

My children, I serve you in love to give you a life that is Mine. Take it and transform the world where you stand in My Name.

Receive My Healing Grace - I

25th August

I chose you…, anoint you and appoint you in My service of love, My apostleship. My calling to you through the darkness of men's souls, despair and doubt. Serve Me in serving them; each other's needs to prefer…

Do not doubt your courage nor ability, for I take care of that problem with My hand in yours. You only have to seek Me in righteousness for Me to come into your life most powerfully. Receive My healing grace that you may reflect it to others who need Me. Heal in love of mankind, bringing My forgiveness and joy. Blighted no more, they will be set free from doubt and despair, dismay and hopelessness – set free to rejoice in Me, be in Me, live in Me. Do as I do.

Pray, and again I say, pray to Me. How else can I tell you of My will and command? Time spent in prayer is time spent alongside of Me. Together we can do so much. A little faith moves many a mountain of distrust and fear.

Serve Me in gladness, knowing that I am there for you. I do not stand alone but with My Father and Our Spirit, all in one power and accord, longing to serve you in love and purpose, beckoning you into Our arms where you will be held safe and secure in Our promises.

Although it will not be easy, the gain is immeasurable, immense, far-reaching, worthy of all effort. As you save men's lives (their very souls) you will rejoice in gladness of knowing Me and serving Me, of belonging to Me and committing to Me and My cause – My just cause, My heart's desire.

Receive now My grace and blessing to do My will in your life, serving as you have been called to do together. Bound in love, held in unity, empowered with My strength and service, I use you in the way I wish to do.

Receive My Healing Grace - II

26th August

Do not doubt Me anymore, although it is right that you should question and ask of My will, seek My purpose. But go now in gladness into this cause of My calling, My planning. Know Me as I know you. Use Me as I use you. Be formed in Me to use My strength, My love, My power of conviction.

My destiny awaits those who seek and find. I would have that be everybody, held together in love of Me. Tell them the glad news of My birth, My new birth, into their lives, My coming when they call.

My purpose and plan is now unfolding in your lives. Live according to My intentions. As you seek Me and find Me, so must others that they may be set free. My joy awaits those who ask for it in My Name; I will not disappoint them nor leave them orphans, but rather come into their hearts where I belong, where I live and serve.

Use Me to know Me. In knowing Me, you will do My will for many, the people to whom I send you out in My Name. Go now in gladness knowing that you do My will.

Receive My peace and prosperity, My calm assurance that all is well in your lives of service. This is My word to you that you may know of Me and believe Me. Have faith and grow in My likeness.

Your Dance of Joy with Me - I

27th August

Persevere, persevere, persevere in prayer, knowing that I stand by to pick up the pieces of brokenness, of shattered dreams. Remember, I know and see all things and will not allow any step on the way to harm or discourage you.

Your plans are unfolding in My Name. Trust Me to do as I say… In trusting, you believe; and in believing I make you Mine, My disciple, My co-worker, called into My service. I will send you where I need you to go. The way will become clear…

Do not doubt Me nor feel dismay. I am with you, working silently behind the scene of your life. But you must keep praying to Me, asking of Me, learning and acting through Me. I come to you in measure according to your desire and commitment. Ask and you shall receive in full measure of Me. Learn of Me – listening and looking, seeking and finding wherever you go.

I will not allow anyone to impede your path, your walk, your dance of joy with Me. When the days are gloomy, darkened, overshadowed by despair, know that I am with you in total recognition of your frame of mind, uplifting you if only you will let Me. Come unto Me, My child, when in sorrow and doubt. Let Me wipe your tears away with the mantle of My loving, My care, knowing that I serve your wishes – and all I ask of you is your service and patience, just a little more patience.

Your Dance of Joy with Me - II

28th August

I take you where I intend you to be, and you will be glad, so glad, you waited. Child of My calling, do not suffer in doubt. Know that I am with you, working on your behalf. You will see My face shine in you like the morning sun as My plans come to fruition.

Take charge, take hold of your emotions, realising that all I do is for a purpose, not yet clear but becoming so. I will not disappoint you. I will not fail your expectations of Me. Thus far have you come, and together we are travelling, hand in hand – My hand in yours, guiding with gentle pressure and steering your course.

Are you ready for more of Me? Tell Me what you want Me to know so there are no shadows between us. I cannot build on you unless you allow Me to make you strong in My image and likeness, knowing of Me and becoming like Me. Give Me those unclaimed areas of your life that we may deal with them together, knowing in so doing you will be made whole again.

You cannot pick and choose parts of Me, for in so doing you water down, dilute, My grace. Give totally to Me in expectant faith and trust. I will show you where things go wrong if you ask Me. Come unto Me and I will give you rest – My rest – from soul searching. Know Me; love Me; serve Me; follow Me. It is quite simple. I beckon; you come to Me to be made whole, secure, safe alongside Me.

Plumbed into My heart you will be given strength to succeed in all that is of Me, My plan. Do not doubt it, for in so doing you are doubting Me. I will handle the difficulties. I will carry you over the boulders on the way, shouldering you high above all that could assail you.

My child, be with Me each step of the way. I share your burdens, your worries, your doubts. I shoulder them to ease the tasks for you. Allow Me to help you. Turn to Me and tell Me; talk to Me; come to Me for comfort and a fresh outpouring of courage.

Go now in My Name of peace, My harmony of intent, knowing all will be well just as I promised you it should be.

My Calling Out to You - I

29th August

Let My conviction reign in your heart, for it is the truth, My truth for all times and in all places. My hand is holding you up in expectation. Be glad and trust in Me, in My Name. Knowing of Me you will come to rely on Me. That is good.

All that I have is yours only if you believe in Me. How else can I share it with you, if you do not want part of Me to be with you, in you? As it is, take Me and hold Me tight in your heart, your willpower, your plans. Make Me your truth, your desire, so you cannot – will not – falter nor stumble on the way.

I lighten your path that you may pick up your feet gladly, skipping along in My joy and knowledge. Counsel of Mine will be yours as you learn to use Me wisely in the way I plan.

My purpose and design are unfolding, a beautiful pattern weaved by Me for many, through you, all of you. Threads of harmony, no discord, as I weave My cloth to be spread out each day; bright colours, vibrant living, glowing with life and love, for that is what I bring to you. My healing grace, anointed for many because you listened and responded to My call to you. Well done, My faithful servants!

Learn more. You can never reach all knowledge and understanding here on earth. You are not expected so to do. But you can learn more of My strength as you practise My teachings and put them to good use. Do as I ask of you, for that is My desire. You will not always know why, but simply trust and allow Me My way. It will become plain to you as time unfolds in My unwrapping.

My Calling Out to You - II

30th August

My hands caress each day into being, folded in My care and comfort – the comfort of knowing Me and serving My purposes; the care of bringing Me, the real and living Me, to others that they too may know the truth, My truth.

They will listen to you when you act in love of Me, when actions speak louder than words. It will not be easy; that was not My promise. But it will be exciting, this walk with Me, for it is the true meaning of your lives – your fulfilment, your destiny, beginning now even as I speak.

My word is plain for you to read. Take hold of it and act upon it in My strength, empowered by My Spirit of love and peace, My Spirit of unity and purpose. You will know when plans are of Me, for you will feel the joy of My presence, hear the word of My calling out to you, see Me in the steps you take as the way unfolds before you, taking away obstacles and illuminating the path without shadows. My calling is yours. Have no doubt of this, but rejoice in My presence, My coming into your lives in this way.

My children, know Me and use My strength for your work, your work in Me. Peace I give you – My everlasting peace sown amongst men where I am. My joy, My peace, My knowing of truth and destiny; no fear, no doubt, no despair, only Me, My Father and Spirit. All of one accord in calling out to you. Calling in My Name, for that was My purpose: to come and know you, be like you, that you may identify with Me and understand My compassion.

My strengths are your weaknesses, made whole again, healed by Me. Allow Me to do this, to minister to you. My healing power and grace is sufficient unto all things. My place in your hearts is assured when you call out to Me, for then I come in power.

My joy is complete when I behold just one of My children safely back in the fold, held secure in My Father's arms of love. For this you were formed. Go now in My Name, serving.

Healed and Made Whole - I

31st August

I set you free to do My work. Fear not the consequences of this change. Come out of the darkness into My light. Step forth bravely knowing this is of Me and My choosing, My calling. Glad you will be that you came to Me and listened, for I give you peace in your hearts – that peace which is only Mine to give. Act in My accord and purpose knowing that it will be well in Me, in My time.

I paint a new picture, a broader brush on the landscape, for there are those who need you and your help, your guidance. As I give you purpose, recognise My will for you… Alpha is the beginning; omega is the end. All that comes in between must be Me, until you reach Me in person.

Become My nerve centre, My pulse, in the ways I show you. It will become clear to you what you are to do, My intentions working out within you ... Serve Me and celebrate Me, My presence, in your lives of trust and serving, of knowing Me more. Learn of Me, My little children, for in knowing Me you are strengthened beyond all your imagining.

Receive My prayer as I stand before the Father on our behalf, longing to serve… you. Be no longer strictured. I bring you freedom in Me: freedom to go where you will under My Name; freedom from fears of failing Me; freedom from oppression and doubt as to the future (recognise your feelings, your release, as you come to believe what I tell you, as you learn to know Me more); freedom to be healed in My Name.

My resurrection was to bring you life in Me, knowing that you can live fully day by day under My calling, My searching for you. Study and learn that you may put into practice what you know of Me as well as what you experience. For in knowing I will become alive in your thoughts and understanding. I will become alive in a way that is vibrant and real, more real to you than the air that surrounds.

Healed and Made Whole - II

1st September

I break all barriers of time and space as I reach out to you. My hand is held out in longing for you to take, to clasp, so I can lead you on into My freedom of choice, knowing that this is of Me and My calling; you will know by the peace that I bring you, My peace of heart, just like I promised ("My peace I bring you."[31]) Do you understand this now? It is of Me when you feel this peace, this inner harmony – leaving the details and the workings of it, the plan, to Me. You have only to take hold of the outline, and I will sketch in the portrait of beauty, the landscape made green by My palette of beautiful colours and intentions.

My calling is to you now to come out of that place of darkness and doubt into My glorious light, My resurrected light, which gives you light and life and growth in Me. Spare not a backward glance, but look forward in your focus. Keep your eyes upon Me, My beckoning. This calling is asking your real trust of Me – your knowing, your believing, that all will be well in My Name. I would not harm you nor disquiet you; that is impossible!

Each day is My day given to you for My work, for a specific purpose. Learn to recognise that purpose day by day and act accordingly. Relax into Me, knowing My joy by thought, word and deed. Rejoice in My Name. That is My intention, My purpose and plan. The essence of Me is distilled in your lives when you listen to My voice and act as I ask you to do, when you do My bidding.

Be not dull but bright in My likeness and love, shining out – My beacon of hope; My beam of light bringing love and purpose to others, bringing My hope, My resurrection, the new life for all.

My nerve centre will pulse with My beauty as you listen to My heartbeat and tune in to its rhythm of love. I formed you for this and bound you together in love of Me and each other, a total unity, each in one, held together, held fast by Me for all times. Relax into My love as it suffuses your life, your lives, all that you do and say – total commitment in My Name, knowing of Me, serving through Me.

---

31 Based on John 14:27

Healed and Made Whole - III

2nd September

I use you wisely according to your strengths. Do not fret about the weaknesses, for those too I use in My way to allow you to learn of Me and to depend. You will see that you cannot manage on your own but must depend on Me ultimately for all things, for that is wherefrom they came and will return.

All I have is yours – yours to give out and share among those to whom I send you. Be released now and forevermore, knowing I have spoken to you, spoken My truth in My Name.

Healed and made whole you will be, as you come to Me and serve – restored, refreshed, remade in My likeness and image; revived, regained in confidence; revitalised with My energy that you may plan your days in Me and with My work. I will show you what, where and how.

Keep asking of Me, making time for Me – time to listen and learn; time to talk and pray; time to sing and rejoice in My presence; time to serve My people in love; time to give.

Much as you give, I will give more to you: more of Me and My plans, My work; more of Myself and My calling for you. Reach out in My Name. Reach out to Me, moving from Me with Me as the axis, the centre. Radiate My love, My vision, as you encompass My strength. Move onto another plane, a higher plane of My existence and strength.

Healed and Made Whole - IV

3rd September

As My heart beats in tune with you, we become a force, a dynamic force in this world, wherever you are; a throb, a pulse of life, a life-giving force of reality, setting men's hearts on fire with desire for understanding of Me. Tune in to that. Breathe it. Live it and sleep it. It is the very essence of your being, your coming in to Me and My kingdom here on earth.

All you will establish in My Name will be good, for it is from Me and cannot fail when My hand of blessing is placed upon it. Receive My love…

Prepare in Me to be strengthened, made whole, taken apart, then reformed in a new and more glorious light, for it is reflecting more of Me and My image, no shadows falling upon you. Be resplendent in My glory, My knowing of you, My working through you and yours.

Be organised in Me, for that is your strength… Be organised that you may serve Me thoroughly, through and through – no corners missed, not slipshod; no misadventure; complete, whole, rounded and grounded in Me; systematic and completely focused; My blueprint stamped throughout in all that you do and say.

Be on your guard for the evil one's snares of doubt and distraction. Believe all that I have told you, for it is My very truth.

Restored and Healed - I

4th September

My child, be sure of Me and My promises. They secure your future happiness and My work for you… to do. I act now that all is put in place, in readiness, for My purpose.

Hasten not – no worry! – but proceed at My pace, under My direction knowing all will be well in My Name. How can, could, it be otherwise so, when you are in Me and I am in you? Obstacles there will be but not boulders. Have no fear of them, for they will not block the way, My path. As they are removed one by one, you will see the way forward clearly, a way claimed for Me.

All will be well and all manner of things will be well when I appoint it. For I work in the greater interest of many influences in your lives – all those whom you touch and reach out to.

The truth of My calling is this: to make ready your hearts for My work; to train you as My disciples, My ambassadors in love, taking My purpose wherever you go. For this reason I bring you freedom: freedom to act in Me and go out unfettered; freedom to use your home as you will for My purposes, a centre of My being there in love and harmony, that which many have not known in their lives. You can bring this to them, for this peace is My gift to you… spilled out in happiness and joy of Me.

Getting to know Me will bring others alive fully, alive in expectation and trust. You are to be instrumental in this in your home of love and good intention. Based on love, grounded in love, you will become whole – whole in Me and My intention; restored and healed (for that is My promise to you and many); a place of gladness, a summer house filled with My joy, laughter and praise, My strengthening love and companionship.

Restored and Healed - II

5th September

All I have is yours to use in My Name – My gifts of the Spirit. Call upon Him that He may come to you in power ... He brings peace and joy that are Mine, that which the world cannot give.

As you come alive in Me – fully alive – great things will happen in My Name: joys untold, marvels unexpected. I increase your faith wholeheartedly. Live it every moment of the day, never ceasing to strive for Me and in Me. Your quest is a hard one but worth the fighting for. All battle is won in My Father's Name. The battle belongs to the Lord.

Give Him all glory and honour. Bow down before Him in praise and reverence for He is your God and King of your heart. All life, all holiness, come from Him to set us apart upon earth – called, set apart, from many who know not, that you may help them to know and understand. For no greater calling hath any man that this: to find themself in finding Me, My Father and Spirit, Our joy, Our life, Our Resurrection, Our peace, comfort and harmony, Our very being in all lives who invite us in.

Take the truth of My love and power to those whom I give you. Make Me real to them. Be patient with them, as they grow only slowly. Remember what it was like for yourselves (still is, in many ways). As you reach out you grow taller in Me. As you trust you grow deeper in Me. As you learn you grow stronger in Me.

Take all that I have and use it – My gifts of the Spirit – that all the fruits may grow and flourish in your lives, a taste of heaven on earth. That is My promise to you which will be fulfilled – is being fulfilled, even now as I speak to you.

Time is no barrier in Me. Know My presence, My saving grace, My love poured out for you that you may have life – *My* life – shared in strength together.

My Joy is Your Joy - I

6th September

Take up My † and carry it with Me, for Me. You are My hands in this place where there is no other to do the task I gave you to do. My calling is just that: My calling to you, each of you individually – individually formed for a purpose in Me.

Know of Me and My will for you, My ways of doing things – so different from those of the world, for they seek not My own gratification. I live for you and all mankind set in My image and likeness. I was formed that you might be – be in Me – totally alive, set free from doubt and worry, released in My Name.

I carry the burden but you must help Me shoulder it, for this is the work I give you to do. The aching of My people must be borne by us, healed in My Name – the aching of desire and longing – for they know Me not. I have come to you and can come to them when they seek and you allow access through your heart, made big in Me. Behold, My children, in teaching of Me, all that you know and have experienced.

My joy is your joy. Share it out. Be confident in the certain knowledge that I am alive and working in you, with you all... called out in My Name and purpose, anointed with one accord of love – My love and that for each other and Me. Unified under My Spirit, although not the same – each different in My strength of being, My fashioning, but bonded together most strongly for all times, for that is My wish, My design.

Those tangled threads are unwrapping in My hands to become a new fabric, a new lustre, more closely interwoven with Me. As I bind you together My seams are interfaced and strengthened by your love for each other, your respect and companionship.

You can teach so many by that, so many who have not known the same nor anything like. Heal them by holding them in your love. Heal them for Me. I need you to act in My Name that they might be convinced of the truth, My truth that I came to set you free.

Be still and know that I am God, for in your stillness you gather speed – speed and strength – sustenance for them as you are fed by Me.

My Joy is Your Joy - II

7th September

Deep peace I bring you in My periods of calm together, that peace which the world cannot bring in all its clamouring and fighting. But My peace lasts, for it reigns in your hearts and minds, knowing that I am there always for you, working on your behalf, that you have not need to worry nor fret. Believe Me when I tell you this. It is important for your own freedom and healing.

As you release the cases onto Me, you are set free to grow in stature and design, My beautiful design for your lives. Live according to My plan, looking neither to left nor right, but straight ahead into My glorious light of the golden dawning – that sunshine beaming into your lives, bringing you strength and growth in Me; healing you and making you whole under My gaze and direction, surrounded, bathed in My light of understanding.

Joys untold shall be yours in My likeness as you reflect more of Me. As you receive more of My light, more will be reflected back into the gloom of men's lives, lighting up their darkness and despair. This is the work I give you to do: to reflect Me and My glory in the Father.

Take hold of My Spirit and make Him your own, for that is what He would love. My gift to you freely given by My death on the ✝ – the ✝ of suffering but the ✝ also of release into joy everlasting. Believe in this; it is My greatest truth and triumph. Oh, that all men could see this – would be *enabled* to see and understand this! Then they would be changed into My reality. My kingdom would come here on earth.

You have your part to play. Go now in My Name, to do My work. I anoint you with My power. I bless you by My grace.

My Joy is Your Joy - III

8th September

I come to you increasingly as you come to Me, to rely upon Me and trust Me more. Then I can use you most powerfully, because you are of Me, in Me, with Me, closely intertwined like a beautiful bound rope of gold and silvered threads burnished with love, harmony and purpose. On that rope I pull you up towards Me, not dangling but feet held firm. My foothold is yours today and every day, evermore. Securely encompassed in My love, you are held safe – safe to set out into My world where I am sending you to teach of Me.

Be glad, My children, be joyful in Me, for this is My calling out to you. Relax in My arms of love in the sure knowledge that they hold you firm. You are supported on all sides and will not fall. You are held erect, head held high in Me, shoulders strengthened, back made straight, hands held out, walking tall and straight, for I take care of all aspects of your life, your lives and wellbeing.

My dear children, walk now towards Me. I wait for you longingly. My destiny awaits you.

My Rainbow of Many Colours - I

9th September

I set your life flowing through Me as My love courses through your veins and sets you on fire with zest for living in Me. I bring you freedom of movement, My discourse of intention, when you plan not alone but in Me, taking hold of My mind and strength, My intentions for you.

My truth is to become your truth for it is all you need to set you on the right path. The journey's direction you can leave to Me. My hand enfolds the plan and compass, set towards Me and My Father's house where joy, untold joy, awaits you and all who journey with you.

Be My guide for those who have lost their way or not even started to walk with Me. Show them how – how to arrive – by way of Me. As I have allowed you to grope through the darkness into My glorious light of dawning recognition and trust, help them to do the same.

Teach of Me; speak of Me; show of Me. Reveal Me in your everyday work and lives, for I am all that ultimately matters – Me, My Father, My Spirit, Our Three-in-Oneness holding you fast.

Formed in My likeness and image you too are gods in My Name for I give you My power – My resurrection power – to bring Me to others in strength of meaning.

Fill their desire for knowing of Me. They do not always recognise this themselves, and yours it is to help them see the light, what really matters in their life and yours.

Splendid is My rainbow of many colours, overarching your lives, everything, with the pot of gold being My truth and reality set at the rainbow's end. Reach out for this with one accord of longing – longing to be in Me and serve.

As you long and desire for Me, I can come to you, for you invite Me into your hearts, your waiting hearts. As I come to you I enthuse you and strengthen you by My very being within – strengthened for all endurance and testing by faith.

My Rainbow of Many Colours - II

10th September

My tests are love stretches, exercises in patience, tolerance and understanding, that you too may use My compassion and outlook. They are not done out of harshness, for I would never harm nor disrespect you. Rather My tests are like the refiner's fire, moulding and purifying. Do not fear My testing times for they bring renewed grace and favour. My trial is your trial but not by jury nor judge, for I provide all means for everything.

I am the way of all things. I am the truth of all times. I am the life given in love by My Father that you may be set free in Me – free to live and love eternally. No greater gift can any man bring than this to others, through Me.

This is My calling out to you, My commission to go out and spread My good news, My salvation into those aching hearts of stone and silence. Radiate, penetrate into the sternest of men's circumstances where they know Me not, nor care. I come through you as you reach out to each other, for that is My choice of working.

My network is human bonds and attachments, My leading strings of love tied together by circumstances of My weaving – thread upon thread interwoven and crossed over by Me into this rich tapestry which you call life. But it is life only if you know Me. For without Me there is no true freedom to live, no existence that is pure and holy.

As I exchanged My life for yours on the †, you became as Me, a holy child of God the Father, with all that entails: all the joy; all the responsibilities of the family of God also.

You do not stand alone but in the mighty company of the array of heaven where My joy awaits its crown of your lives in times to come. For now, your calling is to be of Me, in Me and with Me that through you, all of you, I may act, accordingly.

Go in My Name. My favour rests upon you all.

Come Alive - I

11th September

Be still and know that I am God in all times and places, in all circumstances of your lives as you hand over control to Me. In your relying upon Me, you come to trust. In your trust you come to believe, and in your belief you are strengthened in Me.

My Spirit comes to you all not by chance. He will blow where He wills into men's hearts to bring them alive in Me, to stir their beings into life – true life with meaning, form and intention. As He breathes upon you, you will grow – grow in love and understanding of Me, grow in My strength and likeness.

Fully grown, you become My apostles anointed for leadership and filled by My power. This is My gift to you, that you may use Me wisely and lovingly. I have more to give you as you need and are ready to use this power of influence which will touch so many.

No greater work can man do than that which you are about to achieve in My Name. For in saving others from the blackness of their doubt and despair, you bring them My freedom to trust and know for sure of Me. Their lives will be altered forever because they knew Me and hoped, because they were set alive with the breath of My Spirit within them.

Man without Me is dead. He knows not where he comes from, nor where he goes to. But with Me in him, My breath of life, he is transformed and energised into life – the life I came to give you, each and every one person here on earth.

Come Alive - II

12th September

As you travel back towards Me, the journey is made so much the easier in knowing Me – easier because you are given My strength to deal with all the problems that beset you.

Without Me you are orphaned into anxiety – at a loss, confused, bewildered. With Me, you are set alight with My zeal and fervour; My zest of intention; My scope, wide-ranging scope, of life-giving source.

As you become truly alive in Me, you will grow in an expanse of love. Love you receive from Me, and love you will be able to show to others – all those to whom I send you.

It is no mere chance what is happening in your lives. It is My reality, that which I give you in trust of Me. Many times have I bid you to trust, and again it is My plea. That trust and belief is the bond of growing love between us – that leading string I talked about[32] which you can pull upon at any time. That string of attachment holds our hearts together in unity of purpose. It gives a vein, a channel, for your mind to reach out to Mine, for Mine to enlarge into your space.

Reach out and touch Me. It is My desire that you should do this, that I should be one with you and you with Me. Reach out and touch My heart of love. It is for you today and always.

Come alive – truly alive – in My Spirit of love and life, bringing the peace of knowing Me, harmony and consolation of mind, set secure in trust of Me. Believe, My children, that I am yours. This is My wish and desire.

Do not fail Me. Seek and you will find in ever greater depths and measure.

---

32 See Hosea 11:4

I Call You Not Servants But Friends - I

13th September

Be calm in My Spirit and reassured of My good work in you all. Yours is to uphold the truth of My teaching, that testimony which I brought to earth. Deliver it wholly using My power gifts. Speak as you have been spoken to, and rely upon Me at all times. Do not turn your face away from My direction, but rather look into, at, My glorious light of recognition shining upon you and through you.

Never become disheartened nor dismayed. Those feelings are not from Me. Anything that disquiets or displeases you, hold it up to Me for sanctification and healing. I make whole and mend. I restore and replenish. I weave anew in ever brighter colours when My threads are burnished in love of Me and My Father.

My truth is the totality which sets you free – free to believe more radically in Me and My promises. I will be your guide, ever ready to teach if only you ask and seek Me. I long to share with you My ways and thoughts, My desires and promises, My expectations and hopes. My calling is of you, to you all. As you come to know Me more and more, you are released in My Spirit to serve and delight in Me, all I have to give you.

I Call You Not Servants But Friends - II

14th September

I call you not servants but friends, dear friends and trusted companions along the way of life's journey. It is but a short time until we meet face to face, for life lasts not but many long years. Know My truth before we meet together in heaven; for in knowing this you can sample heaven on earth and help to bring it about.

My realm is a far-reaching one, reaching beyond the boundaries men set for themselves. Reach out and touch Me. Even the hem of My garment was sufficient to bring healing power, grace, to those who held on to it. And I take you by the hand to hold you much closer to My heart of love, My enlarged heart of compassion. My call is to you now, knowing My truth and seeking to stand in it. I will strengthen your resolve and purpose. Ask Me, allow Me, to come in total power into your lives.

My Spirit comes to you all, emboldened by your trust and desire. He blows where He wills according to those who long. He breathes on you now, life, a new life in Me; a joy-filled existence of meaning, knowing the truth, doubting not, alive in praise and proper worship, alive in Me.

Hold Fast to That Which Is Good

15th September

Resolve in My Name. I am with you always, guiding and strengthening, supporting with My life to love. Justify by Me and exonerate yourselves by My love. I will not see you wanting nor in despair.

Hold fast to that which is secure in Me: My truths. Be yourselves in witness of Me and My saving power, that I may strengthen and support you by My real presence in your midst. Where you stand, I stand, when you seek Me and call on My Name, My power. Use Me for all your work but especially this.

My protection is given that you are held in safety, no evil force to assail you. Take courage in Me and hold fast to that which is good. Deliver from evil and stand rock-firm, encompassed in My love.

My children, believe Me! My saving power extends to all situations. I will not fail you. Do not be apprehensive, but rather joyful in My sight, for knowing Me is loving Me, and loving Me is your security, your safe calling.

I will not abandon you nor fail you, for My love for you is ever constant, unfailing in its strength. Be encouraged and of good cheer. I am the God who serves you.

Your Power Will Be My Power

16th September

I will take whatever you have got and multiply it in Me to feed the hungry and poor in spirit. This is My truth, that I feed My people in want of Me by using your power of being real to them. As you come into the darkness of their lives, My light will shine away their fear and doubt.

Love conquers. Love, only love. For this I formed you in Me. Work on yourselves first, moulding to the pattern of My being that you may become as one like Me in all ways. Then you have the power of heaven behind you and in front to beckon you on. Your power will be My power, shared out, 'divided amongst' and 'multiplied by' many times. I strengthen and set free in Me, in My reality. Feed on Me to gain My sustaining power which will embolden you in all things and surround you with the light of My Being, that you may radiate with My energy and joy.

Amazed you will be by all that happens in Me – amazed and overjoyed. Come, My children, into My arms of love where you can rest secure awhile, always held safe, always strengthened. Be built in Me and upon Me for I am your secure rock and foundation, your safe resting place and cornerstone, the One who holds all things together, the triangle of your being – body, mind and spirit – all formed by Me, for Me, My Father and Our Spirit.

Rejoice in your beauty. I, who made you, call you wonderful, a delight to My eye, for you serve Me well. You are My strength and shield on this earth where I placed you, not by chance but to be in Me and of Me in service.

Go now gladly in My Name to do My work and serve many.

I Am the Jewel

17th September

My child, persevere in the midst of this darkness for there you find the jewel in the crown of faith. All these people without Me. They are Mine, and I will bring them back to Me in My way, My time. I use you for this work…bound in My love and longing I give you.

Wait on Me patiently, taking small steps one at a time – looking, listening, learning, reaching out only when and where I tell you to do so. Be taught by Me and you cannot go wrong. My Spirit is upon you… guiding, directing, appointing times, places and opportunities. You have to stay alert to perceive these. I give you counsel and understanding. You must give Me your time and prayer, your intentions to serve and honour Me. In loving Me, many will be made whole by My Name, including those you long for, those you hold so dear. Keep praying for them regularly. Prayer prevents the process of decay. It transforms into new life in Me.

Keep looking to My † of salvation, that saving shape… My Name means 'to save'. Now believe it; believe all that is in Me. I am the jewel in the Father's court, in His hand, a jewel more precious than any gem stone – more beautiful, more solid, worth more than all gold and silver; a prize beyond reckoning but not beyond reach.

Clasp Me to your heart, your hearts, of love in Me. Take Me into your deep – deepest – desire to serve. There I serve you well and always. Do not doubt Me, nor My call upon you… You are My disciples singled out in grace, for this is My desire. In seeking, I find you. In discovery My ways are laid open to fruition. Work in Me, for Me, through Me, completely focused on the prize, the goal, of My calling out to you.

Do as you feel your heart telling you to, always remembering My command to love one another as I have loved you, ceaselessly. By this men will know Me in you – see Me, hear Me, reach out to touch Me. Be constant in your love and support, never failing Me or them. I rely upon you and make you steadfast in Me, My Name.

Take of Me, talk of Me, show of Me and deliver My love, compassion and forgiveness. Heal in My Name all manner of ills and infirmities. Be strong in Me, built upon Me, uplifted by Me until your spirit soars with Mine to the heavenly places where I await you with outstretched arms. Keep coming to Me. I am yours now and forever.

Heal and Be Healed

18th September

You will see things come to pass which you would not have thought possible: healings in My Name; My salvation brought to many through you by Me; healing of body, mind and spirit.

Learn of Me – My ways, My promises – that you may use Me. In your own healing you are able to give of yourself in understanding and sympathy. And as you give, you will receive more: more of Me and My purposes in you. Heal and be healed, restored once more to fullness of life and energy.

You have served Me well over the years but now must go on, strengthened in Me, directed by Me, where I place you. It is no mere chance that takes you into people's lives when they need healing, need Me. I put you where you can bring Me, for the heart is made ready in longing and sometimes desperation. To serve is to be served, restored, forgiven and healed of all ills.

Lead by example and delight in Me. Be resolved in My Name to commit yourselves to those whom I give you. Be steadfast, unwavering in effort and belief. Be restored in My sight of all that assails you. I take it away in My time when you have learnt to carry the † of suffering for Me and in Me. My promise to you was of healing. It will be fulfilled, accomplished by Me.

My child, My children, I love you… with a fire of intensity too bright for human understanding or knowing. That is why you must believe all that I say. It is for your own good!

Belong to Me and no other. Be whole in Me. You are My joy, My treasured delight, forthcoming in My Name and service.

Love Me, and Again I Say, Love Me

19th September

Promise Me one thing: your love for all times. For it is only by bringing your love to Me I know the seriousness of your intentions, your real devotion. This love can be brought in so many ways, by what you think, say and do, to Me and for Me, in others, each other, those I place you with.

Use My love for healing divisions in men's relationships, for healing divisions, fractures in their soul. Help them to turn their eyes towards Me, the great Healer of love.

Show of Me, speak of Me, deliver of Me. Share Me out among many whenever you can – shared in action and direction, letting known what you have learned in Me. The more you give, the more you will receive, for that is one of My laws, one of My principles. You have to make room within you for Me to be there; then as you are prepared to share Me, give Me away, I refresh your spirit by more of Mine.

Your energy is returned in Me. Your desire grows – your longing to give of Me. Thus we have a circle of beautiful light, love, longing – lengthening your days, your lives, your destiny. Regard My words, My children, for they bring healing and wholeness to you and yours, those whom you love so dearly, those whom I gave you to look after, to take care of for Me.

Love Me, and again I say, love Me – through and through every fibre of your being. In My love you will be bound together with each other and Me, Us, My Father and Spirit, a Trinity of love: Us as One, and you and those you bring to Us. An indissoluble love bond, now and forever, made in My Name, to My glory and delight.

You are My heart's desire, a love affair kindling as you come to Me more and more. Like true lovers, set time aside for us to be together that I may show you My ways, My purposes. I need your undivided attention on Me, for jealous love will not share you out amongst distractions that are worldly, not of Me.

Be Mine – altogether Mine – your soul and spirit united in love of Me, blended in My love, strengthened by My love, sustained by My love, certain of My love for you…

My Love Knows No Boundaries - I

20th September

My love for you which knows no barriers, this is the love which you must offer others in My Name. My love is wide, deep and all embracing, not conditional upon circumstances and My feeling. Make yours the same so you can go the extra mile of effort; make the extra pain of self-giving. My love knows no boundaries.

You can take My people anywhere in Me, if only you pray to Me and believe fully. Pray with all your heart, with all your mind, with all your strength, with all your intentions – and be consistent. Lukewarm is not warm! You have to be on fire, with love of Me burning a path in your hearts – a path I may walk upon to enter another man's soul; a path where you can lead Me for you forge the opening.

Do not think this is difficult. Simply trust Me and pray for opportunities to present Me, lovingly displayed in the everyday matters of your life, your lives. Listening and learning of Me, you will become bolder, more certain of My promises. This boldness will give you new life in Me, a sure hope of resurrection for all those you hold dear.

You have to remember that love covers over many a sin – yours and those of others. I can overlook many things, so many things, in My Name of love. And remember, time is no barrier to Me, who am the same today and throughout eternity.

My Love Knows No Boundaries - II

21st September

My healing reaches back as well as forwards. Pray for it to do so. Pray on your knees with your whole mind and body. Pray in My Name of healing that hurts may be soothed, despair resolved, confidence built in Me. Ask and you will receive. Seek and you will find Me for those whom you love. It is My longing to reach out to them through you. For as I put you together, bound you together in your mortal flesh, so My Spirit binds you together in Me for all eternity. You need have no fear and I will displace the doubts.

Give thanks for all things in My Name. Go up with shouts of joy to proclaim the deeds I have done through you. Joy is my heart-warmer, My strength, My reward and delight as I see My children joy in Me – misplaced doubts and fears banished, all because you believed in Me and My promises. Be set alive in Me, your energy infused by My love, your determination strengthened.

My love for you is like the sea water gently lapping upon the shore, waiting to be soaked up into the dryness, to trickle into empty chasms beneath the surface. As you receive Me, My living waters of life, you will blossom and flourish as leaves on the tree in springtime, new life bursting out – beautiful, fresh, a sign of hope, a fullness of life coming from within.

Believe Me, My children. It is all as I have said to you. Take Me now and make Me your own strength, your own power, your own healing, that I may use you for others, those that I gave to you. Do not disappoint Me.

Rejoice in My Name always, and again I say, rejoice! Heaven and earth meet as we come together in love of each other.

A Chosen Path

22nd September

Carry My people heavenwards. Let them know My love, My life in you. Feel My release and set them free from fear: fear of harm; fear of losing sight of Me, of themselves. Freedom from fear is My gift of life – riches beyond telling – won by My precious blood once and for all men.

I came that you might live in Me each day, tasting heaven on earth as you know bread that is broken in My Name of suffering. Eat of Me whenever you can, for I bring fullness of life and strength given in no other way.

Pray each day that you may find your way of knowing Me. I come when you ask. Do you not believe this? Hold on to Me; all that is good, all that is trustworthy, is found there – the rope of life dangling heavenwards for you to pull on and be drawn, like a guide leading his followers through the fog.

The way ahead opens up step by step. You simply have to follow in My footsteps and keep your eyes focused on Me, the way ahead. The swirling mist will not swallow you up, and you will not get lost with Me at the helm.

Trust in Me, My dear children. Come unto Me and receive My life, My way forward. Do not doubt yourselves; rather look to My † shining in glory – the glory of having won you for Me. Do not lose sight of Me, for I need you as you need Me. You are chosen for a purpose. Seek and you will find. That is My promise and it holds fast.

Claim Me that all things may be added unto you. Claim My power, My presence, in your lives – uplifted, strengthened, replenished, My children, My dearly beloved ones.

A mystical union between Christ and His children is a chosen path – chosen by Me and you together. Come, let us rejoice!

My Trust and Truth

23rd September

You must seek more earnestly, more devotedly, putting Me at the centre of all things, surrounding yourself in My trust and truth. Do not be afraid, for I am with you wherever you go. You must know this by now! Why do you see and yet not understand?

Come back to Me with all your heart. Acclaim My victory in your life – good triumphing over the darkness of doubt and dismay. When you think you have lost Me, you have been ill-prepared to meet Me, occupied with your own thoughts. Hand them to Me...

Do not forget My teaching. Become My child once more, in touch all the time. Swim out of your sea of loneliness. Suffering is gain only when shouldered by Me and shared between us because it deepens trust.

"Come unto Me, you who are heavy burdened."[33] I will give you rest for your soul, refreshment for your spirit, new life in your body. You do not have to put up with these ills. Let Me heal you today in the way you think. You have to trust more, be taken on trust, not knowing why and when I will come to you.

"But I thought You were also there, Lord?"

So I am but at times, certain times, I come closer for a purpose. You must learn to recognise when these times are. In all truth I tell you, great things can be done in My Name.

Go out and deliver of Me – My healing power and grace brought about by kind words, actions and prayer of the faithful. Keep searching and you will find My purpose. Look even in unlikely places, for it is there I wait to be found by many. Uncover My truths in their eyes by what you tell them, and always pray to Me in expectant faith and gladness of heart.

Hear what I have to say to you and act upon it in My Name. It is the Lord who speaks.

---

33 Based on Matthew 11:30

Make Me Centre Stage

24th September

"Is there anything You wish to make me aware of today, Lord?"

Myself given in love for you and many – all who accept Me, My children by choice. They come to know Me as they seek and find, believing in My truths. Trust is all that is necessary, coupled with forgiveness. That is the receipt of My forgiveness for your hard-heartedness and mistakes.

No man travels through earth untouched, unsullied by trouble. He needs My cleansing, healing water by baptism and faith. Then he is restored in the sight of God, strengthened to become Our child once more, again walking in the light of recognised love. It never was withheld but so often is not received. This is the great tragedy of earth, of mankind's doing – he who knows Me not nor seems to care. Such a rich treasure house unplundered in Me – untouched, remaining wasted in part; the source of all strength and energy unrecognised, unharnessed.

"Go and multiply!" was My command to My disciples. That meant to grow in both strength and stature – that which comes from knowing of Me, My will, My ways, My teaching, My delight, My sorrow. All can be yours, ours shared together, for I tend My sheep – they who listen to My voice and recognise My call amidst the clamour of life.

Life never was easy but should be meaningful, rich in promise and hope, abundant in blessings and joy when I am involved. Make Me centre stage, and the drama alters plot with a happy ending. Even life's tragedies become cast in meaning when looking at Me – all for a purpose; all to a plan.

You children cannot see the beginning from the end. It was never intended that you can because that builds your trust in Me. And I make adjustments continually for the overall good. Therefore it would be impossible for you to see or even conceive of the overall plan in My mind.

Simply hand things over to Me: trials, temptations, fear and delight, delays, refusal, rebut, jealousies, dislikes, uncertainties, anxieties, hopes and joy – all Mine because you are in Me, of My making; My children formed from love and desire to belong, you to Me, us together, remaining at heart where I am.

The Cross of My Suffering - I
25th September

Uncover, discover the depths of My love where you belong at heart… From the start I called you Mine, but you were too busy to heed. Remember the plea, My plea "Listen to the Lord"? It was spoken then, that you may move forward in Me by becoming pure in intention.

The mention of My Name brings release, a deep, true inner peace of belonging where you were meant to be – formed out of love, for love to be received and given when you make room, empty the space I require to infill, instil My truth. Yes, the truth does set you free indeed.

Heed My loving Word daily. It's all around you if you do but look and see, look and listen, concern yourself with My message. It is sent that you may impart to others the good news of love and forgiveness, healing and glad life in Me – free from worries, concerns, doubts, difficulties, distractions; all worldly matters turned around, upside down upon My † which marks out heaven and earth, pointing the way both up and down, left and right. There is no wrongdoing if you are in sight of My †, where all healing grace is found – hanging there, standing there, waiting to be claimed, named in truth.

You will know the truth which sets you free, for it is My desire. I aspire to use you… For this you must be made ready – willing to give in My Name. Give of yourself, yourselves, for Me in the trust of knowing I have a plan to work to and I need you to conform, adapt, realign yourselves with Me.

Keep trying. You will succeed! Success comes from effort seriously made to persevere in goodness. Listen and learn. Look and see Me there, hanging there on My † of suffering to correct, resurrect you – new life, new hope, new vision, fresh decision, all because you prayed. Well done!

The Cross of My Suffering - II

26th September

Hand over to Me your concerns, anxieties, however small. Remember to talk to Me often. I'm always listening and looking for means by which to bless you!

Inner vision is the result of My Spirit moving in you; and He longs to come in power when I send Him. Ask and receive. He will blow the wind of cobwebs away to let the daylight in – musty, dusty corners, dark and dismal, swept out, swept clean again. Sunshine after spring rain is My warming upon earth and mankind. It brings growth and nurtures the soul into wholeness of being, seeing you decided upon Me.

Make Me yours as you are Mine – together forever in heart and mind, where I'll find you ready and waiting. Inspect yourselves, close introspection brings healing grace, making room for new growth in strength. It takes only love given to Me in intention and effort.

I'll make the decisions. You can rely on that. Simply hand over, rest and relax, My children, My dear and lovely children. I am pleased with the effort you are making.

Give of Yourself - I

27th September

It is for others that I give you yourselves to serve with My love brought to them. It is for you to decide what you can, can't do. But remember to pray to Me for all things. This is the answer for anyone, everyone who seeks to do My will righteously.

Give of yourselves – time and effort – where you can manage it realistically; no stress, no burden-bearing, for that is not My way. I send you out joyfully, expectantly and encouraged – alive with Me, not deadened by the weight of a task to perform. Working, worrying, is not what I want. I am a God of gladness, goodness, and expect you to go in My Name joyfully, rejoicing in the work I give you, choose you to do for Me – My Spirit set free amongst others because you cared to share yourselves enough, sufficiently, to bring about a new release of peace so much sought after.

Everybody needs Me so much to be in touch with their longings, to repair all the damage the world has wreaked havoc upon them. This need not be the case, need not last, for there is always an answer in My grace supplied in love – *for* love – with generosity. Heal My children. Heal in My Name. Recommend My living, loving presence amongst you to be stronger and one.

You and Me together working for mankind's good, where I should place you as My hands and feet; My voice of calm reassurance; deliverance directed through My Spirit connected to My heart of love set deep in the Father's centre. Enter into Me and be Mine. This is when peace is found – the release of anxiety, doubt, despair – repair on offer, freely given.

Give of Yourself - II

28th September

A puncture is a hole needing mending. I'm sending you who know how to act in My Name of restoration, dedication, to do all that is good and can become better yet. Let Me work in you lovingly to make all the difference, take away pain and suffering, offering My redemption, complete redemption. Mention My Name as the One – the only One – who holds the answer to such a dilemma.

Correct; re-connect the soul with the Spirit. Herein lies true healing, appealing to anybody who seeks. Speak of My power, of My forgiveness, of My care, of My fortitude, of My strength, My understanding – demanding no more than a willingness to listen and accept. Then expect My blessings to descend.

I send love (pure love above all that is known or experienced, imagined or desired) hired/lent/sent from My Father's heart of gold.

Know Me, know My Father, know My Spirit as One, ready so We may have begun to hold your healing in Our embrace. "Face to face"[34] will come upon us, and you must be ready, steady in your intentions and promises wherever you go.

Show of Me, know of Me; but let Me be the Doer. It is Mine to give, Mine to withhold, Mine to heed, Mine to hold knowingly, showing you who is sovereign Lord (incredible though this sounds).

It is found easy in Me for you to be faithful, honest, true; the one who I predicted, planned and purposed; My child of love, formed from love for love's exuberance. Go with joy, My children; remember this. It is important to understand what I command and expect. I suspect you do not do so yet – not truly. Let's keep trying. I am a patient God, ready and waiting, your fear abating as you learn to take Me on trust, the 'must' of our relationship – hired help, desired help, given through Me, who can be anything, everything that is needed. Heed My words! They are truth, and life is found within. Begin therefore to live in My Name of glory.

---

34 See 1 Corinthians 13:12

Give of Yourself - III

29th September

Mankind's story must be one of final triumph: triumph of good, complete good, of all over deceptive evil. I have revealed that of My † of crucifixion. It is the † which has set you free to live and come again when you accept Me as your Saviour. My favour is bestowed readily upon those who seek it.

Speak to Me often. Tell Me about your everyday wishes, concerns, fears, worries and sorrows. There's no tomorrow without today bringing what it does – for better, for worse.

Curses are not [permanent][35] for they can be repealed in My Name – the same Name as Truth's triumph, struck down at the hands of Pontius Pilate, then as now. How much, dear children, I carry to your complete restoration, dedication anew to Me, for you will see all the difference it makes when it takes My mercy into this world of suffering, offering a peace hitherto unknown – release of Me in the sea of the world; wave upon wave of new, brave insights. Light of My being, seeing you carried and claimed My Name of holiness, begun but not ended. Lend its power forcefully but gently, calmly, quietly and assuredly.

It is real, you know, when you go forth sent by Me, when you see what you can do. You're who I chose to use in My Name of healing, repealing the ill which makes suffering so senseless. Without Me you are defenceless, so put on the full armour of God; then no harm can befall you.

I call you by name; you are Mine, belonging where I send, lend you My Spirit, to go; as you know My peace is there where we can share each other's power. 'Power hope' is My hope, your hope well within scope of decided discovery, recovery, of the facts which will match, dispatch any evil attack.

Attract goodness, blessings, grace by the repair of prayer where we can share each other's strength and come above and beyond, beneath and below, between and amongst all else.

---

35 Real

Asking About Healing

30th September

Let Me dry your tears, My child, although crying is never in vain. I gave you tears as an outlet of emotions, escape, to indicate the nature of difficulties. Speak to Me about the difficulties so we can sort together – sort the wheat from the chaff.

I love you to laugh, be light-hearted; laughter is healing medicine, and I don't want you downhearted except for sorrow for My pained suffering. You gain much from suffering also – understanding tolerance and need, the grief of others, disappointment in their expectations, their wants, their priorities, their prized attempts to accomplish and achieve. Grieve when it is right to do so, when you know My mission is at the heart of the matter. Then I give you permission to grieve and justify the suffering.

My offering of peace comes upon people unexpectedly. My ways are indeed not your ways. The unlikely can be the most likely. The most likely can bring the unexpected. It's all in God's hands, and He demands you to listen more earnestly, more seriously, more searchingly.

Healing and Wholeness - I

1st October

Never turn Me away. You seek peace of mind. You will find it in Me.

Look at the beauty of Mine in the flowers; the perfection of My plan is seen in such wholeness. Every part matters – stem, stamen, leaf and bud – but none will flourish without the life-giving water at source.

Of course, you need Me, perhaps more than ever before, to restore your spirit, soul and body – united into a harmonious whole person. The relief you seek can be found at My hands if you understand this. Bring the sick to Me, who am the all-time Healer.

Lowering gently through the roof[36] meant just that: the hole is the gap in the circumstances, the chance, God-given, of reaching Me; the lowering is because you need to heed somebody else's assistance; slowly because a jolt would be too much like a force, a bolt of electricity striking you down.

You will get up and walk freely again when the time is ready in Me. Until then be at peace, My child, My children, for I release you from all manner of ills. Ills spill and stain discomfort over mankind, and I find it an abomination that My people suffer.

I offer you life and tranquillity in abundance; the ability to become entirely Mine, chosen before time took its toll; whole children, loved back into being – seeing you trusted, like I said you must.

Blessed are those who believe; caressed are those who come openly, willingly, readily, expectantly, seeking and asking for all that I have to give…

---

36 See Luke 5:19

Healing and Wholeness - II

2nd October

I find you waiting when you are willing to pour out your heart to Me and be set free by the circumstances of My choice. Hear My voice calling you out of the desert existence. There is no need to remain there forever. Endeavour to believe only in My timing, and be patient.

A patient patient is always rewarded in some way, whether by peace of mind, discovery of spirit or whole bodily healing. I offer you all three, to be as fresh as a daisy growing or a walk through the bluebell wood. You should, you know, delight in Me, for you see Me at work readily, steadily doing what needs to be done upon healing and wholeness begun and maintained in My Name.

I anoint you with wholeness of healing, stealing success from the enemy's forces. Of course, you will have to accept, expect and be ready to receive. Grieve no more. It is unnecessary. Time has played its tune and now sings a different melody in harmony with heaven's hope.

You Shall See! - I

3rd October

The emptiness within will begin to undo when you seek My peace through the release of calm trust. That means trusting whatever the circumstances, however they appear to the contrary. Appearances are deceptive, concocted by the world's influence and expectations which you have become a part of. Set aside these and believe more strongly in Me. You know to Whom you belong. Act as if you did, by bringing your heart to Me each and every day in a real way of dialogue.

Don't hide the hurts; it's harmful and useless, as I know them anyway. 'Spring clean' is a breath of fresh air when you take things out of the dark closet to make them bright in the light of My understanding which commands respect, tolerance and sympathy.

No difficulty – I repeat, no difficulty – is too hard for Me to deal with. Don't hide from Me to conceal the truth. It is a useless waste of time – fruitless and offensive to My trust, My love. My love covers many a fault but can only do so if you invite Me in to be part of the 'problem'. I will begin to heal when you hold My hand tightly, trustingly, like a small child looking up in complete belief of goodness, help, love, concern. Compassion will fashion the future just as love can undo the past.

Any length you go to, any strength you find, discover, uncover, will be in My Spirit's name of power. Remember to call on Him often and variously. Fall into His waiting arms to rest there awhile – safe, held secure, with a certain certainty of belonging and understanding (His belonging to you and your understanding of Him and His ways). Remember, He is the power of the Godhead and, as such, should not be ignored.

Power is a magnetic, majestic force working on earth through men who will to believe and receive of it, so they can give and transform the face of the earth. It is not the norm, unfortunately. Not many are ready enough to receive, but to those who do, the power can surge through stronger than electricity bringing light into the darkest dungeon.

You Shall See! - II

4th October

Hope is found in brightness, lightness of heart with hope's longing. And it is your job to share this with others. Uncover the blocks that lock them into insensitivity. It may be you'll see the way forward where they cannot. Stay alert and listening, feeling your way carefully, sensitively. And remember to commit all things to Me, who can see the beginning from the end, in between as well.

Unlikely are the turns many a path can take. It's all a matter of God-given or God-letting when the way is right and cannot happen until man is ready and willing and waiting. It takes much patient, slow preparation for it to happen, and often life is too much of a rush – a rush of lost opportunities where something went unnoticed, unsaid, unfelt, not thought about, because of the busyness of mankind – a cutthroat industry churning on relentlessly without My guidance. It is foolhardy and risky, dangerous and will bring darkness. Only My children can have the ability to switch the light of truth on.

Through their own suffering they come to understand how I can command peace at the centre when they enter into Me, who suffered more and beyond anything you will ever know. Grow tall in Me, My children. The way is hard, the path is long, but it is not for nothing that you did ever belong to Me and My vision, My decision.

Live and let live – slowly, gradually – reforming errors, conforming to truth, performing only when I say so to guard against mistaken decisions, however well-meaning. I hold the answer to everything. Ask Me; seek Me out; speak to Me more often; and of course don't forget to listen to the reply. My answer is life-giving to all those who will accept and correct the error of their condition.

You Shall See! - III

5th October

God is a graceful guide and teacher. His preaching is never in vain. The same yesterday, today and tomorrow, He remains constant in the 'sea change' of your lives. Hold your heads high above the storm waters. They do not come to drown you but to teach you to look up expectantly, and in looking, see – see Me walking across the water to you, arms outstretched in longing. Our belonging together is the best that ever will be. You shall see! You shall see!

In Me is found everything worthwhile – all hope, all happiness, contentment, joy – lent not just for a season but as a reason for being; becoming the person you were made to be in Me, of Me, for Me, with Me; complete, replete in My care and calm. No harm will befall you, My children.

All will be well in My Name which conquers the world with victorious calm, the banish of harm and hurts. Healing is in the appealing to Me, who paid the price already – a steady force at work gladly, readily, for those who seek and ask. Don't be afraid to do that. You won't overload Me. That is not possible, not even probable, for I am the mighty, everlasting truth of God.

Yet Better - I

6th October

I acknowledge your acceptance of the fear of looking inwardly at yourself. I will help you if you just appear before Me resolutely, trusting the way will appear to ascend, not descend into a valley of despair. Repair is around the corner.

Christ's calling is a real 'calling out', shouting to you to come who are heavy burdened and receive of Me: My care; My forgiveness; My help; My support; all that you have been taught about. The likely outcome is 'good' to 'getting better, yet better, yet better', if you let truth flourish and grow, to know its complete impact and transforming power.

Simply employ your heart more. Banish the heaviness by truth at work; then reach out complete in My love of acceptance, accepting the truth for what it is, what it was, what it stands for to take you into the future. Back into the future – travelling back to go forward; travelling down to go up; travelling under to go over, to overcome anything that's a problem – but always in My Name of truth. The same now as ever it was, it must remain close in your heart's centre. That is where I enter man's soul.

Yet Better - II

7th October

Whole force of My being given to you for sharing with others in their difficulties. Repair with care, concern, compassion – lent from Me, sent by My Spirit, bent upon the Father's glory. The story of mankind is to give and let live, to go and forego, in My Name of truth. You will be glad you did; you can and you will come forward in My Name of truth. I repeat this as it is vital teaching, reaching into the innermost part of man's convictions. Predictions will come about honestly only when you, man, have received of Me to be My trusting children – searching, ready, waiting for the starter's orders to go out beyond their expectations or even imaginings.

Such it is with you who trust and believe they must do something for Me. Called upon to be Mine to serve in gladness of heart and find complete fulfilment when your life is shared fully with others who need you. Intercede for them – the 'greed' in your heart growing more rapid, more earnest, as you wish them too to heed My voice calling, no longer falling on deaf ears, but eradicating fears and fusing, enthusing new vision, fresh decision, complete revision in Me.

You will see – you *will* see – the difference it makes when I break man's heart of stone to own it as Mine own – cherished, complete, contracted to be in Me.

You are My song of delight, and we belong together eternally, made for each other – each for the other to uncover the best. The request of My heart is you continue to believe and receive of Me, My child. Hide not away.

I come in the day's brightness that you may have sight of Me – light of your life and your loving.

Thou Hast Searched Me and Known Me - I

8th October

Love is of the essence of life, overcoming strife resolutely if allowed to do so. You who trust (or try to) must let this flourish anew in strength. It is the length of your recovery and the discovery of what lies ahead, awaiting for when you are ready.

Man's discovery, the recovery of My plan, is dependent upon four things: trust, obedience, self-sacrifice, effort – but all in Me. It must be in Me to be effective at all. Seek Me, speak to Me, heed Me, then go forth, walking before you can run even in enthusiasm. There is so much to learn on the way forward in Me, who directs and inspects the contents of your heart to see what's genuine and what's manmade or illusionary, founded on pride or possession or gain. Remain in Me, My children. It is the only way to be secure and ensure progress as I planned it.

Coming is going. That is coming to Me – to be sent forward by Me out into the world's community of suffering where support and encouragement are needed in large measure. This you can give when you have understood the first lessons in love: giving and forgiving by the force of love – a ticket to ride somewhere glorious, somewhere beautiful into the realms of peace, content, practically given in the everyday things of being rather than doing, seeing rather than looking, or striving for more, ever more.

My rich store is already set up for sharing amongst those who wish to partake, make it theirs – ripe, rich and ready for those who at heart believe but are perhaps waiting to perceive more of Me. That's where you come in: for you can begin to share your experiences in whatever way you can. Just speak the truth, painful though it might be. Let others see how you came through the hurt by My side of hope, on the side of optimism, knowing you will win because I am there to share everything – yes, everything – with you.

Thou Hast Searched Me and Known Me - II

9th October

Children of Mine, fine is the waiting when it makes you ready. Be patient and willing, honest and open, ready to commit and submit to Me. Obedience is all-embracing, all-encompassing of My mission. It gives Me permission to use you as never before.

Folklore determines that good comes out of the bad or troublesome, getting better all the time. Believe this and receive its truth in the telling, welling up inside you like a fountain of hope's holding, enfolding the beauty of tomorrow. A bud unfolds but slowly when nurtured, when the condition is right. You are the same, gradually increasing in size and stature of My making, taking you onwards to fruit in time, in season. The reason will be of My making before the fruit is shaken to the ground to feed.

Man's greed is for the wrong thing. But you can bring sense to some who are ready and waiting. That's My job to sort out. Yours is to be the provider of fine food in season. It's not like the warehouse where everything is always readily available but is selective, corrective even, under My influence. Much always has to be prepared, got ready, to be ripe for the picking. But My harvest field needs workers like you who will do as I ask, go where I send, and lend My Spirit of Truth's power, however unlikely the situation seems.

Thou Hast Searched Me and Known Me - III

10th October

Trust Me, My children. I cannot say this strongly enough, often enough. Your very life depends upon it, for without, I cannot send you. It would be ineffective, maybe useless. And I want you to be powerful, productive in Me, who hold the keys of the future kingdom. Unlock the future by your willingness to go in My Name and accomplish the unlikely – finding, seeking and speaking in places unsought-of, unthought-of except by Me.

You will see what a difference My lightning strike can make, take. Only believe this of Me and be ready. You will not know the hour of My calling. Appalling is the condition of mankind's motivation, movement, to seek and find Me.

A new way must be found, ground in the truth of exercised discipline – trusting and trying out that trust to see its effectiveness and the direction in which it will take. That leading string of love, long ago discovered, uncovered as if by chance, was a fresh glance My way, where light always shines brightly – no day, no night, simply pure, bright light of knowing, understanding, existing, showing, going in My Name set forth.

Claim My Name, My Spirit's power. He is your ground force at work, hoeing and pruning, chopping and weeding and seeding the fertile patch made ready for spring – the time of fresh enlightenment; slow but healthy growth; steady and secure because it is firmly staked upon the ground of My making. You know the tallest oak tree can come from the tiniest acorn. So it is with Me that one grain of truth can open up, mushroom, into a forest field flowering in the beauty of knowing, just knowing, this splendour.

Thou Hast Searched Me and Known Me - IV

11th October

The Sender of all life, all love, waits and is ready. Are you, My children? I hope so; I pray so. I need you as you need Me, and togetherness in a team is a winsome combination, a collective force – of course, to triumph eventually.

Battles are not won victoriously, readily, but steadily by ground planning manoeuvres and shifts of armaments to where they are most needed. You must listen to learn this. Claim My battle plan. It is no forlorn hope but well within scope of your achievements if guided by and under the flagship of all My authority.

Do nothing on your own. It is fruitless, pointless, a useless waste of time and energy and resources. Economy is Me at work successfully, efficiently, wisely – giving to give, living to live fully.

You will be glad, My children, that you learnt this lesson, even if it takes a lifetime's learning to respond properly, exactly, coherently, correctly, directly when you hear Me call out to you. Do not doubt My calling. Simply listen attentively, all eyes as well as ears, any fears put aside in My Name. The gain is recognition of Me whenever we be together – Me calling out to shout My business, My intentions, to you, sometimes silently. Your conscience, your brain, your imagination, your intuition, your thoughts and feelings, hearts and minds combined together will find the answers.

That is enough for now. More than this you will not cope with. I speak as I find you: ready, waiting and desiring to receive. Go in My Name of grace, a fond embrace of love, given to be shared out amongst My children who mean much to Me. You will see this in My continuous commitment to you. Believe in Me and trust My truth unfolding before your very eyes. The size is enormous and will certainly take your breath away – panoramic beyond belief and wider, wider yet, when you get going in trust of each other, of Me and My, our, planned victory.

My Reality - I

12th October

The reality is there when you share your cares with Me. You know I cannot come as an uninvited guest. It would not be right to do so. Gate-crashers are never welcome; they are regarded as a source of disruption. So I can come close only when you want Me to. Do not keep Me at a distance, at arm's length, for our strength combined together can tackle anything, any problem however great or small or seemingly insignificant. Nothing is beyond the reach of My influence and compassion.

Remember, Who made you in the first place did fashion you for a purpose and breathed into you the very life you have. Life-giving is for living with Me, in Me, through Me – Me by your side where you can even hide if necessary; Me to carry you when the going's too tough or rough; Me to share with you all the secrets of intimacy; Me to hold your hand like a trusting father or a lover completely taken by you.

You will never know this side of heaven the great, enormous, immense, eternal love I have for you – a love which will go to any length to set you free from misconceptions, misapprehensions, self-preoccupation or dedication to the wrong thing. Any of these can, may, and often do, bring calamity; and really, the way forward to live your life is quite simple if only you would see it by being living in Me. I can set you free if you allow this to happen – free in any way you ask.

My Reality - II

13th October

Remember, it is My task, My God-given task, to serve. For this I came; for this I continue to be your Saviour… Salvation means 'spiritual health'. Can you not see a wealth of opportunity awaits you and others through you when you come to be set free in Me – free of your concerns, emptied out so I can fill you afresh with Mine?

No wonder the world is in such a mess when men insist upon going solo, sailing along single-handed until almost inevitably they are shipwrecked by circumstances, the unexpected, or things running out of their control. If only they had handed the control over to Me in the first place, the whole encounter and result would have been different.

My influence is a steadying, calming one, making you (mankind) ready for all manner of greater things; but these can only happen as and when you are prepared, willing, wanting to be made ready in Me. Seek the answers in Me. Speak to Me often, but listen more frequently than that. Do not drown Me out by your (or the world's) busyness, clamour, shouts, demands, commands. You must set time and space aside where we can be together in quality of your making and My taking up the invitation that we meet.

I long to greet you with love, My child, My children. It is the desire of My heart to impart much wisdom and strength to brighten your days, let you amaze at My ways of working. Together we can do so much. I hold the keys to your future.

If getting on your knees means to pray, do so (metaphorically speaking) – anywhere, anytime, anyplace, anyhow, any means by which you can reach Me – until we are one in the communion of constant communication. Always openness is necessary – openness, willingness to give; openness, happiness to receive and believe what I am showing you, telling you or leading you into.

My Reality - III

14th October

My riches await those who are prepared to be dressed in the royal robes of expectation: expectant hope, belief, of what can be, is to come, in Me. However fast or slow the progress will go depends to a large extent on your gratitude, attitude of mind and strength of belief. That belief must be founded/grounded in the trust which cannot see but believes what is to be because I said so – going in My Name of truth, seeking the right way, speaking in honesty of clarity, of judgment, because you sought My Spirit's influence.

He it is who takes you forward in My Name – that very same Spirit that brought Me to birth, directed Me whilst on earth, and raised Me from the dead. I promised to send Him to you. Claim and name that promise so you share in My Spirit's power. Then compare your life before and after His influence. You may be shocked at the difference you see. I can be all things to all men, in all places, as and when I'm required, because My Spirit is spirit and can go and invade men's hearts, persuade them onto the path of righteousness, working in so many places at once. He is My earthly force, My energy, My working and is of course in constant, continuous touch with Me.

You see two triangles at work: the Trinity you know of (our Father, Myself and My Spirit) and the triangle you understand less well of (Myself, My Spirit and yourself). These two triangles interlock with a star-like quality of brightly shining mystery. We can lighten any darkness, penetrate, reach, anywhere on earth. Nowhere is too distant, lying without Our sphere of influence.

It was all set up, intended, this way before time began that man should meet God, that they may work for good, for better, for the best together, whatever, wherever, whenever the circumstances dictate – and, in reality, that is everywhere all of the time! Mine and your influence is needed. Heed this, My child, My children. It is an important truth, not to be overlooked.

My Reality - IV

15th October

You, in Me, can make a real difference. You need to believe this and perceive how to progress. All you've got to do is ask and wait, listening and looking and thinking. Then follow My directions precisely, concisely and accurately – no more, no less than this is asked of you if you want to make a difference, a real difference, in the world.

You do not need to take the world by storm but by My still, 'remaining quiet' voice offering calm peace – the release of all manner of hurts, troubles, inflictions, addictions, resentments, discontentments which tear man apart at the heart. My heart is a healing heart of pure, self-giving love, uncovering joy, deep contentment, hitherto not known; yet it can be shown through man at work with Me. You see, I choose it to be this way so I can have eyes and ears and hands and feet everywhere at once brought alive by My Spirit to inherit all that is good – all that our Father wants to give.

Live and let live in Me to set the prisoners free. Let the lame walk and the silenced talk. Peace and justice, justice and peace; the release of food for the hungry; healing for the hurt; agreement between enemies; land for the homeless; all needs met in Me as part of the Trinity of pure love and affection.

Dedication is Our connection to mankind and is made all the easier when We find you ready, willing, able and prepared to help by acting in Our Name by claiming Our strength and living within the sphere of Our perfect promises never to be broken. Speak these out to mankind so they will find a new way of looking at things: fresh understanding, commanding they think and act differently – not in the 'instant gratification', disposable way of the world but in the patiently waiting, planning, perfecting, correcting, re-planning way of divine life, that divine life which leads to eternity.

The maturity of your understanding and actions does matter because that will be the attraction to others, to our way of living and forgiving. Go forward as you best know how to, under My guidance. Do not hide your light under a bushel! For the darkness of the world needs many bright pinpoints of light to illumine the way forward. You are part of this – My calling, your response, our working together.

My Reality - V

16th October

You may see only one small speck – one tiny beam of light – but I see forwards as well as backwards and can see how tiny beams become brighter, further reaching until they arch over a wider area illuminating with My truth. And like the fabled rainbow there is a pot of gold at the end. That is what I send My people in search of: gold so rich, so precious, so beautiful it is to you unimaginable and beyond compare.

This is what I want you all – My children – to share: life in all fullness, gladness of joy, the best you can possibly imagine, become yet more glorious, more lasting, more beautiful, more fine, more wholesome, more enriching, more rewarding. The affording has been done by Me. All you need to do is agree, then we will see what happens!

You are caught up into infinity, playing your part even now. How the future might be changed, the knot… to untangling slowly, carefully, gently but relentlessly when you pull in My direction! This is up to you to choose and use with as much dedication and influence as you can muster, make, to take the world forward.

The Fruits of the Spirit - I

17th October

The fruits of the Spirit are: "Love, joy, peace, patience, kindness, goodness, faithfulness, gentleness and self-control"[37], to be used in My sense for the good, for the uplift, for the healing of others who need Me to be at work in their lives consciously.

Admit to My presence, and use it joyfully, not sparingly but generously, giving of all time and effort without compare; for we share this destiny, this purpose, together as one. Close upon My Father's heart I lie. Close upon My heart must lie the direction My Spirit takes – will take you, if you are but willing.

Concealing Me is no use. Revealing of Me is power in action. Put into action, placed there by the trust which must give the force of propulsion going forward – always forward – without a backwards glance, is the direction I like to take you.

You must make it a possibility by prayer to repair any earlier or possible current damage to our relationship. Our relationship must be of oneness – trust, openness, love and belonging, each to the other completely – until you reach My heart of love, of loving service, giving and receiving of Me.

You will not be as I intended (reach your full potential in Me, planned with a purpose, slowly unfolding) only as, when, you let Me take hold of the situation – the invited Guest who is welcome at table, at hearth, at the heart of all decision-making. And I mean *all.* The best friend is not excluded from certain selected parts of your life but is included in every joyful celebration, sorrow, hurt, risk, doubt, despair – or simply the everyday mundane happenings when he (or she) will remain constant in their affection for you, ready and willing to support or hold or help. Such am I but so many times over, more magnified in intention for your good.

---

37 Galatians 5:22-23 (NIV)

The Fruits of the Spirit - II

18th October

Simply the mention of My Name makes a difference. Don't be afraid to name Me when you claim My power. It is insulting to talk in generalisations when you know the truth by conviction. Share it, declare it, compare it with the world's empty philosophies, and you will see such a difference that will never be (could ever be) manmade in imagination or portrayal. The greatest betrayal of My people is to hide from Me or to hide Me from others who long, wish, desire, seek to discover the truth. Speak to them about Me – how you have found Me. Human-to-human contact, narration, makes sense and impact in the telling, sharing, comparing of one person's experience to another. There you will discover, uncover, recover mysteries of many kinds.

The history of mankind is made up of manifold mysteries, some of which will never be understood. Others simply need the God-light shining in on them. Man can do this by his ardent desire, intention, effort, willingness to seek the truth of Me. I am the Way, just as I said. I am Truth, and I am Life given for you that you may enjoy it fully. Fulfil your role and purpose in it. However hard this may seem to be, remember, I am there for you.

Self-sacrifice is not a current, fashionable notion/event, but it always was My Way. You will be asked to give of yourself and that may be until it hurts. But there is power, a powerful force, at work – a release in any suffering that is made into an offering, whether specifically for an intention or generalised, leaving the choice up to Me. My benevolence, love, compassion, desire to help, support, lift up high again, knows no limits, and I will use any means available to Me offered by My people – their intentions to love, to work out of love, through love, for the betterment of another who may be held dear to their heart, or may indeed even be a stranger.

The Fruits of the Spirit - III

19th October

Man is a community, the whole of mankind a network of support, which sometimes sags because each did not pull up the strength to play his part. Then it becomes like a kitten playing with a tangled ball of string tossing it about, pulling this way and that randomly. But I am not the kitten! The confusion ensues because there was no mother or father, no leading figure there to stop the entanglement in the first place. Confusion can so easily, so readily, breed further confusion, a mess running out of control.

Any order, sense of progress, needs clear, decisive, decided, worked at, believed in and followed organisation. Rules which are to be heeded, obeyed, respected are drawn up for the greater good. They are there to guide and safe-keep in comfort and common sense, respect and convenience. Rules are not to be broken without some dilemma, dismay, distress, or worse occurring. I give you sound, simple, straightforward rules for life. Heed them! Proceed to live by them. They are life-giving, life-saving, life-fulfilling, life-enriching, freedom for all who obey willingly. If you find this hard, ask for My Spirit, My soul-seeking Spirit's guidance, help and support. He has fought many a battle to win over souls to My side where the victory lies eternally.

It is important that as many as possible join our forces. Of course, My real desire is for all of mankind to hear of Me and find Me stirring in their hearts of love – self-giving, forgiving, 'letting go and living' love; that love which can conquer all sin, which began with the long shadow of My † and will end with the victory when all men belong to Me.

I it is who set you free to find your way home with Me as Guide at your side to our Father's home of beauty beyond compare where we will share eternity (or, if you prefer, infinity) together. And it's a very long time! I know, for I made it to be so that we may be together in free expression of love always.

The Fruits of the Spirit - IV

20th October

Worship is at the heart of thanksgiving – worship, adoration, admiration and awe. These I cannot earn nor demand. They must come – need to come – from a genuine heart of painful progress towards reality, where I let you see that all is all only in Me.

Your earthly expectations, hopes, desires, memories even, will often disappoint, dismay, but remember to return to My safe haven of rest where peace will be found completed, dependent upon the depth, breadth, length of our relationship – walking together, talking together, being together, because that is our choice of how to spend your time (yours and Mine in fact). But I always give you the choice. Don't lose it (the time) or abuse it or dispute it, but dedicate to spending it wisely, decently, honestly, openly, compassionately for Me. That is service, and each of you is called to serve differently according to your God-given talents sent to produce something good, worthwhile upon earth.

Give and take, offer and receive; it's all part of that great and glorious network, the inner working of which you cannot understand, the outer workings of which you see and will be – are already – part of.

How much I use your involvement in the future depends upon how much you want to serve in obedience, how diligent you are as a student wanting to listen, to learn and to put into practice the teaching. High achievers are the result of high strivers who work gladly, willingly, relentlessly, committed to a purpose, a goal. If that goal is Me then you will see – you will surely see – what a difference you can make in this longing, aching world, taking a little portion of it to pieces to rebuild, remould, hold (or rather be held) in the power of love, almighty love, that which conquers everything. Every ill, every inconvenience, every harmful intent, all can come under love's flagship banner. It is the winner in all situations of conquest.

The Fruits of the Spirit - V

21st October

Rest in Me; remain in Me; revive with Me; be restored by Me, replenished; then reassess the future's brightness in the light of love known, shown and lived, more and more. More love, more power. More power, more love. It's a circle of My influence – neat, rounded and always ready to roll forward gathering speed! It can roll in any direction according to the connection you make.

But just remember to ask for My guiding, leading light to be shown. It is the torchlight to bring men safely home through the dark, a light beam leading the way, Christ's light – insight, powerful and penetrating, able to pierce any gloom or confusion, for it lights the way so readily.

I long to see My people safe and secure in Me.

Let Go and Let God Work - I

22nd October

Hold up to adversity by My strength. It will repair the world's damage if you let the Spirit in to begin healing. 'Let go and let God work' is a true saying taking up, opening up, enormous possibilities for the future of mankind. He who finds himself in a dilemma, a doubt, a disaster, a disgrace, must pray – for apart from Me you can do nothing. I am the fuel to ignite your passion, to make a difference in the world, My world.

Grief – oh, so much grief – comes from separation between man and God. When the women stood at a distance away from the †, how much grief they felt! If they had come closer, perhaps I could have spoken words of comfort, reassurance, to cut through the blackness of despair.

Repair is My business, My mission, My commission, My longing so that you (mankind) are then belonging to the Father, the Spirit and Me – the Trinity who sets you free to be triumphant over evil; triumphant over troubles, despair or doubt, that you may shout My Name in glory. Mankind's story is one of falling to rise again when hearing My calling to get up and walk, for you are healed in My Name.

It is not the same for everybody nor ever can be, for this is the way I intended it to be. You have to leave the healing choice to Me, for mankind needs all kinds, all manner, of healing. So deep is the damage sometimes, the repair even is hidden from normal sight and understanding. A new repair may be invisible but nonetheless real, vital, and life-giving (eternal-life-giving, that is). For that, happening in My Name, I work the same miracles – far-reaching, life-changing, opportunity-rearranging miracles – as those performed in the biblical narrative.

Let Go and Let God Work - II

23rd October

Everything is comparative, and sometimes man sees only what he wants, chooses to see, but if you are in Me – truly in Me – then your range of vision, your every decision, your attitude and gratitude is (has become) life-changing in its implications and intentions. The mere mention of My Name brings power to your elbow instantly – My Spirit's power, Our power, yours and Mine to share.

He is beyond compare in His ability to produce, to change, to alter radically, even to turn the world (whether yours or global) upside down, on its head, simply because instead of fear, doubt, mistrust, apprehension, that mention of My Name of love (Jesus, meaning 'Saviour') buys the grace for you to move forward differently with other insights and understandings – a whole, fresh, exciting, wider, clearer vision and vista opening up because you claimed My Name and shared in My mission to bring God to His suffering people waiting anxiously on the sidelines.

To come centre stage is to come into a blaze of glory beautifully, wonderfully, mercifully, fully alive as I intended. Mankind is given an amazing power share if he but chooses to tune in and take it, make it his own, used for the good of others. He can uncover the depths of mysteries and recover some of the sense that has been lost in recent times.

Let Go and Let God Work - III

24th October

I'm the same today as yesterday and My power does not diminish, however often it is used or however strong, forceful, incisive it needs to be. See Me at work; be Me at work. You hold the key to open up opportunity when you work gladly, joyfully, with Me, for Me, for others to uncover life as it should be (as I intended it to be in the fullness of man and God united as one, close upon – very close, resting upon – each other's heart).

There testing knows no gain, for if we remain locked together like a reef knot we can move comfortably, held securely and neatly but not so tightly that the breath of individuality, creativity and man's spark is struck out. There will always be a space between us, a holy space where man on earth cannot enter; yet centre your affections/focus/intentions on Me, and see how comfortable the knot of love is. Most people would not describe it as a knot – more of a bond, a covenant of love, encircled by My Spirit's revealing, healing truth.

He it is who makes all the difference in the world. The very name 'spirituality' arises from the power source of the Godhead, always ahead of man's understanding, wants or needs. He heeds My instructions, impassioned pleas even, to move into a situation and life-change. Spirituality at source means allowing, helping mankind to connect with, tap into, God's almighty, mysterious, ever further-reaching, radically uprooting, transplanting, fruit-growing force of power.

Let Go and Let God Work - IV

25th October

He who made the moon majestic can do all manner of things, all manner of beautiful things, in men's lives. It is like a prism or a diamond reflecting many colours of the rainbow – the faceted colours of hope shining, combining, arching together. Like the sunbeam's dance, you can too, filled anew with a joy so glorious, so beautiful, it is unlike anything you have ever compared life to – a new you in Me set free because you listened and learned and looked and did see My promises coming through, through our prayers together, the source of all that is good and growing in the knowing of Me and My ways.

Man set on fire with love for Me is ablaze with something different. You only have to look at history to see that, to see Who changed the world into a beautiful, better, restful, harmonious place. You are part of a calling to bring about such change by helping men to open up their truth in Me.

I wait patiently – oh, so patiently – looking forward to the day when we all are as one. Not many are given a Damascus experience. On the whole it is 'slow and steady wins the race' of progress. Accepting some setbacks on the way, taking these as cul-de-sacs of learning but yearning to go forwards, will always take you forward if you let Me be in charge of the route. We must travel the journey together. Any other way is not only hazardous but useless in the long term and unfulfilling.

Let Go and Let God Work - V

26th October

Man yearns for God. Whether he recognises it or not, God yearns for man. It was made this way since time began, and your mission, mankind's mission, is to make the connection in the best way that he or she can. Differently for each one of you, as I intended that to be part of life's rich pattern. Knowing must be the showing of God; reaching must be the teaching of God; sharing must be the comparing of life with or without Him to see the difference it makes.

Man is losing his vision amidst a rise of false philosophies, the greed of gain and merciless usurping of arrogant power. Our destiny depends on enough men opening eyes to see, ears to hear, minds to receive and hearts to love whatever the uncomfortable circumstance. Love is the essence. Love is the truth, My truth. Love is the conquering, all-powerful force. Ultimately love, and love alone, will make all the difference in the world.

A world curled up in upon itself needs to open up like the petals of a flower to receive sunlight. Bright light of truth is bright, life-giving, life-fulfilling, life-sustaining.

Remain in Me My child, My children. Together we can do so much: the battle won together; correction made together. Protection, protection, protection is the by-product of your trust in Me. I will hold you safe, securely, in My hands, and then we can move delightedly, unitedly together – giving and receiving, receiving and giving, living each for the other to uncover the joy.

Words of Comfort - I

27th October

I speak words of comfort to you when you sorrow, that your heads may be held up higher in hope of seeing Me. Be reassured by My presence supporting you in all times but especially when in difficulties.

My love carries My children like the love of a mother carries a baby in her arms so no harm can befall. You can be, will be, cradled in love if you allow this. It needs human adult humility to accept dependence, to acknowledge how frail you are and how much in need of support and My help. My help comes full of love, gladly.

I seek to speak to you through all happenings. What can you learn from the current situation of difficulties, the struggle (it seems) to simply survive? Can you thrive in the knowledge, certainty, of My love and help, care, or especially in the midst of things you don't understand?

Without a clear picture to go by, you have to rely more on a map which shows tried and trusted ways of moving to improve (make a difference to) your life. You are wayfarers through life. Use the map I have given, drawn up for you to plot the way forward.

Resting is testing by the wayside, waiting for a signpost of further instructions not knowing when this will come, how this will come, or in what direction you will be taken. Much has to be made ready within yourselves, reaching a deeper level of trust, of belonging to Me wholeheartedly. Much has to be made ready in others if they are to discover, see, uncover My hand at work in this situation. Dedication is your keynote – dedication to progress in Me. Regress is when you turn your back on Me and doubt.

I am the God who made the very world you live in, cohabit, by My grace. Can you not see that I can do anything – anything that I choose to do – for the good of many?

Words of Comfort - II

28th October

No man is an island, and one person's experience, even the suffering, will reach out to teach, show others something – something good, something unexpectedly, something worthwhile, something previously hidden from human sight of understanding. Growing in experience is coming to know, understand or simply believe what you did not know before. It takes you where you could not, would not, or cannot go because the circumstances were not right, were not prepared sufficiently to allow you to make the discovery. Like little children, much teaching – the best teaching – comes from finding out for yourself through experience, the experience of Me, when others have done the preparation by providing the necessary tools.

I am known as I am known by those who show Me, love Me, celebrate Me, rely on Me in every way through their day-to-day. I am the gentle, patient Healer, never in a rush to push forward, because time is of My making and therefore need not be an anxious element. Time can be 'the standstill' and yet hurried up into speed even at the same time/possibility/occasion. It's all in My hands, you see, but you must use the time I have given you to make ready, be prepared, to receive more of Me.

It is in receiving, only in receiving, that you can give. The more you empty out of yourself – your own pre-occupations, misapprehensions, misguided thoughts, mistakes of the past, concerns for the future – the more space you create, the more there is for Me to fill up. Emptied out of doubt is to be ready to receive more because you believe in something better waiting round the corner.

Words of Comfort - III

29th October

Being patient is a life's lesson. It's hard but worthwhile, for when determination is there I can sow seeds to take root. Roots go down into Me, holding on strongly, firmly, gathering nourishment. The roots of the person safely anchor, stabilise the growth of soul and spirit within the body, so whatever buffeting and blowing about the body is called upon to take, to endure, the roots hold it firm. They are twisted and combined like sinews of strength. Roots are absolutely essential to growth. The taller, further-reaching, the growth is, the more roots have to go into Me deeper. You must not let doubts or difficulties come along to cut you off, chop at the roots, for without Me you will do nothing, My child; you will even fight to survive.

Life is the learning, the growing, for knowing Me, in living and loving. I came that you might have life, and still I come for the same reason when asked. Seeking is to find. In finding, hang on to your prize of faith which is of inestimable value – a treasure, but not a treasure to hide away, bury, or let stagnate; rather a treasure to celebrate, give joy to you and hope to others.

Words of Comfort - IV

30th October

To discover Me and My way is a light of hope shining through any darkness, however bleak it seems. You will be amazed at the difference I make to your life to take you to unimagined places of joy, fulfilment and, most importantly for you, peace. The peace you seek can only be found in My strength shared with you.

The repair of fractured lives, hopes, dreams, ambitions, wishes, targets is awaiting. My dear child, I long to stride through your life, riding high with confidence. Choose to believe in My sincere desires for your good, your better good, and then you should be able to see the way slowly but surely, securely unfolding in Me.

Yours it is to remain patient that others may see the difference belief in Me makes. I take you not by storm but by a gentle hand – gentle but firm; holding your safety, your recovery, in love; awaiting in love.

Give Me thanks for the day I give you whatever it may bring. Never fail to give thanks. By this I know I am not taken for granted. You know how good it feels when someone thanks you. It is the same for Me: heart-warming, love-bonding, helping the relationship to sustain and grow stronger. That is why thanks is essentially important.

I have given you much, My child, and await to give you more when you are ready to receive.

Belonging to Me Is Paramount

31st October

Belonging to Me is paramount. Blessings follow accordingly, according to My grace and timing. Rely upon them, My dear children.

The truth reaches you through perseverance and trust, making you take hold of the unacceptable so that it may teach you one of life's lessons: that is, relying upon Me. It is not an easy, comfortable way forward, but comfort and cushioning did not necessarily do anyone everlasting good. Endurance, courage and the strength to overcome in My Name did and does still today. Remain with Me, My child, accepting, not kicking against the goad nor shouting defeat.

Be still and remain still until I come in My Spirit's power of replenishment, complete replenishment. Let go of the fear which binds you, holds you captive. I come to set the captives free, to give strength to the weary and hope to the afflicted, all those restricted by pain and suffering. The offering of My life upon the † was complete victory, overcoming mankind's darkness, even darkest fear, all hostility.

Time and again I come to you when you call upon the mention of My Name as Saviour. Remember, saving means spiritual health – complete spiritual health, spring-cleaned, adjusted, re-focused, re-vitalised. The length to which this happens is dependent upon faith, your putting one foot forward knowing the other will surely follow, not knowing where I take you, why, or even how – and especially at the moment it may seem impossible and against the odds of reality. That's where the trust must enter into action and not be just a word spoken or a plea. It must be a real encounter with the living, life-giving Me.

My choice is to give voice through such as you who can understand something about pain, suffering and difficulty, knowing that through these doubts, through the dismay, beyond the burden, shines the true light of love, beckoning, attending to your every need.

Feed upon Me, My child. True spiritual nourishment is all you need to progress. I remain with you. The gain of trust we share together.

Life is a Journey - I

1st November

Let the Spirit flow, free flow. He is the healer reaching places which, humanly speaking, are impossible to access, buried deep inside – the hurts you try to hide, the agonies of doubt, the conflict which restricts your belief and your trust in Me. This must be removed by My Spirit, the power of His searching like a spotlight reaching into the darkest, hidden, even forbidden, places.

Man struggles to become whole, one in unity of spirit, soul and body, combined and refined by My influence and teaching when it's reaching into his heart. It is only My Spirit that makes this possible. That's why I sent Him as My gift, like I promised to do. He can search out anything, everything which fractures or tears apart. He searches, looks for, finds, uncovers the heart of the matter. Ask Him to help. He is My light of truth shining, combining the love of the Father with the will of Me, the Son.

I showed, when upon earth, what My willpower can achieve. My Spirit's share is to allow you to do great things in Me, for Me. Repair is in My Name of love, holding out the olive branch of healing in broken lives or circumstances.

Chance is not chance at all if you look at it closely. It is a set of circumstances unfolding in My holding power (or not, as you choose). Use it wisely, guidedly, usefully. In helping yourselves, you help others too, in the learning of one of life's valuable lessons.

Life is a Journey - II

2nd November

Journeying is travelling onwards. It consists of starting, stopping on the way, remaining for rest and replenishment, looking for signposts, following directions (or re-directions if you take the wrong route), and eventually arriving. I am the map; My Spirit is the torchlight compass pointing in the right direction. All journeying leads to making a home somewhere, whether temporary or permanent. Life is like that: one long (for some, *very* long), twisted and tortuous journey homewards to Me. Travelling light is My way, not confused by doubts, fears, inner turmoil, confusion or delusion.

I cannot put it more simply than saying, "I am the Way."[38] I am the Way that leads to truth, and it is that truth which leads to life eternal. You must travel. There is no option about this. Life is a journey from the moment of conception into the everlasting. It is your task to learn and practise and portray/teach/share as many God-given truths en route as you can.

Mankind is sorely, desperately in need of teachers who have personally experienced the difference I make. 'Two travelling as one' (you and I) is the fusion, infusion of God-power to make sense of what happens on the way. All events looked at in the light of My teaching, reaching the heart rather than the mind, makes the difference to how you view life and its rich possibilities or restraints, constraints. Like a child, a toddler child on a walking rein, sometimes you need pulling back, turning in another direction or even halting for your own safety. "Stop still, stand and reflect!" is no bad maxim to heed. Too rushed! Too busy! For this is so much – too much – of daily life.

---

38 John 14:6

Life is a Journey - III

3rd November

Time out, time apart, time still in the being of your soul's search, is time well spent if it is meant to open up new possibilities, new routes, new pathways in Me. I come to a busy world that so often, sadly, is too busy to see, hear, feel or approach Me. You cannot connect readily with Me whilst on the run of the treadmill because the sheer pace pounds in your heart, your mind, your ears. "Be still and know that I am God,"[39] are amongst the wisest words ever spoken.

"Know" means "to know with, surely", not think, imagine or suspect, but to *know* because you have seen, heard, felt, experienced the reality. Life's reality is more – much more – than the daily grind, find, for survival and satisfaction. Look inward to discover, uncover the deepest levels of meaning. Modern man and woman is making the mistake of increasingly looking outwards for their wholeness; whereas they need to turn inwards to connect with Me. Yes, I can be everywhere at once, both within and without because that is part of My supernatural power, but it is the being within each individual which provides the place where I can most powerfully and directly speak to each person alive.

'Knowing me, knowing you' was the title of a song. It holds true for what happens when you know Me. By this I mean when you know Me you begin, increasingly, to know yourself, and this is such an important, essential part of life's journey. In the coming and the going must be the knowing, and in the knowing must be the growing in truth in Me. Can you not see how vitally important this is?

Without Me you will not find, discover the direct connection with our Father in heaven. God made it this way, so it must be so. You cannot counteract it except at your own peril, loss and distress. Tragically that is why there is so much trouble in the world – trouble, strife, misunderstanding, heartbreak, misrepresentation – all because man journeys his own foolhardy way without reference to Me.

---

39 Psalm 46:10

Life is a Journey - IV

4th November

I told you for good reason, "I come to set prisoners free, to give sight to the blind and to comfort the afflicted."[40] Look at that in the widest sense in which you can understand it, and then ask what you can do about it to help, heal an aching, breaking world forsaking My way, My truth, My life. Vital, urgent, life-giving, life-living, life-saving work is waiting to be done by My fellow key workers – those who will shoulder the responsibility and humility of admitting mistakes, past errors of judgment, wilful ways of looking and thinking; those who will give up their self-sufficiency, be emptied out so that they can be filled by My Spirit's power. He is the electric, magnetic, atomic, nuclear force, all fused into one supercharge. 'Large' or 'enormous' do not describe His power!

Just as I said, "Taste and see that I am good,"[41] I now say to you, "Plug into, fix upon, the Spirit's power, His magnitude, His supernatural force, and you will be amazed – truly amazed – at what will happen." "In My Name," is not just a phrase to trip off the tongue. It is like the plug entering the socket to turn the electricity on – beaming, streaming out with such force. No pylon on earth could ever contain or carry it.

Remember that teaching, "Ask and you will be given."[42] Ask to receive and share My Spirit's power, Our love (and that means the Trinity, for Father, Son and Spirit are indeed inseparable). That power will take you further than you ever imagined or dreamed of. All you have to do to start the flow is go on life's journey seeking, open to receiving, acknowledging and thanking Me, then asking for more of My power to be shown – the gifts I long to shower upon you.

---

40 Based on Luke 4:18

41 Based on Psalm 34:8

42 Based on Luke 11:9

The Light of My Truth - I

5th November

Learning of Me is a long process whereby you need to absorb a little of My truth at a time in a way that you can understand for yourself, so then you become personally involved and need to practise the truth of what you have learnt; that is the testing of your faith. At times you will be able to rest, remaining secure in your progress. At other times you will be pulled forward rapidly or slowly but always steadily if that's what you seek and ask for. Speak to Me about it. Be specific and tell Me what you want. Although I know already what is in your heart, the speaking out helps you to discover, uncover, more about yourself.

Check your words against the tenor of your heartbeat, emotions, to see if there is discord, discrepancy. If there is unease, ask Me about it. Ask My Spirit to enlighten you with Our meaning and understanding.

We do come to give you the light of truth. Now, you know light shines in many different ways and can be broken up into the colour spectrum. On one occasion, the light will shine from one direction, on another occasion it will come from elsewhere, and sometimes it will appear warmer, softer, more welcoming than the somewhat harsher, clearer, brighter light which can show up blemishes, faults or mishaps. But even that is good, although it may feel uncomfortable and disconcerting. But what will ultimately matter is the truth – My truth, God's truth, revealed as consistent, compact, directive, corrective and uncompromising.

You may have to weaken in your resolve to know. I do not give you – anybody – the ability to know everything, for if I did how could you trust Me and if you did not trust Me how can our relationship grow? Learn by looking and listening to the silence within, when you begin to communicate – really *yearn* to communicate – with Me. I will not withhold Myself from you, for I long to be in close touch – the closest touch – even more than you do.

The Light of My Truth - II

6th November

Prayer is our conversation together and your conversion, gradual conversion, to My revealed truths. These I reveal as and when you are ready to receive and understand. You can make yourself ready by the humility of admission – admitting that you know nothing except through Me; that you achieve nothing lasting, worthwhile, eternal, except through Me; by acknowledging that all good things in life are My gifts of love to you.

Look at your current situation. Can you not see this plainly evident? Proclaim, name, claim the blessings I have honoured you with. There is a way to give thanks and bring delight to My heart of love. Lovers always want to please and thank each other. It is no different for us. If you are to become My closest friend, ally, confidant, one upon whom I can rely, you must show the patience and respect of one who values, and admire and is grateful for what the friendship has to offer, wanting to sustain, maintain it at all costs.

There will be some personal costs involved. Look at what it cost Me to gain, to win, man's forgotten friendship with our Father in heaven. It cost Me everything – yes, *everything* – I had to offer. Little, by comparison, you will be called on to give, but called on to give you most certainly will be. You cannot be My disciple without full giving of yourself in commitment – as much time, energy, effort, dedication as you can muster.

Do not attempt to do this in your own strength for you most surely will fail. Knowing this is why I promised to send My helping, guiding, protecting, connecting Spirit. Call upon His power, His strength. He is so ready to help you, to heal you of former hurts, to harbour you in a safe port as you prepare to set sail under His power, His breath of life.

Life is for living, living for Me to the full in complete happiness. Come, My child, let us succeed together.

Healing - I

7th November

You are the building blocks of healing . I am the cement that holds it all together by the power of My Holy Spirit. You, My people, who live in love, to give of love. Love is the ultimate healing force. I share it out amongst you richly that you may richly give. Living for Me means partaking, sharing of the gifts I long to offer. Healing is high on My list of priorities. How many remain unhealed because they did not seek and ask, did not trust sufficiently, did not truly believe in My power, My capabilities and therefore block Me off!

The † – My † – is like a giant key to unlock this problem, for upon the victory of the † the world was turned round, upside down, inside out by possibilities. Things hitherto seemingly impossible now become possible in My Name. Yes, it is by the † that you are healed. Its influence is so far-reaching it stretches light to every corner of the world. My heart, pinned there, was such an explosive heart of love. When it was shattered it fell apart to be spread everywhere for the good of mankind.

Healing - II

8th November

Mankind's most urgent need is usually one of healing: healing from the negative, destructive influence of the world; healing from self-deception; healing from all manner of inner sickness which will manifest itself by outer infirmities. I am not saying that physical illness is a punishment but rather it works to some extent under the restrictions of cause and effect, just as you see how addictions can take over and control both mind and body, completely influencing their wellbeing.

True healing will always come from Me working from the inside out. How can the body and soul be truly fit and fine if the spirit is in some way afflicted? Affliction is always restriction. It can cut back to the chase. Sometimes it lets, allows, My people to see and understand more of Me in their stillness and thus in this it serves a very useful purpose. But I would rather it happen the other way round, whereby mankind's frenzied activity does not wear out the working parts of the mind and body. I did not design it so (for life to be so demanding) but man has taken his own wilful route, and in separating from Me you see the rise of many ailments.

My †, however, is a horizon of hope when its implication, its restorative power, dawns in man's understanding. The light of the Father shines from behind the †, making it stand out in stark but dramatic relief, an ugly but beautiful symbol standing both for torture and for healing, so clearly visible to those who want to look in that, My direction. Look closely and move forward; then the † with all its healing power becomes tangible, tactile.

Healing - III

9th November

Reach out to Me and feel My very real, near presence in your heart. That is love – My love – reaching out to touch every nerve, fibre, joint, bone and sinew of your being. As I knitted you together in the first place, who better to know exactly what consolation, comforting, healing you require, just as a mother intuitively senses for her child and aches to the point of heartbreak when something goes wrong and her child is hurt. So it is with Me. I long, My dearest children, to put you back together in the broken places of heart, mind and body.

Find Me and you will find true spiritual healing. Discover spiritual healing and you will be amazed, truly amazed, at what else you uncover in the way of needing prayer for complete healing. Powerful, devoted, dedicated, decided prayer is always the channel I use. It is the means whereby My heart enters into the human situation to transform, reform or newly form possibilities. Prayer is at the root of the †; the power of prayer moves into the † to gather the effectiveness, all that I gained there – to claim this and name this, the full range of the †'s triumph for mankind's benefit.

Imprinted there upon My heart, a part of the prayer remains whilst part is reflected back in the signal of My response – the response made out of pure love, nothing but love. Love is what I live for. Love is all that I am. Love is the bond, the relationship of Us, the Trinity, and it is this very love that We want to give out, to share, to repair Our people in whatever way they are broken. Prayer perfects and connects with what I started on earth during My lifetime. You now are given that same healing power that you saw Me use on earth. We share the same Spirit, therefore the same power, therefore the same possibility of miraculous results.

Believe this, My dearest children, and use it fully. By My mercy you were saved; now use the same mercy to help heal others' hurts of mind and body. You will always find Me more than ready and willing, waiting to relate to you.

Healing - IV

10th November

Never underestimate the power of prayer. Expect miracles, then name them and claim them for My glory. Man often needs dramatic happenings to help him believe. You can be part of this miracle-working, dramatic, life-changing process.

Trust, believe, act, give thanks and remember always to praise as best, most meaningfully, as you can. Praise is an outpouring of love in appreciation. It warms My heart and stirs yours to even greater things. Praise always!

You can offer praise by the healings you see come about. When Saint Iraneus said, "The glory of God is mankind fully alive in Him," it was an apt and perceptive description. "Fully alive" means without hurt, without the restriction of ailments. Pray with praise; see the answers become manifest in healing; then pray once more simply to give praise! This is an effective, simple sequence. Use it and teach it – solitary, silent, still praise or shared praise which can be exuberant in enthusiasm and excitement. There is a place carved out for both, but never ever underestimate the importance of meaningful, heartfelt praise.

Herein lies the strings which, when touched, play tunes of everlasting joy. Heaven is a non-ending crescendo of such joy, and I long for you to experience the taste of heaven.

Don't Lose Heart - I

11th November

Don't lose heart. You stumble and fall only to get up and try again. However many times, I am with you always.

Patience and understanding are the essence of love. Love is action in waiting, and waiting for perfection takes a very long time! I showed the way for My children and send My Spirit's support, but only too well I understand their frailty and tendency to fall, collapse under strain.

Look to My †, the emblem of victory overcoming anything that assails you. When you stand in its shadow, you also stand in its glory reflected, reaching out to touch and influence you. From this you can draw daily, hourly, strength if needs be. Such was the power, influence of that occasion/event, its source can never run dry. Cataclysmic in effect and result, the † remains the source – My source – of overcoming all that assails, assaults you as difficulty.

You will overcome with Me by your side and My Spirit surrounding. Together, sent by the Father, We are a force of dynamic power, more than earth can hold. Ours is the influence, the force that connects heaven and earth together. Neither is ever separate, for they are fused invisibly but tangibly by Us. My people are part of the electric current which gets things done by moving through mankind radically, efficiently, although not always quickly.

Don't Lose Heart - II

12th November

Preparation has to be made for anything life-changing. When you rearrange your time, effort, intentions, thoughts, to give Me priority, much has to be done first and on the way. The journey is long and arduous for it is one of giving up of self, dying to human ways, wants and needs, to rise to a new, full, glorious life in Me – one where great will be your peace and joy in fulfilment.

So try not to worry about the stumbling blocks on the way. I do understand and sympathise with the difficulties. All I ask of you is effort to try again and obedience to walk/talk/think/act My way of righteousness. This means admitting mistakes (that helps to develop true humility), asking forgiveness to clear the path, asking for My Spirit's help and guidance, then setting out, non-defeated, once more. You will succeed in time, however arduous the task now.

And remember, the longest, hardest preparation is set for those who are to achieve the most. More is asked of those to whom more is potentially given. Life is not equal in that respect. My Father has His own choices, known only to Him, not set in stone but set, cast, in the hope of His heart. And hope always allows room for change and improvement until success is met, like a long distance runner striving, practising, until he succeeds in breaking his own barrier of previous achievement, all because of determined effort to succeed. We need such as this to build the kingdom on earth – no easy task in the face of strident opposition. Therefore the workforce needs to be well prepared, armed with righteousness, imbued with diligence, sound in knowledge and strength of endeavour.

There is always a right way to proceed to ensure the best. This We ask of you. Do not give up nor fear the setbacks; they are merely part of the course of training and all will be well with you remaining in Me, My dearly beloved child of effort.

I Came to Make a Difference

13th November

All that I am is yours, My child – all that I am in love for you to guide you through life and its many difficulties, dangers, pitfalls. All is safe passage with Me at the helm, for would I ever see harm befall you? No, that is impossible, not just improbable! But you have to believe this and claim that belief to put the promise into action. A promise is not a promise until it is claimed and implemented. I designed it so.

Much that comes under My jurisdiction is alien to man's way of thinking and doing, for his very being and seeing has lost touch with reality – the true reality, that is, which is Me; the unseen to be seen, the unheard to be heard, the not noticed to be noticed.

It was for this I came to life on earth: to make a difference. And how much difference did My life make? A difference of heaven upon earth to those who accept and believe. No difference at all to the indifferent. Some difference to the serious doubter still seeking.

Yet I came to speak to all men, and all men need to hear Me for their own destiny and fulfilment. It is an important, life-giving, life-saving mission given to those who know Me, to allow My light to shine brightly wherever I deem it necessary.

Mine is the choosing, yours is the using, to trim the lamp and make the light effective. Together we stand to hold the world in our hand of possibility – possibility of new life with joy and hope, all because you believed and spread the gospel, the good news of My truth. Earth holds no more important work than this fundamental sharing of divine truth.

It is the key to being, the key to becoming rich in Me, My Father and Spirit. Trinity is a power of holding – holding out arms of love towards you, Our mankind, Our very own people, formed for a purpose, formed for Us. Is the truth of life so very difficult to grasp? Does anything else make any real, lasting sense into eternity at all? I think not.

Fall into the arms of your living God, My child, and there be safely held clasped to the bosom of love and healing itself. It is all you need; it is all I long to give to you – doubts forgiven, uncertainty destroyed, all because you came to Me in trust – open, longing, searching, asking trust.

Go now in peace, the peace of Christ, My peace to give you.

Show Us the Way - I

14th November

Tethered to the dual harness of resentment and jealousy, resentment gives rise to bitterness, souring the heart. Jealousy gives rise to feelings, false feelings of insufficiency, souring the mind. Be cleansed by Me to become free. Remain close by Me to be free into the future. This is not a 'once only' step. Your propensity to fall back must be guarded against by prayer, close prayer of a repentant, aching heart – aching to the point of shedding tears. This will release fears pent up inside where you try to hide from Me and yourself. We have much to deal with here; but you have made a good start, My child. Feel your heart's ease lightening, brightening. "Come to Me all of you who are heavy burdened and I will give you rest."[43] That's My promise.

No failure is a complete failure beyond hope. For where I am, light and healing love are waiting to flourish and abound. All perfect restoration is found in Me. Come, My child, My lovely child of seeking truth, speak to Me about everything but especially that which is heavy upon your heart and will start to grieve you and Me. Together we can be the solution, resolution to progress. Inner healing is the appealing to Me, the great Physician of love – loving understanding commanding that all things work for good and should always get better.

Dark is only dark if you allow it to be. Switch a light on, and it chases the dark away. You know I am Truth, and truth is light in any situation. Resolve to live in darkness no more, for it does you no good. Like a plant, darkness can provide for gestation; but growth, strong growth, comes with light and the right nourishment and feeding in strength - borrowed strength to begin with, maybe a weak strength that needs something, someone to lean on, like a climbing plant upon a stick, but growing stronger with inner strength the more the plant (and you) reach out to the light of My life – life lived in holiness, the holiness of purity of intention and deed. My truth is agreed between us, so why don't you act upon it? What stops you?

---

43 Based on Matthew 12:28

Show Us the Way - II

15th November

I understand those hurting feelings you are thinking about but, "Come to Me," is a decision you must command. Remember, faith not feelings, at all times. Yes, I gave you strong – the strongest – feelings, but these belong always within the realm of My influence.

In Me you begin; in Me you continue throughout your days, until that glorious day somewhat far away yet when we meet face to face to greet each other in unreserved love. Don't you want to be able to say to Me, "I did my best for You, Lord"? Well then, you must learn these lessons we are working on. You cannot arrive until you've started, and you cannot start until you decide to. Yes, it takes courage and perseverance and determination, but all of these are gifts to you if you do but ask Me. Ask and receive from your generous Giver of love – full love, all love. It is more blessed to give than receive, but you cannot give until you've received, and all My work involves giving.

Living for Me is fulfilling to the utmost extent of your ability and time and willpower. Ours it is to transform the world; you're part of today's world. Never miss an opportunity to set others free in Me. But first you must be set free, completely free, yourself.

Trust Me - I

16th November

Let Me be free to help you. You bind Me up by your disbelief – a lack of trust. I cannot come to you unless you genuinely believe in My powers and desire to come to you. Why do you doubt Me when you have so much evidence of Me at work in your life and the world? Why hesitate and prevaricate needlessly?

I am not surprised to hear all you want to tell Me. My heart is big enough, strong enough, deep enough and sufficiently caring to carry all your troubles and sorrows. I do understand when you doubt, but unless you come to Me, sit with Me and we reason together, how can I let you know and understand, really grasp, My viewpoint? A silence between us is a shortcoming in understanding, a discrepancy of love and is not helpful nor gainful. You must, My child, believe in all I tell you, even when storm clouds gather and the horizon is thereby lost, shrouded in dark mist of confusion.

It is I who sees the whole picture – something you can never achieve whilst on earth. Just as a parent takes a wider view, perspective, on anything for their darling child, so as to prevent them running into danger or stumbling in the unknown, so it is with Me. My way is one of merciful understanding. I know it takes time – a long time – for you to grasp all of My truth, to be really certain of Me and My workings. I keep telling you to trust because you will never be in a position to see the beginning from the end of a situation, so complex and somewhat devious are the many parts of any situation, interwoven like tangled threads. Pull at one thread and you may tighten into a knot another thread or threads. Only One who can see the beginning from the end – and you know that is Me – can successfully untangle the mess and confusion life lived without Me gives rise to.

If only all of My children would listen and learn from Me, asking what they are to do in the day, day by day, many errors and much false fumbling would be avoided. Why don't you seek always to speak to Me early in the morning? Why still act so independently when you know this is not the best way?

Trust Me - II

17th November

Do not let your head be ruled by your heart! Emotions are good and worthwhile and often can be used as indicators. But beware of the times when they play false with you and dictate actions against My truth, My gospel truth, unfolding clearly before you. Do not let yourself be swayed away from Me by your feelings.

Faith is, remember, fact not feelings, certainty not uncertainty, discovery not hidden, understanding not confusion, action not inaction, all summed up in that one short but challenging word which says, "Trust." Unless you trust Me, how can I be fully, effectively at work within your daily situation? Trust means handing over to Me without doubt – I repeat, without doubt – and letting Me be free to do whatever is necessary and needed. I can see the answers. I can see the solution. But your resolution to trust plays its part. Perhaps this is one of the most difficult lessons (trust) that My people have to learn.

Remember how Peter denied Me three times, then feared in his failure he had lost My love? All that time he had been with Me to learn first-hand from Me, and yet still he had not learned to trust in the overwhelming power of My love and influence – the absolute certainty of Me, My constancy, your security in Me and through Me. 'All put in place by Me' cannot go astray, for it receives heaven's blessings.

Trust Me - III

18th November

Our Father is a constant deity of protective hope and healing. His encouragement, His love, is manifest and made secure in Me. Surely you see and understand that by now? I came to earth for one purpose only – to reveal the all-powerful, complete, total, *utterly* complete, nature of My Father's love and compassion for you. The best parent that anyone could ever wish for, He can want nothing other than your total wellbeing and has provided every answer, every means, for this to be achieved by Me, in Me. Come to Me, My child, and believe this as if your very life depends upon it. Your very wellbeing does.

Nothing has gone wrong which cannot be put right. Nothing has caused hurt which cannot be healed. Nothing has gone astray which cannot be straightened out and made secure for the future in Me. That is My job, My role, My calling – a reason for My visiting upon you to let you see this, My ultimate truth and reality. God is good, so very good; not only will all be well, it will become better!

Trust Me - IV

19th November

Yes, you are being tested. But testing produces endeavour and effort to meet success. Then success can build upon a sure foundation and move forward to greater, stronger triumphs. My way is one of everlasting truths and triumphs. I look to the future as well as the present and ensure all will be well in Me, built upon the sure rock foundation of My truth, My teaching reaching into the very core of your being to make a difference – a real, lasting difference. You see, I in you and you in Me will weather any storm, any trial.

It is your denial of Me at work which stops progress. Realise this and claim My success; name it, proclaim it, even when you don't feel it because you cannot see anything happening. The dark can hide all manner of workings, but the dark of your indifference or uncertainty drive Me away. Act as if you can see even when you can't! Accept My truth, My way of working; there is no better way for you. Indeed, there is no other way to success – everlasting, complete success.

"Come to Me you who are heavy ladened and I will give you rest,"[44] was and is My promise. It stands fast for all times and all people who trust and belong to Me. Let Me be powerfully at work within you, My child, and you will come to see all the difference in the world taking place. This is My promise. This is My truth and I will not – cannot – fail you if you turn to Me in complete trust. Honour Me by this trust. Do not just pay lip service nor fluctuate day to day.

I am the same yesterday, today and tomorrow. Spend more time with Me, consciously aware of Me, concentrating upon Me, and you will see. You will see all My plans and promises hold true for you and for all My dearly beloved people who trust in Me and invite Me into every situation, dark or light. My bright light will shine in radiance, penetrating the darkest corner of the hidden soul to set you free – free to be in Me, with Me, fully for Me, so together we can achieve so much.

---

44 Based on Matthew 11:28

Trust and Truth - I

20th November

Fairness is My justice and peace put into action by the power of the Spirit. If your spirit is agitated then you are not in the place of My peace. My peace releases fear, doubt, uncertainty, indecisions and confusion. Confusion is not My way; it is the result of man's activities without My involvement. Clarity and truth of purpose come from Me. Have I not promised to set you free in the world?

Take My promises and claim them as part of your prayer. This is important. When you do, it shows Me affirmation of your belief and hope founded upon the sure certainty of My promises. As My word is the living word, alive and active, it holds fast every day for you.

My way is always the right one. In My way, on My path, you cannot falter if you stay close to Me – close enough for us to talk together. It is in the receiving that you come to understand and in the understanding that you come to ask even more. 'Ask and receive, ask and receive' is the pattern. It is the 'seek and find' that you have been promised. Seeking and finding must involve looking, listening and learning with your heart and mind, your feelings and thoughts fully, sensitively awake.

Trust and Truth - II

21st November

I did not give you a spirit of timidity to fear Me.[45] I gave you sound sense which recognises readily the full light of My truth and will not be happy, not genuinely happy, with anything less. Anything less than Me and My guidance, and you will never be free to act in all wisdom, for where but from God our Father does wisdom come from? Certainly not from mankind and his vain imaginings!

Truth is the reflection of the life, the full, beautiful, fulfilled life, which is the purity of the Godhead at work at nothing but love. Love comes to its perfection in Us, in Our way of working. It is this very love, this connection with Us, that mankind must seek after, hold onto, own, share, celebrate, dedicate and venerate. I cannot stress this enough to you, My dear children.

Ultimately, nothing matters but love, and all truth is founded upon, grounded upon, that love which seeks to give nothing but the best – Our own, God's very own, best. Blest indeed are those who come to grasp and fully understand this within their earth's lifetime. For this appreciation changes all manner of perceptions, both widening, deepening and rounding the outlook of your understanding and your willpower.

You know that dying to self to grow in Me is another important – vitally important – part of becoming free: free to be whom I desire; free to be My child, active and purposed in love; free to serve Me and do what is right for Me. You cannot do this unless you listen constantly and learn willingly.

My expectation, My hope, is for a pupil alert and receptive at all times; one willing to own up to mistakes and learn from them; one not afraid to venture forth into territories unknown; one not reluctant to re-visit troubled areas of experience, to re-invest time and energy in these, but with Me very close on hand, this time to illuminate your darkness and clear the way for your understanding.

---

45 See 2 Timothy 1:7

Trust and Truth - III

22nd November

I never leave My children as orphans to struggle on their own. Those who come to Me will always be helped, supported, strengthened, consoled, comforted and guided by My Spirit of truth. You must trust Him. He is a taste of heaven upon earth, a foretaste of the glory – My glory, which is yet to come upon you who seek Me and love Me.

I love you so much, My darling children. My heart overflows with feelings for you – good, honourable, wholesome, happy feelings, of course. Those things I will gift to you in order to bless your coming in, your going out, walking in My way of truth. You can see how important – critically important – this matter of truth is. Without it I cannot function. It is one of the sources of My energy, the power which connects Me to you and, on a wider scale, heaven to earth.

Truth is the only way forward or, where necessary, backward. Truth is in the standing firm and waiting. Truth is in the standing still, reflecting upon what is happening. In My Name you must proclaim and act in all truth. I will have nothing less. It is one of the hardest lessons for mankind to learn: this complete, open, pure, honest, direct, effective truth of plan and purpose, willpower and action, thought and decision – no bends, no variance, no digressions, no hidden agendas, so nothing of self at work, only truth, My holy truth, giving you right standing before our Father; that is what matters.

Working in truth you can trust without fear, you can hope unalloyed. Trust and truth go comfortably hand in hand. Love and life are to be illuminated and inspired by the quest for them. Then all else follows on. Do you not see this, My beloved children? Think about it, and it should become evidently plain to you.

My Purpose - I

23rd November

Rest in Me, rest in Me, and you will see the glory of My light shine in your confusion when you are with Me, understanding My principles, how I work, why I work and what for.

Love is always a guiding light of My life in you. I designed you for this purpose. I hold you safe and secure in the palm of My hand for this purpose, this God-shaped purpose, My Father's plan in Me, in you, together – fused together and enthused by the Holy Spirit.

He it is who uses to the full and effectively all of God's power and might working with God, for God, through God, by Me, that you may be free in My love to serve obediently – looking, listening, asking, taking on board in your life all that I will, all that I want, to show you, to let your love, knowledge, and understanding of Me grow.

For therein lies your life's meaning. My purpose come to light in you, through you, with Me at the helm steering, negotiating, navigating the way – day by day, one day at a time, unfolding in all its possibilities or probabilities.

Keep the sinful one, the evil one, the deceiver, at bay. He is all mischief – nothing but mischief – and will impede your work if you let him. All too readily he gains a foothold, a strong foothold. You must not give him an inch, *not one inch!* Call upon Me – the majesty of My supreme love at work banishing him and his influence. My good, powerful love at work will always triumph over evil. Satan has no power except that which you give him. Give him leave to act, and he will take a mile, making inroads on your life to disrupt and destroy. Do not let him get a foothold. His stranglehold is death to love's opportunity. Deal with any elements of selfishness within yourself that might invite him in to begin his devastating work. Once in, he triumphs easily, all too readily. Banish him in My Name of truth, justice and love.

I have conquered all sin by My righteousness. The † was a complete victory once and for all people who accept Me in faith. Faith makes miracles happen – some spectacular, some small, some even seemingly insignificant, but miracles nevertheless.

My Purpose - II

24th November

I long to bless all of My children if they will let Me become involved in their lives. Do not be careless and forget Me. Do not be so busy you leave Me behind or drive me out.

Do nothing without thinking, "Is this to my Lord's everlasting honour, praise and glory?" Then you cannot go too far wrong.

You belong to Me, My dearly beloved child. Claim your place in My heart in My Father's family. He will let you be a full member with all the family's privilege of membership and closeness, close support of each other. The Trinity is there, each in its own distinct part and character and together as One in love, to share and provide for all your needs. Simply, you belong to Us and We belong to you.

Therefore I, your Christ, will intercede to the Godhead for you, adding My prayers, My plea, to yours as long, of course, as you are working within My Father's will. This is vitally important. For without that (without Me in Him and Him and Me reaching you) we can do nothing.

Invoke His Spirit, God's almighty power at work, at all times. As you ask, He will come with healing in His wings. Ask for His wisdom and He will not disappoint you.

Look at your feelings instead of your thoughts (or perhaps *rather* than your thoughts). Whereas thoughts are a yardstick, a measure to work by, feelings are a barometer, an indicator to go by. Heed this. I will be there in your feelings. Share them with Me by telling Me all about them.

I will come as to one who is hungry, famished for the truth. You have to need Me – really need Me – and acknowledge this in all humility, for Me to come readily. I stand and wait, oh so patiently! Do not delay. Your needs are ever pressing. Let us forge ahead together.

Switch off the red light. It spells danger! Let My light, My green light of love, take you forwards. Love is the way to travel. Love will cut through the swathe of difficulties. Love will forge a new path in its purpose to serve kindly and generously.

Do not hesitate. Act now in the way you know to be right; then leave the rest to Me.

Search, Seek Listen and Find - I

25th November

Stress is self-inflicted when I am not part of the plan. Did you ask Me for guidance before making your decision? My permission is vital in all things at all times, for I am the God who knows and wants and will ordain the very best for My people. Refrain from your independent decisions. How often have I told you this already?

I who made you, formed with loving, careful thought, know what is best for each of you individually. Yes, it is more difficult to decide when others are involved, but you must trust Me to make the best arrangements in My perfect timing for everyone involved. Each of you is equal in My sight; no one has the right to demand of Me more than another.

Heart-centred is where you find Me in residence. Look at your heart, the seat of your conscience. What is it telling you?

You may go in My Name only as and when it is My choice. My voice should, must, be heard above the world's clamour, saying, "This is the way; walk in it. This is My desire; remain in it. This is My truth; walk away with it."

What matters is what I want, for that is always the very best, the optimum possibility, to bring you complete happiness. In My directed happiness therein lies peace, the peace of knowing that you do My will to the best of your ability.

Uncertainty should always make you look at the situation again. Stop, look and listen for a word from Me. Then you will clearly see the way forward.

Search, Seek Listen and Find - II

26th November

Too many of mankind's mistakes are made simply because they did not consult Me, heed Me or involve Me. Would any loving father allow his young, immature, inexperienced child to wander off without guidance? You, My children, are those young people, immature in your experience of looking and listening for My directive word. Practise this! Practise this until this is as natural as breathing to you and as vitally life-giving. Practise it for everything, for every decision you make, even the seemingly insignificant, for I am Lord of all things in your life and want to be – *long* to be – closely involved with you. But I wait – wait patiently and politely – to be asked and invited in.

You must begin this side of our relationship, and I will help you to develop the skill until we are constantly, continually in close touch. As now this may seem impossible to you, rather like a dream of hope; but believe Me, My children, it is part, a very important part, of our ongoing, growing relationship. Just as husband and wife grow closer and closer and can come to know – just *know* – what the other is thinking or feeling, so may it be with us.

Keep the lines, the channels, of communication always open between us. You never know when I will call out to you – maybe in a special way, maybe amidst the most mundane thought, but you ought to be ready at all times, ready and prepared to act upon My Word. Anything less I regard as disobedience and am displeased and disappointed.

Search, Seek Listen and Find - III

27th November

The Holy Spirit has been appointed as your Counsellor, Guide, Friend, Supporter. You need never be without His holy influence working for your good, indeed for your best. Blest by Him, you will succeed in every need of yours, for you will find your need and Mine become inextricably entwined together. Does this not please and excite you, My child of love?

The powers of heaven above are searching to influence and appoint your actions on earth below. Then your reactions will succeed to joy. Joy, true joy, is My measure of success. Unless you receive this you have not heard Me aright. It may be like Samuel, when I was calling in the night, that you do not recognise My voice immediately.

If in doubt, ask and ask again. When I come to you it will be clear, for I do not make a mystery of My desires and wishes. I repeat for this is important: *"Listen to Me, My children."*

Search, seek, listen and find. Find the treasure, the pearl of greatest price – yours for the asking, Mine for the giving, when you are living out My word of instruction, direction and request. This is My behest to you: *"Look, learn to listen and respond in prayer."*

The time we share is so vitally, essentially precious. It is life-giving indeed – health, hope and happiness for you – for in our time together lies the heart of God.

We Count in Measures of Love - I

28th November

Do not judge your effectiveness; only I can do that. Simply trust in Me to be the Way, the Truth and the Fullness of Life – your way, your truth, your fullness of life guided by My hand as you come to understand of Me.

Be alert at all times, ready and waiting for My call to service. Service is found in so many a different way, not only by what you think, do and say but by your intentions placed before Me so I can turn these into reality. Place everything before Me: all ideas, hopes, aspirations, any failures, fears, disappointments. Let Me work on them, through them, to teach you by My insight of experience.

God's way is My holy way forward – yours to obey and learn from. This is all you need to discern. Ask yourself the question, "Is this from God, my loving Father, or not?" If it is – when it is – it will have a profound, holy and complete truth that resonates in your heart without a doubt.

Never doubt yourself when you are in Me. Together we can be such a powerful force, effective into eternity. All you need to do is to surrender your will-power, your intellect, your interest, your enthusiasm and your commitment to Me. Let Me work in you, with you, through you, for you. Never try to do My work alone. Partnership with Me is essential. Recognise, name, acclaim this God-given partnership. It makes you into the person you were planned to be. It sets you free from all manner of doubt and the stress of struggling and striving. You can leave the effort to Me and simply be responsive.

Listen, always listen, to My Word of truth given for your direction. Connection to the almighty God is a most powerful thing. Let it bring you confidence; let it bring you joy; let it bring you purpose and persuasion. Speak of Me as though I am real in your life, for indeed I am! Listen and learn continually.

We Count in Measures of Love - II

29th November

Open your eyes wider and the horizon extends. You never know what is beyond the horizon until you walk towards it. Make Me the horizon. Let your sight extend as far as Me but no further. Beyond Me is darkness where no man should safely go.

You know My Way is always forward in love, in light, in truth, in goodness. No dark thing will enter into My plan and purpose. I am the living Word of God the Father; I bring life and hope to a darkened, disillusioned world.

Have regard for Me and you have regard for hope, a God-given hope man cannot achieve on his own. You must stay connected, fully connected, to Me by My Spirit of life – the Spirit who brings all manner of good things, connecting heaven and earth, the holy and divine, with the mundane and the everyday.

The Spirit's way is to proceed with power as and when you are made ready by inclination and intention. I will always use those who give themselves over to My purpose. The gain for mankind can be enormous, beyond your wildest dreams or imaginings. Trust Me to use you.

We Count in Measures of Love - III

30th November

Rely upon Me and I will rely upon you. Be confident in Me and I will return the honour. Can you not see what we can be together, My child? Hand over to Me and do not doubt Me. Any doubt puts a brake on our progress, to halt it albeit temporarily.

I wish our progress to be steady, increments made day by day, sometimes in so small a way they are hardly noticeable to anyone except Me. Other times more major events occur, but usually My pace is a slower, surer, steady pace for there is much to get ready, to be prepared in My people's thoughts, their lives of understanding. Progress is measured not by you but by Us, the Trinity of life.

We count in measures of love, for this is what ultimately matters. Love wins through all difficulties and dilemmas. Love is the solution to all of the world's problems. Seek Me and you seek love. Seek love and you seek the completion of the purpose for which mankind was born into life. Love as best you can, whenever and wherever you can. Love in Me; love through Me; love with Me; love for Me. This is your calling, your keynote, the harmony in your God-given life: love. Love at all times in the very best way you can.

Many will be the opportunities and openings I provide for you. Do not fail Me by being too busy about your own business. Heed Me; you need Me! Love to live for Me and live to love for Me. That one mission will see you free to be always acting within our Father God's purpose.

Yearn for Him, yearn for Me, yearn for My Spirit – the Trinity of love. Yearn Us, but you do not have to earn Us! Let love have its everlasting way and you will live in hope.

Advent

1st December

The reason for the season is Me, that My people may receive Me to bring glory to God. The angels sang at My birth because they rejoiced at the possibility of what could happen when My people become free in Me – free to please God by taking on My uprightness. To be upright is to live in the light of God's teaching obediently. I am the revelation, the clearest revelation, of that teaching, but also I am your strengthening because I send you My Spirit as I promised.

Ask for the Spirit this Christmas that He may enlighten your lives by My truth. It is the Father's truth emanating from the Father heart of God. That is where I reside. Will you come too, come to Us to be held safely in that love?

Love came down at Christmas – yes, in a very real way, tangible to you in its fragility. It is this fragile nature of love which necessitates your need of My Spirit. He, only He, can do what you cannot do alone. He is My wisdom and truth, that which comes from the Father's heart.

Start a relationship with Him, My Spirit, and you will not lack clear spiritual understanding. He is My favour to you. He is My promise to you, and you need Him more than ever if you are to grasp the full meaning of Christmas.

Use Advent as your preparation time, a time of deeper, more reflective prayer. I come where, to whom, I am welcomed. Do you want Me to come in to your heart to start a new – newer, fresher – way in your relationship with God? If you do, pray.

Pray as never before, not just earnestly, sincerely, but confidently – confident in My grace and goodness. This is love sent to earth for a reason, not just for a season but that man may know life eternal.

Yes, you have every reason to be glad, to be joyful in anticipation this season. Much is awaiting to happen. Will you let it?

Holiness - I

2nd December

There are no 'perhaps' or 'possibilities' with Me. I work with that which is probable, the certainties of My time, My arrangements, My willpower and intention.

That is why it is important to rely upon My Name. Using My Name, a Name so special, releases the power of sanctification which our loving Father offers to all who believe in Me and will become ready to receive My teaching. My teaching is full of God's complete wisdom and truth as is no other. My teaching contains all the inspiration and motivation, all the knowledge in faith which you need to live and succeed by.

And I call you to the fullest of full lives imaginable in Me, graced by the riches of the goodness of our Father's love. It is to His complete joy that you remain in Me and I remain in you as a dynamic force of truth to touch a waiting world.

The strange thing is the world does not know it is waiting, but you who know Me understand the lack of the world's wisdom and knowledge. True knowledge is bound up with, found in, faith. Although discernible, it is not measurable nor quantifiable in a scientific way for God did not make it that way.

So faith, trust and hope – these three interrelated acts of the conscious mind – remain interchangeable, closely bound, wound together in My truth. My truth is given – *always* given – to those who want to receive and wait to receive. I give them the fullness of truth that they can understand at that point in time within My universal truth. Do you see, do you understand, do you appreciate, do you follow how I come to each one of you separately and individually, so that collectively you who bear witness to Me, faithful witness, bear out My truth?

Science cannot substantiate Me, neither one way nor the other, but you can by lives given over to following, abiding by My wisdom, My truth, My way for God.

Holiness - II

3rd December

Ask the Holy Spirit; reach out to Him. He will always gladly, willingly, joyfully (it is His greatest joy) teach you in terms you understand. His command is only that you try to remain open to all I want to show you. This requires effort, time, the tranquillity of silence, your ability to listen, and the humility to put Me first in your life. The reality of your life is not in the seen 'everyday' about you. Your reality is in an entirely different realm of which you as yet taste and see but a little bit in Me: that which I purpose and plan to give you; that which you humbly ask for and endeavour to work towards.

I always esteem effort and applied concentration, dedication to the task in hand. Too many of My people are distracted in the everyday, running hither and thither, busy about tasks which I did not ask of them. Life can thereby be filled in a somewhat meaningless way.

Meaning in life is what is of everlasting, eternal value. This is the connection between heaven and earth, for that which is begun on earth can be, will be, continued in heaven to My purpose, for our Father's full glory and honour. Mankind must, should, live for this purpose, and this purpose becomes not possibility but certain probability, full potential in Me by the unlimited power of My Holy Spirit at work in you, with you, for you.

Through time you will see this happening if you ask Me to reveal to you My truth, known, shown, in the way I work. I never work in isolation but always through My full commitment to bring to earth My full spiritual healing which is the clearest possible revealing of the Trinity's power – Our power of everlasting, all encompassing, life-transforming love in all its beauty of holiness.

Holiness is you and Me working together, influenced, guided, led by My Spirit to the splendour of My Father's will. Let Him instil the fullness of Me in you in all you do with Me, through Me.

Holiness - III

4th December

Living for Me will let you see the way forward, full in God's grace of wisdom and truth. This is His love shared out amongst many, any who care to believe and receive from Me.

Receiving Me is one sure step in the right direction of connection to God in all holiness. Out of holiness He formed you. Out of holiness God desires you. Out of holiness God hopes for you. Come, My child, be holy as I am holy, the source of God's given goodness. Come to the Father through Me, with Me, in Me, for I come to you for this and no other purpose.

It is My plan, My Father's plan, the Spirit's plan, begun back in a time and place beyond your imagining, that you should be made completely holy in Me… You can receive and live of Me now, transformed, reformed, conformed to My holiness. This above all else is the love I long and choose to share with you.

Use Me, My child, more than ever before, and you will stand surely secure in the Trinity's grace and love. Feel Our embrace of love empower you now as you submit to the wisdom and truth of Our holiness. Let love shine through your holiness. Let love conform you and combine us. Trust Our love given in holiness, where Our truth will abide in all you think, say and do for Me as long as you let My purpose be at work.

Go now, My child, in the holiness of love, and do not forget My teaching, reaching out to you. I am the Way forward; see this. I am Truth; have regard for this. I am Life in the fullness of love lived for you, in you and with you. Come, My child, let us always be together in this self-giving love, living for each other and thereby those you know.

Love does 'make the world go round' when it is found in Me. Take My hand and you will see! I will lead you forward – always forward – in My Father's truth.

Listen to Me - I

5th December

My Word is everlasting, abiding truth, holding firm for all people in all places at all times. I am the God who changes not, except when petitioned by My people for mercy or help. But essentially in character I never change for there is no need. Perfection cannot be bettered or made more complete or more beautiful. My way is perfect. My plan for My people is perfect.

If only they would heed Me by listening more for My voice, whispering words of loving encouragement. Even when the truth hurts or threatens to destroy, My special love wins through the quagmire of men's doubts and deceits.

I came once upon earth, to save all – all of mankind – from their own sinful wilfulness and false pride. Both of these are big enemies fighting a fierce – the fiercest – of lengthy battles to win over body and soul.

But My Spirit in you can remain impregnable, when [you are] in touch with My Spirit of truth and protection. Connection to Me through Him is vital, as vital as the air you breathe, for like that very air it is life-saving and energising, renewing the very mind, will and emotions and thereby strengthening the body itself.

It all stems from hearing, seeing and believing: hearing My Word daily; seeing Me at work everywhere; believing in the best and that the best is yet to come. My truth is a profound, life-changing, life-saving truth, too valuable to be wasted by falling on deaf ears!

Listen to Me - II

6th December

Listen to Me, My child. Come to Me today in any way you can. I am not a prescriptive God. Come to Me as best you can; spend time with Me; set time aside and listen. Listen hard, listen long, listen with concentration and awareness, but above all, listen with expectation and intent.

Be assured or reassured that you will hear Me in some way – not the same way for everybody, for I am a God of immense creativity and capacity, but hear Me you will. Then you will know I am real and you can reach out in hope further.

Explain to Me everything: your reasons, hopes, fears, delights, dislikes, wishes, problems. Nothing on earth is too large for Me to handle! Hand over to Me and listen for My advice, My solution. Learn too to look at your feelings for guidance. I gave you feelings in the first place, and I will use these as a thermometer to let you know if you are hot or cold and a barometer to gauge your actions in the way ahead.

'Changed from glory into glory' is My way, My path. It means letting My light shine through you, penetrating, then driving away the darkness. Light travels rapidly in straight ways, as do My directions. Listen out for them. Seek these directions with expectation of My speaking to you.

Listen to Me - III

7th December

Seek and you will truly find – find Me ready and waiting, only too ready to converse with you, My darling children. How else can we grow close, become ever closer, unless we converse together? Seek in earnest to speak to Me. Speak then listen, like in everyday conversation. It is no different. Leave spaces between your sentences. Ask questions; receive answers! Sometimes you will have to wait, for I have much to do in readiness to answer you, much to put in place elsewhere. Then, simply be patient and believe in Me.

Keep seeking, keep speaking, keep asking and you will be rewarded. Believe Me, it is My truth. (S)he who comes to Me will never be disappointed. Seek My Word and listen for My voice, spoken directly, through others or through My living Word heard expectantly, received thoughtfully, prayerfully.

Glorious will be the result of us being together. Glorious, I tell you! Believe Me and act upon it.

Call Upon My Name - I

8th December

Wait, wait, wait upon Me. I will set you free from the snares of "the devil who stalks around like a lion waiting for someone to devour".[46] Call upon My Name of protection. It is your safekeeping – guarding you from harm. Evil will pounce on any hapless victim.

Be careful; be vigilant; be watchful. By calling upon My Name at all times, My Name will always overcome the evil one, for yes, I am stronger than he who is in the world. Although satan has the keys of the kingdom of this world, I hold the keys of the kingdom of heaven, and it is to that kingdom of love and mercy that I call you now.

Step out in My Name of grace. Step out in faith to embrace My love – the power of My love which is beyond anything that you can ask or imagine. Call upon that God-given power to transform your situation from fear to hope, from doubt to certainty, from despair to expectation – the expectation of belonging to Me by the desire to be made whole, to be healed in My Name of love which conquers all evil intent. Call upon the power of My Name; it is incontrovertible and indestructible.

Yes, "I am with you always even to the end of the age."[47] This is one of My greatest promises which you must proclaim – proclaim to Name Me Saviour, Lord of your life, of your hopes, of your dreams, of your ambitions, as yet unfulfilled.

Plans of My working will always come to fruition when you call upon My Name of goodness. For this is the Father's goodness found alive in Me, promoted by My Spirit. It is Our duty, Our bounden duty, to reach you with this message – this message of Our love and regard for you. Will you accept and believe?

---

46 Based on 1 Peter 5:8

47 Based on Matthew 28:20

Call Upon My Name - II

9th December

Believe in all I am telling you; believe in all I am showing you. Believe in all I am directing you towards; for this is the light of My love shining amidst and through, piercing your darkness. Love, My love, alive and active, will chase the darkness away, will put it to flight. Your might will become as bright as day when the daylight of My truth invades your heart and mind so you find Me real, as real as the air which you breathe to keep you alive and just as vitally, essentially necessary as that air.

I am the source of life – life lived in all full goodness of the Father's love, mercy and grace. Embrace them now in My truth, My dear child, and suffer no more.

Turn to Me, yearn for Me, call out to Me and believe in My Name of healing love, repealing all manner of ills. Nothing is beyond My redemption. No one is beyond My love.

Be honest before Me, transparently honest, and tell Me all that troubles you. Talk to Me. Be free in Me. I understand your needs, your doubts, your difficulties, your dilemmas. I sympathise in My Name of compassionate love springing from the Father's mercy, the grace of His reaching out to you in Me, through Me.

Together We, the Trinity, long to come into your life, to restore you and make you whole – whole in Our holiness of love, perfect love. This is the love you need that you are seeking, albeit subconsciously. Only We are able to supply your every need.

Come now, My child, without fear. Let Our love appear to you as never before. I wait for you, you wait for Me, so what is the delay? Trust Me and act! Turn to Me with all the longing of your heart and see what belonging to Me will do for you.

Trust: the 'Must' Of Our Relationship - I

10th December

Trusting is believing; believing is trusting. Hand everything over to Me without reservation so I may see your trust. This is the building of our relationship, the firm foundation of love. Love asks for trust. Love demands of trust, else it is no love at all. Love is built on believing the best the other will give, even to full giving as necessary.

I relied on trusting My Father when I was sacrificed on the †, believing this was His will for Me. That trust set you free from sin to begin again.

When you trust Me much happens in My Name of love, in My Name of truth. For love is My truth, but you only know this to the extent that you trust in Me, believe in Me and accept all I tell you without question... for you cannot make sense of My ways which are not the human ways you are familiar with. This in itself requires a deep level of trust, handing over to someone greater by far than you are. Does this not comfort you, My child, that I am in charge and not you with all your shortcomings?

My rule of merciful love is far reaching for those who trust Me and invite Me into this situation to begin My work. My work is always a healing and holding work – holding the enemy at bay that you may walk in My way of truth, the truth of the Father's love. If I had not trusted Him, for His purpose, His holy purpose, where oh where would you be now?

You call Me Jesus, Lord, and indeed I am, but you must trust Me to enable Me to be Lord of your life. Lordship means over-ruling your ways, your inadequacies, your misunderstandings, and your misapprehensions for My much better, holier way of truth.

Trust: the 'Must' Of Our Relationship - II

11th December

Walking with Me, talking with Me, is the way forward for you who trust Me to act in My Father's Name of love and mercy, understanding your every need. Plead with Me to give you this greater understanding of the need for trust – trusting in the truth; trusting in the truth of My way bringing you forward gradually as and when you are ready to go further with Me. To be with Me you must trust in Me and act as if you did.

Speak of Me, your confidence in Me, for as speaking forms the words of your thoughts, trusting forms the basis, the ground-rock, of our relationship. Without trust we cannot move forward for there is nowhere to go. With trust we move forward into My Father's arms of love keeping you, holding you, safe from harm. Trust is as necessary as that.

Trust Me, My child, and move forward in My love which is the Father's power of love overcoming your difficulties and hesitations. I came to set you free from those when you believe in My Name by trusting Me fully – trusting Me to be merciful, compassionate and kind so you may find the fullness – the full fullness – of My Father's love living in you. Then you too can act in My Father's healing Name of love helping in My world, helping through Me because you trust in Me and all I allow to happen to you.

Believe Me, My child. Trust Me, My child; it is the freedom from harm, the harm of insecurity. Those who trust in Me fully are fully safe, held, embraced by the power of My love holding and honouring their trust. Can you not see, now see, that you must trust Me more?

Trust: the 'Must' Of Our Relationship - III

12th December

Call on My Spirit's help, His guidance, His assistance, His support, His strengthening, allowing you to see, to understand, all that I am telling you. Work through Him. Do not work alone, for in that way lies failure. Work in My Spirit; believe in My Spirit. He is the revealed truth to those who trust in Him.

Trusting in Him is trusting in Me and My Father bringing Ourselves to you, making Ourselves real to you, as never before. You need more and more of Him to begin My work of restoration, healing your hurts, your doubts, your insecurities, even your indifference. His work is a great work of restoration done in My Name of love. I send My Spirit to those – *all* those – who ask to receive of Him, believing they will and trusting in the outcome. I will not take you where you do not want to go, for that is not My way of working. I take you where you are prepared to be led in love, trusting Me fully.

Look at the difference in the lives of those who trust Me and those who do not. Look at the measure of My love they can call upon – My love far reaching to the innermost parts of the human soul, the psyche, where nothing but My love can reach to mend, to mend the damage of the time when you did not trust Me because you did not know Me.

To trust someone you have to know them very well indeed and that is how it is to be for us: you, My little child, held safe by My love, waiting to grow in Me, to grow fully in faith that I may use you for My purpose, My healing plan for others who are learning to trust.

Trust: the 'Must' Of Our Relationship - IV

13th December

To believe in Me is to receive of Me, and to receive of Me is to believe yet more. But you all have to make a start by trusting, letting Me take hold of that trust to do whatever I will. Until then there is no movement forward, no real movement, for you have blocked My progress. When you trust Me you unlock the door to a better, happier, holier future, building trust upon the step of trust.

You must trust Me now, My child, and let Me take you forward into the infinity of My love – a love infinite in its scope and purpose, its effect and result for those, and through those, who trust Me fully. Ask the Spirit, My Spirit of truth, for the gift of such trust to enlighten your life; then and only then can I take you where I want you to know Me completely.

You are My child of love growing in that holy love I give to you, to live by and flourish beneath. Receive more of Me. Believe more in Me by practising trust, the 'must' of our relationship.

Preparation - I

14th December

Making your heart ready to receive Me is the most important thing you can do to make ready for My coming, realising that I come to you in the everyday in those who are wanting, willing, ready to receive Me. I come into the depths of your being where I can reside or not according to the preparation you make.

Would you receive a special guest, a royal guest, without the vital, necessary preparations? That would be careless – foolish in fact, for unless you are ready, have made ready, how can you sit down with that guest and enjoy a meal together? Am I not offering you the richest banquet imaginable upon earth? My banquet is a foretaste of heaven, the full joy that awaits My people. It is given to you as a gift of love to help you understand, to savour all that is on offer – on offer through Me, the invited Guest coming to your home if you make your heart My home.

The stable, crude and bare, was made bearable because of the welcome for Me in Mary's heart. She truly believed the words, "Let it be done to me according to Your heart, O God."[48] Will you, can you, do the same for Me?

I can only come to set My people free through the lives of those who know and welcome Me in amongst them. My saving grace is given that you may embrace My love and live it out, give it out to those in need. Kindness and love are for sharing in Me, through Me, with Me. But you have to be ready to receive Me by heart preparation. Look what is there. I do not choose to share where I am not wanted. I am not wanted when you will not take the time, make the effort, to prepare for Me.

---

48 Based on Luke 1:38

Preparation - II

15th December

What is important – really important – you will always do. Is prayer that important to you? Do you really believe in its effective outcome in Me? If you do, most surely the time will ensue when we can work together for My Father's glory. Will you make this your life's story, to prepare for Me that I may do in you, through you, all I plan to do? You will not know this until you make ready. Then steady is My influence upon your progress.

Holiness is dependent upon preparation and reparation – repairing the faults, the fracture lines of faith, that you may be emboldened for the future. When there is a break in our communication – always the result of sin which lets evil in – your heart is not strengthened, nor secure to hold Me. I can slip through the break of trust.

I need to trust you. You need to trust Me. The freedom of faith depends upon this. Trust is built upon layers of prayer, asking, seeking, finding, realising all the truth, God's truth, I speak to you. This cannot be done unless you prepare to receive Me. In the preparation I see your desiring. In the desiring results My coming – My coming to you that we may work together in a new way – always a new way – of deeper faith built on more trust.

Have I not told you that trust is a 'must' of our relationship? Now I say to you, you must make ready to receive My trust and believe in all I say. That is to trust Me fully. Make ready, prepare to share your life – all of it – with Me in an even greater way today. Christmas is waiting as a great celebration for those of My children who make ready to receive My love by preparing.

Preparation - III

16th December

Pray and prepare; prepare and pray; then obey all I ask you to do. Do not be so busy about the everyday matters you do not hear Me. Yes, the tasks are important, but only to an extent. Do not let them crowd Me out.

Let Me prioritise for you and prayer will always be at the top of the list. Do you use – usefully, really gainfully – all the time I give you? Ask for My Spirit's supporting and strengthening to guide you. Ask Him to make your heart, your mind, your entire life ready to receive Me. Listen to Him. Listen carefully to all He tells you to do. His telling is My asking of you. Do you realise this?

I am asking you now to prepare, to make ready to receive Me, not just at Christmas, but each and every day in the special way I choose to come into each individual life. Reach out for Me, and I will reach out for you. Come, My children, make ready for Me.

We will not look back but forward with hope, for the future is sound in Me, is found in Me. Will you help shape that future?

Make ready then to receive Me, and neither you nor I will be disappointed. This is My promise to you. Make ready to receive Me that you may believe in all the fullness of life I offer.

Come, My child, now today and pray some more. Prayer never fails. It is the source of our communication together. It is where reparation and preparation both lie.

Come, pray to Me, then obey Me. Make ready to receive Me. The world is waiting. Are you?

Get Up and Give to Live to the Full !– I

17th December

My guidance on how much to give is not rigorous, but what you give should meet the need and be given gladly.

To give is to get better. It gives Me more space to work in your heart. As you start to be generous I can be generous too, and you know what that means: manifold (layer upon layer of) understanding will unfold when you decide to act in My Name, in the way I called you to do.

Listening is about learning to receive instructions and act upon them gladly – going out in My Name to serve, support and strengthen.

Decisions taken in Me will always be guided aright and give you fresh insight into My way of working. All children are loved and desired by Me whatever the circumstances of their birth's arrival, and survival is so often dependent on the compassion which flows as men know Me in their hearts. That is the start and continuation of God-given generosity, whose life force will flow with vigour when the way is opened up by removing the boulders of selfishness; greed, gaining for the sake of it; making a mark, a statement to the world about one's own status, security, strength in society. Succumb to Me, My ways, acting, knowing, going to any lengths to succeed to any need most felt.

I will always give you the help required. You do not stand alone or apart. Ascend to My heart of generosity's giving, living to let others know the reality of Me which can be seen alive in you if you choose it.

Get Up and Give to Live to the Full! – II

18th December

'Lose your life to gain Mine' means giving up some of what you value: time, effort, energy, intention. Trust must let you act willingly. Singing songs of gladness is for sharing, comparing how good God is, how gracious, how generous, all loving, all knowing, all showing His presence here upon earth. Dearth of existence was never part of His plan. It simply overran because of man's own need, greed.

Get up and give to live to the full! All I have given to you is of Me to be shared. Start with your family also means the wider family of those adopted into your care to share in the responsibilities of living within My sphere of influence. Calm destiny awaits those who fall in, begin to adapt, adopt My way of thinking.

All of you are children, most real and dear to My heart. Impart towards each other the grace of My love; embrace of My power to shower you with blessings – all of you, not simply a selected few. You who knew Me before must share of this Good News. It is the repair of broken, fractured hearts where I can start to mend and heal.

Concealing My presence is no good at all. You must reveal My wealth of bountiful goodness, My store of riches awaiting plundering. I'm wondering what you will do next. Text upon My heart of love this message: "Live to give, to give, to give." It's all I ask. As I gave to you, give of Me freely, willingly, gladly, generously. No struggles, for when you share from the heart you can repair all manner of damage and evil.

My rule over the world is of love, above and beyond everything else that matters. Shatter any misconceptions applied by My hand held out in love, when you are hand-in-glove with Me, and see the difference it makes.

Get Up and Give to Live to the Full! – III

19th December

You can take Me to others in many ways. This gifting is one of them, lifting them up higher without the strife of everyday financial concerns and stress. The mess may be of their making – or maybe not. It is not for you to sit in judgement.

I sent My Son that all sins might be forgiven. All means all – a fall away from evil's power to shelter the earth from sin's reign of disaster. My light is now shining, does shine, as bright as the Christmas lights, to celebrate a season, reason for being here.

Go in the light of gladness to give of your heart. In joy you receive; in joy go out and give generously – not lending, but sending the gifts I wish to bring.

I did receive from the three [wise men][49] the gold, frankincense and myrrh they desired to bring, but far more important was the love offering made from their hearts of conviction: prediction of the Christ Child's influence upon the world, a portent of giving. And far they had travelled to do so, to let the world see how to be living within My reach.

You must put your actions where you find your heart and mind are in My truth. This I ask of you – no more, no less. You can indeed bless by Me. Give to live joyously.

---

49 Kings

Life Is an Adventure - I

20th December

Ask of Me to get to know Me more – My will for you, for all of you. Turn to Me at all times to know the truth of My calling out to you, My intentions for your life. As I plan, My plan unfolds steadily according to your intentions to act in My Name and purpose.

Lovingly I use you in My service, My love poured out on you and through you that you might manifest Me to others - those to whom you meet and work with. My calling into men's hearts falls on deaf ears unless they can see Me and you in action together. Take Me wherever you go. Go in My Name of truth and freedom.

My love sets all men free if only they will allow it to permeate their souls, deep into their hearts. Together in My Name you will work powerfully, effectively, as you learn to trust and ask, as you learn to be in Me each moment of your day, never failing to recognise My face, whatever the situation, however dark and despondent.

I use you … in the way I intend, formed together, bonded together in love. In My love you will become powerful, an effective tool forged by Me, striking like an arc of steel, cutting to the core of problems, but gently because you are of Me. Hewn away, chipped away, chiselled gently, I mould you into My intention, My form, My beautiful children.

Bonded by love you can act together as I show you how and where and when. But you must keep coming to Me in expectant faith, not looking to right nor left away from Me.

Bold you will be in recognition of Me – bold and assured as you see My plans coming to pass. Learn of Me in meekness and gentleness, humble of heart and burning with desire for My gifts. My gifts are given where they are needed and will be used. Seek of them in My service – those gifts so freely given of Me for your use for many.

Life Is an Adventure - II

21st December

As I use you all I will freely maintain My promise of coming to you in power. All that I have is yours in abundance. Use it wisely but, as I told you before, not sparingly. This is important to realise, for the more you give out of yourselves and Me, the greater the space there is created for Me to fill with My love and power, My plan and purpose.

Seek and you will find Me in your every day. Knowing Me you will be filled with joy and gladness: that gladness that comes roots deep in the heart of your soul; that gladness which speaks of the purpose of your lives, your very calling into being, your purpose here on earth as you pass on your way to Me, bringing others along with you all.

My intention and purpose is made plain in your eyes as you pray and know Me more, as you ask of Me and believe all that I am telling you, have told you, can tell you. My children, know that I am God and no other. Know that I am yours and call you. Know that I love you with the fullness of My being, My whole self. I cannot love in any other way.

Take hold of Me totally that I may take hold of you securely, leading you on in strength and delight. Believe that I have called you. Believe that I use you. Believe in Me as I have in you. Dearly beloved children, you are My delight for all that you do in My Name and purpose.

Amazed and amazing you will feel as you shoulder My † with Me. The burden will not be too heavy for it is under My control. All is under My influence.

Life Is an Adventure - III

22nd December

Be still and know that I am God, the God who cares and comforts, who reassures and holds truth, who creates and comes when you call on My Name. Call out to Me often; cry out to Me if in doubt. Seek of Me, ask of Me, and anything done in My Name will succeed when it is of My plan and purpose. You must try and discern that plan and purpose by eagerly seeking, learning and listening.

Make Me your life's intent, your goal. Come in gladness and joy into My kingdom where I await you, knowing that all will be well in My Name and service, My bonding with you in love and unity, My forming of you for action and delivery.

Doubt Me not, for I am the truth, the ultimate reality of all you see, hear and seek. Know Me now that you may know Me more in the future. Stronger and stronger you will become as you seek and find Me, as you walk hand in hand with Me, My guiding of your footsteps on the way. Life is an adventure of excitement with Me beside you each day. Take of Me and hold Me tight in longing to serve, learn and grow closer.

My child, this Christmas, know that I am yours – that Child born in Bethlehem so long ago, yet still the same throughout eternity. I was born and died to give you life – a life of freedom in Me – that you too may know and serve My Father, that you too may live forever, for all times, in My Father's house in that special place He has prepared.

But there are many steps along the way: steps of My calling and guiding, My forming the way, the walk, you should take. Do not listen to those who defy Me, for they must not cloud your judgment. Simply know Me, that I am there. I am there for you at all times in any way you seek.

Come to Me, My children, and rest in My peace and joy.

The Victory of the Cross

23rd December

Trust Me in all things. Trust Me in the fullness of life in My means and methods. Trust Me amidst the difficulties even though these come daily for I have taught you My truth that "when you are weak you are strong in Me"[50]. This is an affirming promise; name it and claim it as you name and claim Me as your Saviour.

My saving help is offered in accordance with your prayer where we share life together. Do not doubt amidst trial for there I am carrying the heavier end of the burden. Can you not yet feel it – My hand at work uplifting?

Light shines when you receive My grace by fully believing My best: My best intention; My best outcome in the working of grace. Grace is the gifting of God unfolding in ways unsought, unmerited, not dreamed of but there for the asking, taking, making My way of the Father's love plain, opening out before you.

As you believe you receive; as you ask I act. Presumption is in doing what I do not ask or not doing what I ask. So I say to you, "Ask and receive, receive and believe, and go forward."

The truth of healing lies in the repealing – My repealing of all that has gone wrong with the world because you belong to a God of great grace, our Father of mercy. Mercy is His steadfast loving kindness poured out over us. That includes you and Me through the victory of the †.

The victory of the † is far more outreaching than man has ever yet imagined. The glory you will see is dependent on the victory – this, My victory of love, conquering all sin. It is sin which lets illness creep in. I overcome by the work of the †. The victory is won – death, disease defeated – when mankind meets with his God trustingly, believing in this His ultimate victory.

Satan's defeat is in the place where we meet.

---

50 Based on 2 Corinthians 12:9

In Giving You Receive

24th December

My child, I am yours today and every day to use wisely as you bring Me to others and serve Me. In truth I tell you all that I want you to know at this time, believing in your trust of Me, your dependence upon Me.

Go forward in My Name, expecting of Me even more than before. Take hold of My very life for it is the blood which was shed that you might live in Me in My Name and calling.

'Go for gold' in My Name, plumbing the depths of My calling out to you – not the depths of despair but those deep rivers of peace and joy where My life-giving waters flow, loving sustenance to all those who need Me. Drink of Me and you will be strong in My Name. Eat of Me that you may be replenished and made whole again.

My just cause is your calling, your mission – knowing Me. I suffuse you with My life and strength, My peace and knowledge. Those gifts you earnestly seek will be yours to have and to hold. Take them gladly. I offer them now to you, to use of Me and for Me.

"Be still and know that I am God"[51] in all times, places, situations. There is nothing I cannot handle nor control, for all is of Me in the first place.

Put in My hands all you own and possess that I may multiply My blessings to you… My cup and portion are your share, to share out amongst those to whom I give you. Bless them accordingly with your riches and joy.

All that I have is yours to use for Me. Do not possess alone, but share out wisely and discriminatingly. My loaves and fishes can be multiplied many times over. See My miracle at work as you hand out your share. In giving you receive; you receive more of Me.

Take Me wherever you go, whatever you do, knowing that is what I ask and expect of you. Do not be afraid of failing. All is possible in My Name and season. When the time is right I will show you.

Have no doubts of Me. You are learning fast and becoming Mine. Keep it up! What joy – joys – you will behold in Me and Mine.

Glory be to the Father whose Name is above all names and to Me, His Son, together with Our Spirit of love, peace and harmony!

51 Based on Psalm 46:10

Freedom

25th December

Recognise My voice within you, speaking out that others might hear Me, hear of My good news, My freedom brought to you all by My Spirit. He releases you from fear and doubt for He sets you free in Me, free to rejoice as you believe My truth.

In Him you become truly alive as you breathe in the breath of My life-giving strength – that strength brought about by My death on the † and My resurrection which gave life, My life, to all that seek it. You only have to turn to Me and ask. Ask for a fresh outpouring of My Spirit.

That which was won in My Name was for your freedom: freedom of access to the Father, My Father and yours; freedom to be yourself in Me, now truly alive; freedom to come to Me at all times and in all places, whenever you choose. I wait only for the invitation.

I live in your hearts as you become alive in Me with the breath of My Spirit. He it is who brings you fresh hope in My freedom. He it is who anoints your purpose and My calling. He is of Me and from Me, held fast for all times in our Father's love and destiny.

The journey to My Father's house is a long road – but not winding, for My Spirit guides and My light shows the way for you. Come, My children, come alongside Me and dance for joy as we journey together.

My freedom, My life, is the most precious gift you will ever possess, and I give it to you now. Released and restored you are, in My Name. Be like the caged bird set free in the glorious sunlight and warmth of My love.

My Calling - I

26th December

I give you My peace at all times. Be of Me and in Me, knowing My will for you by asking of Me. You must set time aside for us to be together. I cannot find you easily in the rush and we need to grow.

Being of Me you will become secure in My certainty of plans and will learn to trust to a higher degree, a greater level. Then I can use you more, fired up with My certainty of purpose and plan.

The secret is to be still and know that I am God, to let My presence be the filter in all your thoughts and actions. As you desire, it will be, become. Be careful therefore what you desire, long for. Seek Me first that your wishes are directed aright, in accord with My plan.

I can bless only what is of Me, according to Our intentions. My hand is upon you guiding the way forward. You are My child, held safe and secure in My love, but you must recognise what is of Me and what is not. That means tuning in to all your thoughts and feelings and asking yourself is this of Me or merely yourself?

I would never do anything at all to disquiet you. If it is of Me it is good in essence and intent, bringing peace to your soul, joy and harmony. Your conscience is My sounding bell of authority, My touch fuse to ignite your doubts. When it flickers, stop, think and pray. Most importantly pray, that I may speak to you directly.

My Calling - II

27th December

You are of Me and from Me. It is only natural that I should want to tell you of My plans and intentions, that we should act together. But this I can do only as and when you are ready to seek, to listen, to learn of Me and become what I call into being, what I ask of you. Then you will be united in Me, My bright light shining all around you. You will be My lamp in the darkness of men's souls, a beacon of hope and certainty, an anchor of trust and assuredness to those who are floundering.

Believe Me, My child, My children, for it is the One who speaks who knows all things. As I was formed before time began, I know all that is and was and will be. I see the entire and you fit into it – a rounded whole of existence in Me, to the full, life lived out in joy of purpose as I am served. This is My promise to you all. Take it now and use it for My glory, your greater gain.

I thrust you forward onto My path but with a push so gentle you barely perceive it. Feel My hand upon your lives, knowing I send you where I want you to be, where I plan. Rejoice in this. It is My truth of existence, My reality of happening, more solid than the ground upon which you now are, for it is My next stage for you.

The stage is set ready and awaits you, the players, My performers. The drama is My life in you, your life in Me, about to be played out to a wide audience. Come, My children, the curtain rises and the lights are low in expectation. Step into the spotlight of My calling.

Love Me as I Love You Today and Always

28th December

My child, be Mine now and forever in this newness of life I give you – this fullness of love, My fresh outpouring. Be humble before Me, renewing your spirit. Wait on Me patiently to reveal My plans to you, My intention and purpose for your life, your lives, your new growth in Me.

Keep coming to Me with longing in your heart, determined to do My will and asking. You do not ask often enough of Me. Clamour like a small child wanting to be carried, then reach out and touch Me. I hold My arms out towards you, lovingly, tenderly – those arms which can carry you, transport you heavenwards.

Glorified you will be by My presence in your lives. Seeking, you will find. Knowing, you will be known for My love of you, your love of Me. Determine in Me. My strength I give you – My resolve to serve our Father through Me and My, our, Spirit.

Rejoice, and again I say rejoice in Me always, for I am the source of your lives, the reason for your being, the aim of your becoming. Know Me as I know you. Love Me as I love you today and always. This is My truth – that which I want you to know and understand in Me.

God grant you My Spirit of love and life, My power to transform situations. Come to Me and learn of My heart, My mind, My will for you and others whom you influence. I bring them to you for a purpose in Me. Seek and you will find it. Ask and it will be shown to you.

Much has happened. More is to come. Believe Me when I tell you this. Believe My Word. It stands firm like the rock upon which I build all My foundations. Be built on Me, in Me; then you can reach out through Me, secure, held fast in My arms of love, the certainty of knowing My will for you.

Desire and Belong

29th December

The more you trust in Me, the more I send you deliverance, for you have freed Me to act. It is not so much about a date – an actual day – but more about your state of mind, readiness to receive in belief.

I give. I am a generous giver and cannot wait for this healing grace to be received, given in My love. Ask and receive, seek and find and you will surely discover Me and My righteousness overflowing in love. You can be filled head to toe when you are ready in heart and mind, when I find you obedient and ready to receive, perceive more of My ways. Gladly you come; gladly I give.

Live in Me, My children. You'll be glad you came this far, ready to travel on – bright star of My making to set the heavens alight with hope and expectation; worldly issues set aside in the light of My presence.

Prayer is the answer. Pray, pray, and again I say, pray, as best you can. It is the preparation and the perfection of what happens to please Me, placing you apart from others in your expectations.

Dedication matters at heart. That's where things begin, and it is the seat of hope, desire even, although you have to be careful not to mix that up (desire) with worldly ambitions.

I call you by name to claim you as Mine – to serve and be served, belonging together. Children of My choice and forming, go where and when I send you. In the meantime, trust and hope. Desire and belong in faith. It is your strengthener.

Commit yourselves daily, darling children. Protected, corrected you can travel far in faith's activities. Desirous of Me will set you free to be as I made you… Belonging, belonging, belonging – that's what matters to Me. We must be as one in mind and Spirit.

Full Fullness - I

30th December

Rely upon these words in all their fullness because they are My Truth and you must recognise the Truth to set you free from your own misconceptions. Walking the wrong way is a walk away from Me, and I call you back to My fullness of life where every hope and joy is found in Me, through Me, by My Spirit.

You will be able to impart this to others, to those I give to work with you. As you work you must work through Me without doubt or reservation or complication of deviation onto other paths.

Take My Gospel Truth for it is the fullness of God's Truth, His revelation to you that you might understand and expound it to others. Note I say "expound it" not "expand it". For the full fullness – God's fullness – is already there enclosed, encompassed, in My Word of Truth. I say, "encompassed," because you understand that a compass will always point you in the right direction. This is the way I want to take you. Will you be led?

Pray for My Spirit's guidance, His enlightenment, His teaching, written into the core of your understanding and commanding obedient compliance. Do not look elsewhere for you will be compromised by diluting My message. Pray; pray earnestly to seek, to hear, what I am saying to you that I may speak to My children through you.

My love is waiting to be revealed in all that you do for Me. But you have to rely on Me completely and no other to discover what it is I am asking you to do. In this way you can serve God completely to the fullness of your destiny, God-given. That lies in Me – no other way; no other influence; no other voice; no other choice to make – I chose you. Will you choose Me without dilution? The resolution of your work depends upon this, or you miss the point.

Listen to Me, My child. Listen and learn from Me and no other, and you will most surely discover for yourself directly from Me all that it is that I am saying to you, showing you, revealing to you by My Spirit. My Spirit is key in all of this. Pray to Him every day, first thing in the day, asking Him to bring Me, the reality of Me, fully alive to you in all that you do. Then obey what He tells you and submit your way to following Mine. Mine is the Way I want you to go, to know the fullness that is waiting to be found by you.

Full Fullness - II

31st December

I gave you enormous capabilities. Use them in Me, through Me, by My Spirit. Come fully alive in Me and you will not look back, for there will be no lack of My favour, My fine favour, given to you that you may bless others through Me. Spiritual work is heavy indeed, a heavy responsibility, a burden of care I want you to place on My shoulders, nowhere else.

Let Me carry you forward into that place where you so long to serve God. As you recognise how much you belong to Me, how much I have done for you through My †, you will come to realise all that our Father is longing to show you.

You have travelled so far in this but you need to move on and leave some misunderstandings behind. Ask Me to show you what those misunderstandings are. Although searched for in good faith, they are still misunderstandings when they do not reflect the full fullness of My God-given identity. You must recognise this if you are to succeed in all that God needs you to do for Him.

Begin now, My child. Do not delay! Do not lose another precious day, but turn to Me unreservedly. Turn to Me; return to Me completely, and see what I will do for you, what I will do in you, what I will do through you.

Go on bended knee and ask. Ask for a great measure of My Spirit of Wisdom and Truth to teach you directly. You need not look elsewhere for I give you of Myself if you seek Me.

Speak to Me about any problems. I will not fail you. Please do not fail Me! There is much, much work to do together, and it is time we moved on forwards.

1 Thessalonians 5:19-21

Do not quench the Spirit.

Do not despise prophecies.

Test all things;

hold fast what is good.

Also by Sue O'Donnell

This heart-warming devotional was birthed out of Sue O'Donnell's daily journey with the Lord. Perfect for daily readings and quiet meditation, these morsels of wisdom and worship will inspire and grow your own personal relationship with Jesus.

In Short: Poetry, Prayer and Scripture for Daily Meditation
Published by Onwards and Upwards Publishers
Available from **www.onwardsandupwards.org**
and **Amazon.co.uk**

#0001 - 220818 - C0 - 229/152/21 - PB - 9781912419371